WOMEN

AND

MONEY

WOMEN

AND

MONEY

The Independent

Woman's Guide to

Financial Security for Life

FRANCES LEONARD

ADDISON-WESLEY PUBLISHING COMPANY, INC.

Reading, Massachusetts   Menlo Park, California   New York
Don Mills, Ontario   Wokingham, England   Amsterdam   Bonn
Sydney   Singapore   Tokyo   Madrid   San Juan
Paris   Seoul   Milan   Mexico City   Taipei

Library of Congress Cataloging-in-Publication Data

Leonard, Frances, 1939–
    Women and money : the independent woman's guide to financial security for life / by Frances Leonard.
        p.   cm.
    Includes index.
    ISBN 0-201-55097-0
    1. Women—Finance, Personal.   I. Title.   II. Title: Women and money.
    HG179.L442   1991
    332.024′042—dc20   90-25060
                                                                         CIP

Cover design by Janet Halverson
Text design by Janis Owens
Set in 11-point Goudy by Shepard Poorman Communications
Indianapolis, IN

1 2 3 4 5 6 7 8 9-MW-9594939291
First printing, April 1991

For my parents, Richard and Doris Leonard,
who opened the door.

And to the memory of Tish Sommers and Laurie Shields,
who showed the way.

CONTENTS

ACKNOWLEDGMENTS / ix

INTRODUCTION: A SECOND LIFETIME TO ENJOY / 1

1   MAKING THE BEST OF YOUR MIDLIFE DIVORCE / 7

2   FACTS OF LIFE AND LAW FOR MARRIED WOMEN / 35

3   SEX, AGE, AND YOUR JOB / 61

4   HOMEMAKERS AND PAID WORK / 91

5   WHAT WOMEN NEED TO KNOW ABOUT PENSIONS AND

     SOCIAL SECURITY / 111

6   STRAW INTO GOLD FOR THAT SECOND LIFE / 153

7   MINIMIZING THE GAPS IN YOUR HEALTH

     COVERAGE / 181

8   CARING FOR DAD, THE KIDS, THE HOUSE, THE JOB—

     AND YOU / 199

9   CHECKING UP ON THE REST OF YOUR LIFE / 233

APPENDIX I: DO YOUR OWN LEGAL RESEARCH / 241

APPENDIX II: RESOURCES / 251

INDEX / 255

ACKNOWLEDGMENTS

My warmest thanks to Donna Ambrogi, founder of the California Law Center on Long Term Care: Nancie Fadeley, former assemblymember from Oregon; Lou Glasse, president, and Joan Kuriansky, executive director of the Older Women's League; Dorothy Jonas and Bonnie Sloane of the National Organization for Women's Task Force on Women and Marriage; and Lillian Rabinowitz of the Gray Panthers, who supported this project from its earliest stages.

The hard work, research, and exceptional insights regarding divorce which underlie the first chapter are based on the work of my friend, Harvard sociologist Lenore Weitzman.

I am indebted to my agent, Sandy Dijkstra, and my editor, Martha Moutray, for their vision, enthusiasm, and encouragement.

Finally to my husband, Richard Best, and our children, Sam, Zak, and Gabrielle, who put up with me during all of this, all my love and thanks.

A SECOND LIFETIME TO ENJOY

You are one of the most fortunate women ever. As an American woman today, you can expect to enjoy an abundance of years all but unprecedented in the history of the world. You can plan on nearly one-third more retirement years than men of your age. Compared to your great-grandmother, you have a full second lifetime to enjoy—a kind of rebirth. What the caesars and queens of history couldn't buy with all their power you've got a shot at—one more chance. And with the proper planning, you can make your second life even better than the first. You have a giant head start.

First time around, you had no control. You didn't choose your parents or your economic circumstances. You couldn't read or write. You took what you got and made the best of it. This time, you're far better equipped. You know a little something about the world, about who the players are in your life.

You are also entering midlife at a time when it is fashionable. Elegant magazines cater to you, advertisers woo you, and fitness mavens like Jane Fonda may be older than you. For women, there has never been a better time to be entering midlife than now.

Making your second lifetime as wonderful as your dreams takes planning. Financially, midlife is different for women than for men, and women must plot a different course. There are critical differences between your life, your work, your family roles, your life expectancy—and those of the men in your life. Subtle though they may be, such differences add up to different planning strategies for women who want to come out economically on par with midlife men. Experts agree that, without such planning, even if you are well paid, your second lifetime will almost certainly be substantially poorer than a man's.

There's an assumption that the crevasse that has long separated men's and women's lives has now narrowed to a puddle jump. After all, more women are in the paid labor market, and many employment barriers have fallen. Yet important distinctions persist—the Commonwealth Commission, the respected Johns Hopkins–based research institution, predicts that, by the time today's 35-year-old retires in 2020, poverty among older Americans will be confined primarily to *women* living alone.

Surprisingly perhaps, the biggest problems are nestled in the folds of progressive laws. Good laws, like the civil rights laws, which intend to protect against employment discrimination. Reform laws like the federal pension laws, and the no-fault divorce statutes. Old friends like Social Security. These and other good laws enshrine policies which fit the *male* work pattern or family role. For women they come out just a little wrong, like an ill-fitting garment you yank and twist, but never can make just right. As a result, women must chart a separate course to reach the same end.

You cannot escape these gender-biased laws. But you *can* work around them—and showing you how to do that is the purpose of this book.

Let's see how two women managed their midlife years, with very different results:

Meet Ellen, an advertising agency receptionist with eighteen years on the job. At 41 Ellen was moved to the mail room—her boss said the agency wanted a "fresh" image, and gave the receptionist job to a 22-year-old. When Ellen was 42, the agency dropped its fringe benefit package, and she learned that health insurers wouldn't cover her on her own. At 45, her husband left her—his earning power went with him and Ellen was left with little. At 46, Ellen went into debt to pay for her children's college education, because child support stopped when they were 18. At 48, Ellen's brothers pressured her to quit her job to care for their father who had Alzheimer's disease. She soon learned that caregiving twenty-four hours a day cost her all of her friends—and very nearly her sanity. At 50, in reviewing her retirement options, Ellen discovered gaps in pensions and Social Security which especially affect women—and looked forward to an old age on welfare.

Michelle did things differently. When she found her position being marginalized at work by up-and-coming male colleagues, she recognized the hallmarks of age and sex discrimination, and filed a claim. When her company eliminated health insurance as a fringe benefit, Michelle used her savings to pay the first premium on the conversion policy offered—a good move, since she subsequently learned she was medically uninsurable for any individual policy because of a history of benign cervical disease. Through her fifteen years of marriage, Michelle had carefully established credit in her own name. She bought an hour of a lawyer's time to learn what property rights were hers as a wife, and took steps to ensure that her name joined her husband's on their marital assets. When he died suddenly at 51 without a will, Michelle received the entire estate. Because she and her husband had been careful to preserve her pension survivor's benefit in the event of his early death, she could expect something from his pension in time. Term insurance on her husband's life secured the kids' college educations. When Michelle was 47, her elderly mother needed help. Because she lived across the country, Michelle arranged for a geriatric care manager to coordinate the various services her mother needed to remain independent. At 49, Michelle contacted her pension administrator and the Social Security Administration to secure estimates of her retirement income at 65. This shocked her into fully funding every tax-deferred device available to her. By planning ahead, Michelle faced her second lifetime with a rewarding job, an adequate health insurance policy, a mother well cared for, and a more secure financial future.

Ellen's plight was not her fault. She was a hard-working woman, and biases and circumstances preyed upon her. But we women come to our second lifetimes with many wisdoms, and two of these are: "Life isn't fair," and "You have to watch out for yourself." No, you *shouldn't* have to plan and strategize to protect yourself from inequities, and that's why throughout this book you'll see how laws and practices that create bias should be changed. But until these changes come about, forewarned is forearmed. This book is about changing Ellens into Michelles, about making the most of your second lifetime.

Along the way, you will learn how to set up retirement savings plans at your workplace even if your boss doesn't want to provide a pension. You will learn how to protect yourself by handling Social Security intelligently, ordering priorities, commandeering windfalls, and using life insurance to maximum advantage. You will learn about health insurance for the medically uninsurable, respite services for caregivers, and how to salvage as much as you can financially from a midlife divorce. You can protect your marital property rights, and your rights to inherit, as well. You will learn how to recognize employment discrimination, and how to prove it even without a "smoking gun." You will learn how to recognize problems before they become unsolvable. Understanding the system is the first step. In the Appendix is a guide to researching the law yourself.

Throughout this book are "quick tips" and strategies, presented with the special needs of midlife women in mind—a departure from "unisex" economic advice books. The tips and strategies are meant to supplement standard works, not supplant them. Along the way you'll find checklists, and, in the last chapter, a detailed assessment of how you stack up for that second lifetime.

About terminology: In this book we'll assume that midlife for women begins at around 40, and that an "older woman" is one who accepts that description of herself or perceives that others are applying it to her; for statistical convenience, we'll call a woman aged 65 or over an "older woman." All women work, but I will use the term "working women" to mean working for pay.

This book is for men, too: men who would like their wives to earn more, or who wish their mothers were financially independent, or who are among the millions who face some of the same difficulties that women do (low pay, or job mobility, or family care). It is for men who understand that a fully productive society benefits every one of us.

We all run a financial marathon if we live long enough, but in this race there need be no losers. Leveling the track benefits all the runners. Everyone can reach for the grand prize—a second lifetime full of health and the means to enjoy it.

Let's get started.

1

MAKING THE BEST OF YOUR MIDLIFE DIVORCE

"The Law may not be used as a handy vehicle for the summary disposal of old and used wives. A woman is not a breeding cow to be nurtured during her years of fecundity, then conveniently and economically converted to cheap steaks when past her prime."

These words were written by a California appellate justice seven years after the advent of "no-fault" divorce in that state. The justice thought he had spotted a trend. The new no-fault divorce law had made it socially and financially possible for a man to end a lengthy marriage without the expense and scandal that were inevitable under the old "fault" standards.

The justice's sentiments were seconded by noted divorce researcher, Judith Wallerstein (*Second Chances*), who observed from her long-term sample:

> Many of these husbands who pull away after fifteen or twenty years of marriage talk about their wife's age as an important factor in the decision to divorce. They admit that they are repelled by the changes in her face and body, by the inevitable sags and wrinkles. I have the sense, as they speak, that they are frightened by an indirect vision of their own mortality. In seeking a younger woman, as many do, they seem to be trying to delay their own aging and eventual death.

At the end of World War II, only one in twenty-five divorces filed in America involved a marriage of longer than fifteen years; a decade after no-fault's debut, it was one in four.

Midlife economics are different for women than for men, and never is this more true than during and after a divorce. This chapter presents strategies for women survivors of divorce, as well as those currently or soon to be involved in the struggle. First, no-fault divorce is examined, and its unanticipated negative consequences for women explained. Then, support and property awards are considered, along with collateral matters such as health insurance, delaying the sale of the house, Social Security, pension rights, and college costs. Finally, lawyers, fees, and the array of available divorce "packages" are analyzed with explanations of which would work out best for you.

THE FAULT WITH NO-FAULT

 The way things were.

Divorce in America changed in 1970 when California enacted the first no-fault statute, and the other states quickly followed suit. Prior to no-fault, when the couple made their vows promising their union "until death," the law took them at their word. They had made a contract, and like any other contract, it was binding unless breached by one of the parties to it. Each state had its own conditions for breach of the marriage contract; you had to have *grounds* for a divorce, and they were usually along the lines of adultery, desertion, and physical or mental cruelty.

It worked like this: Tom and Sally were married in their local church in 1940, both age 22. Tom served in the war, and Sally stayed home to care for their first child, born in 1942. On Tom's return in 1945, he joined a small business in town and they settled down in suburbia to raise their family, which eventually grew to four children. In 1960, Tom decided he wanted to marry Joan. He asked Sally for a divorce, and she refused. It was not a broken heart that caused her dismay; it was that she had looked at her prospects as a divorced wife, and they were not good. Tom was proposing to pay her one-fourth of his salary to support herself and the four children. He was suggesting they sell the house and divide the proceeds in half (for a share of $6,000). He would give her one-third of "his" bank account ($5,000)—after all, he could afford to be generous, because he had a good pension to look forward to, as well as his Social Security. Tom's terms were generous for the times—but Sally saw that at age 42, twenty jobless years after her education, there would be no employment for her. One-fourth of Tom's salary couldn't begin to support five-sixths of the family, and a "nest egg" of $11,000 would hardly compensate for a future with no home, no Social Security, and no pension.

So Sally refused to go along for the ride, and Tom began to look for grounds to force a divorce—in other words, find her in breach of the marriage contract. But to sue Sally for divorce, Tom would have to bring evidence to court that Sally had committed adultery, or deserted him, or, in some states, that she had been mentally or physically cruel to him. And because Sally was guilty of none of these grounds, a divorce over her opposition was not possible.

But Tom still wanted to marry Joan. He continued to bargain with Sally. "How about this?" he said. "You can keep the house, and I'll agree to give you one-third of my salary until I retire, then half of my Social Security."

"Getting better," said Sally, "but I can't raise the kids on one-third of your salary—what about college?"

"Okay," said Tom. "I'll settle a college fund in trust for the kids right now, and, because it's tax-deductible, I'll pay half my salary to you and the kids for alimony and child support. Joan will have to work, but it's worth it to us."

"Throw in life insurance for my benefit when you die, and you've got it," said Sally.

Sally and Tom hired a private detective to photograph Tom and Joan in bed together, then Sally sued Tom for divorce, using the photos to "prove" adultery. The children were aghast to learn of Tom's affair, but it had to be made part of the public record, for, even with Sally's consent, divorce was not possible without grounds.

Now, the ugly word for Sally's bargain is *blackmail*. Tom could not have Joan until he bought Sally off. When Tom paid Sally's price, he was free. Pretty sordid? This is exactly what parties to a commercial contract do. Let's say two businesses make a deal—Greenacre Store will buy a hundred widgets a month from Blackacre Suppliers. When Greenacre wants out, it cannot just walk away from the contract. If Blackacre has performed its end of the deal, it is entitled to bargain to protect its interests. So Greenacre must buy Blackacre out. It happens all the time, and it is considered a good thing. The law encourages amicable adjustments to unworkable contracts, because it favors the free flow of commerce. The law continues to bind the parties to the contract until they reach an agreement and mutually agree to terminate the contract.

This is where no-fault missed the boat. Millions of women who thought they'd made a binding, legally enforceable contract when they married prior to no-fault, discovered the rules had changed on them midstream. The contract that was enforceable when they made it, was no longer enforceable when they divorced.

If you married before no-fault (in most states no-fault was enacted between 1970 and 1980), your situation has changed. The rules changed for those married forty years just as much as for newlyweds. Either you or your husband can get a divorce now, virtually for the asking. Property and support awards differ widely by state, but the fact that your marriage can be dissolved upon the say-so of one partner is a fact of life almost everywhere in the United States. You will not be able to show the court your long history of fidelity, or his of skullduggery, in hopes of influencing the property or support awards. The court will not even permit you to try. As a result, you should rethink your situation to minimize surprises down the line. They probably won't happen—more long marriages survive

than dissolve, even now—but it can't hurt to have an accurate understanding of your legal position.

▶ *The way things are.*

No-fault dissolution works like this: Elaine and Roger were married in 1968. She was a homemaker their twenty-three years together. Roger discouraged her every time she proposed learning a trade "just in case."

"I've got life insurance 'just in case,' " he'd tell her. "No need to worry."

But in 1991, when they were both 45, Roger said goodbye. He wanted a different lifestyle, he told her, and was gone. Elaine's lawyer said there was nothing she could do to stop him.

When the law removed the dissolution itself from the bargaining table, it devastated the bargaining position of the economically weaker spouse—generally the wife. No longer could Elaine withhold the divorce until her needs were met. She and Roger could still negotiate such matters as support and property division, but the dissolution itself would be granted no matter what. In short, Roger no longer had to buy her out. If they failed to agree on the economic matters, the court would decide for them. And in every state in the land it's usually the Rogers of the marriage who walk away with the lion's share of the fruits of the marriage. Even in the handful of states which purport to divide the property equally between the spouses, the partner with the higher earning power—almost always the husband—leaves the marriage with this invaluable asset intact. Midlife wives, with their earning power devastated by years of homemaking or secondary jobs, descend the economic ladder.

Elaine was awarded one-third of Roger's salary for one year, one-fifth for the next year, ten percent for the third, then nothing. "It will be good for you," the judge told an ashen Elaine. "You can learn a skill, get a job—all kinds of opportunities for women these days. It's an opportunity for a new life. You'll see."

Elaine saw only too well. No job history, no skills, plus

age 45 equals no job. No welfare, either, because she did not have minor children to qualify for Aid to Families with Dependent Children (AFDC), nor would she be old enough for Supplemental Security Income (SSI) until age 65. Although she had worked productively in her home all her married life, there was no unemployment compensation for her. She was not old enough to receive divorced wife's benefits from Roger's Social Security.

The house was ordered sold by the judge, and the equity was reduced substantially by the attorneys' fees. She received one-third of its remaining value as her "equitable" share. The judge ordered Roger's pension plan to pay her one-third when he reached his plan's retirement age of 65, but that was twenty years away.

Roger, on the other hand, did quite well. He got most of the proceeds of the house and pension, which, along with his earning power, were the primary assets of the marriage. And of course, because his earning power didn't count as property, he walked into the future with it intact, except for some nuisance alimony the first three years.

The children were ages 18, 20, and 21—all in college. Roger saw no reason to pay child support or contribute to their college expenses. Why should he? The court wouldn't order him to support legal adults. Because they lived with Elaine, their support would be on her shoulders. Since Elaine's marriage was dissolved in 1991 after a change in the law, she was entitled to stay in the group health insurance plan at Roger's job for up to three years, but since the premium was over $2,000 per year, it was out of the question for her. Elaine's standard of living plummeted; Roger's rose.

Of course, Elaine was luckier than many American women her age. Not all states permit alimony, nor do they all divide pensions. Many women don't have equity in a house to divide, either. And women divorced before 1988 were immediately thrown out of the health insurance group policy from their husband's job.

So this is the fault with no-fault. With unilateral divorce, the law took away the weaker partner's bargaining chip. Then it compounded the error by limiting the chips remaining on the table to those recognized by the state, rather than those to be agreed upon by the parties.

Women, especially those now over 45, are almost always the weaker partner economically, so legislatures in most states decreed that property would be divided "equitably," that is, according to what the court thinks is fair. But this seemingly compassionate system is fraught with differences among the states, and even among individual courts within a state.

No-fault fails most by dictating a definition of marital property. Partners in the commercial world are free to define for themselves the property interest of their partnership. If the principal asset is leaseholds (leased aircraft, offices, and departure gates, for example, can amount to millions of dollars to an airline), then those intangible assets are given a prominent place on the bargaining table when the partnership is dissolved.

No-fault removed that freedom from the marriage partnership. If the court does not recognize an intangible asset as part of the marital property—say royalties, copyright, or goodwill—it is not permitted on the bargaining table. The wife lost her bargaining chip when she could no longer hold up the dissolution until her future was secure; she lost again when she was denied the opportunity to negotiate for certain assets. The husband often keeps 100 percent of the intangible property, including pension rights and business goodwill, while the rest of the property is subject to the equitable-division rule. And the greatest loss is the enhanced earning power the husband gained at his wife's expense while she stayed home or otherwise stunted her earning ability and he proceeded apace with his.

THE IMPORTANCE OF SUPPORT AWARDS

Since the average marriage lasts around seven years, let's agree that fifteen years constitutes a lengthy marriage.

When such a marriage breaks up, custody battles are usually not the problem they are in younger marriages, because older children and teenagers enter into the negotiations themselves, and generally find ways to be quite persuasive about their preferences. This is not to say bitter custody battles never happen after long marriages, but if custody is disputed, the teenager is generally going to make the final decision, anyway.

Child support, on the other hand, is of crucial importance. Teenagers are *very* expensive people—clothes, housing (high resistance to shared rooms), perhaps car/gas/insurance, entertainment, and food, food, food!

In addition to child support, spousal support increases in importance as the years advance, and performs a very different role for the long-time homemaker, newly displaced, than for the younger wife.

▶ *Supporting the older child.*
When states lowered the age of majority in the 1970s, the age at which child support ceased fell from 21 to 18, in most cases. Child support was for children, the reasoning went, and 18-year-olds were now adults. For divorced mothers, the effect was to thrust the cost of financing the college education onto their shoulders, since fathers generally could not be ordered to pay support for legal adults.

☑ **Under the federal Consolidated Omnibus Budget Reconciliation Act (COBRA) (for companies with at least twenty employees), your kids can remain eligible for the family's group health plan for up to three years after losing their eligibility due to age (or many other reasons) even if you or your husband leaves the job. You'll have to pay their premiums, but these are generally cheaper than individual policies, and groups usually offer better benefits. But you must act fast— usually within thirty days of the disqualifying event. Be sure the health insurance is discussed during divorce negotiations, because the premiums run in the thousands of dollars per year.**

Women who manage to hang onto the family home by signing off almost all other marital assets get a rude shock when college time comes for the kids. Since equity in the home is counted when establishing the child's eligibility for financial aid, a single mom with a modest income can find her child disqualified for financial aid because of equity in the home. Financial aid officers assume she can borrow on the equity and finance the education herself, even when a low income would make repayment of the loan impossible.

☑ **Fill out financial aid applications as soon as they are available in January, and submit them at once. Do not wait to see if the child is admitted. Many colleges distribute their own scholarship funds on a first-come, first-served basis—you want to be among the first. When the acceptances come in, in the spring, you'll be in a better position to make an informed choice.**

Partly as a consequence of support ending at age 18, many children of divorce face a lifelong lowered standard of living. Judith Wallerstein's sobering findings were that, among her affluent, educated Marin County (California) sample, only one-third of the fathers who were financially able to assist their children with college tuition did so. The remaining two-thirds contributed nothing. Wallerstein found that, ten years after a divorce, "60% [of 18-year-olds] are on a downward educational course compared with their fathers, and 45% are on a similar downward course compared with their mothers." Downward economic mobility for the children of divorce is unexpected and deeply troubling, especially from a public policy perspective. No longer can it be hoped that divorce is a private tragedy, from which the people involved ultimately recover (or at least have the decency to cope with unhappily but silently). If millions of individuals face compromised futures because their parents' divorce diverted them to the slow track, then society suffers grievously from the undereducated talents of its labor force.

Many lawyers advise the newly divorcing mother to keep relations between the children and their father as good as humanly possible, including the warmest possible relationship with the stepmother—not because this is the most "mature" way to handle the situation, but because it is the most likely way to encourage the father to help with college costs (although Wallerstein found that even fathers with wonderful parental relations did not see funding the college education as their responsibility). This approach is not only distastefully obsequious, but also dreadfully chancy. Better to negotiate a college-funding agreement at the time of the divorce, and have it made part of the court order.

A few colleges will let you "freeze" tuition at the current rate for an admission years down the line. In other words, you can guarantee a 1991 tuition rate for your 2001 matriculant if you pay now. If you are getting a divorce, this might be one way to get your husband to fund a future education; perhaps he's more amenable to paying for it now than he will be after his family bonds loosen or he becomes involved in a new family.

Spousal support.

The divorced woman most in need of spousal support (alimony) is the midlife or older homemaker. Even if she can retrain herself for the job market, age discrimination and her lack of paid experience will work against her chances of landing a job she can support herself with. There is little chance that she will remarry (only 11 percent of women who divorce after age 50 remarry, as opposed to over 76 percent who divorce before age 30). Yet, according to Harvard scholar Lenore Weitzman, author of *The Divorce Revolution*, fully one-third of older homemakers are not awarded spousal support. One state, Texas, does not provide for alimony at all. In others, there is a statutory limit of one to three years, although permanent alimony is making a comeback for older homemakers in some places. In most, it's up to the discretion of the judge, who is often bound by guidelines determined by the legislature or judiciary. Military wives are especially hard hit. Because of frequent transfers they have been unable to build equity in a home, or develop a career, and whether they get a crack at the military pension is up to the state. In addition, many retired servicemen can structure their retirement benefit to include a high proportion of disability benefits (instead of 100 percent retirement pay) and the disability share is not split between the parties.

States differ profoundly on such things as spousal and child support, division of marital property, and recognition of assets such as pensions and business goodwill. It is possible to "forum shop" to locate the state with the best laws for your circumstance. You have to establish residency in the intended jurisdiction, which can be a matter of weeks, months, or even a year. Unfortunately, getting the comparative information is not easy, since most lawyers know only the laws of their own state. (Appendix I shows how to research the law yourself—your local law library may have the statutes of all the states.) If you have moved recently, you may not have lost your earlier residency; if you find yourself in a divorce situation, you should ask your lawyer to compare the two jurisdictions with your best interests in mind.

How to keep health insurance.

In 1980, when 41-year-old Helen divorced Chuck, she learned to her horror that she no longer qualified for his health insurance from work, nor did she qualify for individual insurance because of an earlier breast biopsy (benign). No amount of money could buy insurance for her. Because of harmless breast or cervical conditions, many divorced women over 35 were joining the uninsured by the millions. Congress finally arrived at a partial remedy for the situation (the aforementioned COBRA in 1988). Now, under federal law, you can remain a member of your husband's group plan for up to three years after your divorce (or widowhood). There are conditions, of course, and the cost is high— between $2,000 and $4,000 per year—but groups are usually cheaper than individual insurance, and no medical examination is required.

☑ **You must act fast to secure this protection, usually within thirty days of your divorce or widowhood. Scrape together the money somehow. Later, you can decide if you qualify medically for a less expensive policy. If you don't sign on, you may very well find yourself unable to secure medical benefits until you get a job which covers you, or you qualify for Medicare at 65. Don't chance it.**

▶ *Protecting your post-divorce retirement.*
In some states, you may be entitled to a portion of your husband's pension after he retires (see chapter 5). Your share can be awarded as a "cash-out" (meaning you'll get its equivalent amount at the time of your divorce, either in cash or as an offset against other marital property, sometimes the house), or it can be deferred until your husband reaches retirement age. If he chooses to work beyond his normal retirement age, he will have to pay you your share anyway. Be sure your attorney looks into survivor's benefits.

A wife's share of retirement income can be ludicrously small. Here's how a court divided Bruce's $400-per-month pension when he and Jayne divorced after eighteen years (Bruce worked twenty-five years for the same company): Jayne was awarded one-third of the pension earned during their marriage, so she gets one-third of eighteen-twenty-fifths of his pension, or $95 per month.

☑ **If your share of the pension will be deferred until your husband's retirement, be sure your attorney has the pension administrator pay you directly. You don't want** to have a collection problem with your husband years down the line. If it's to be paid as a lump sum at divorce, it may be ordered paid into an IRA, or paid in installments. Be sure you discuss these alternatives with your attorney, so he or she can negotiate the best deal for you.

In many states, IRAs, Keoghs, 401(k)s, stock options, ESOPs, tax-sheltered annuities, and other retirement savings vehicles are divisible marital property.

☑️ **You can help your attorney negotiate your share of the property if you can provide him or her with the right papers. But even if you can't, tell your lawyer about everything you know about, or have a hunch about. Perhaps an investigator can come up with the particulars.**

If you were married at least ten years, you will qualify for a Social Security benefit, equal to one-half of your ex-husband's in most cases. Your benefit does not diminish his. You can collect it as early as age 62 (60 if he has died, 50 if you are severely disabled), but if you do, it will be reduced for the remainder of your life. When your former husband dies, your benefit increases to 100 percent of his, no matter how many former wives he leaves behind. But under the "dual entitlement" rule, you cannot collect on your own Social Security account *and* his (see chapter 5).

☑️ **It's easier to apply for divorced wife's benefits if you know your former husband's Social Security number, but you can apply even if you don't have it. If you have lost touch with him, and don't know if he has died or retired, Social Security can probably help you. If you believed you were married, but later learned he "forgot" to divorce an earlier wife, you may come under Social Security's "good faith wife" rules and still get a benefit. It's worth checking out.**

▶ *Support versus property.*

Let's say you've negotiated a settlement with your former husband, a 55-year-old retiree. For one reason or another, the $700 per month available to you (one-third of his pension) has been characterized as "spousal support" rather than "marital property." The lawyers have told you this is just a technical distinction. But is that really all there is to it?

No. Marital property is a right—spousal support is not. The $700 spousal support might be lowered if he falls upon hard times, or needs more of his income to support a second family, or has high medical bills. It will almost certainly stop if you remarry, or even live with someone. It will likely be lowered or discontinued if you get a job. It is subject to modification in most cases—according to your needs, and his ability to pay. But if the award was property rather than support, it will continue whatever you do, whoever you marry or live with, however much money you earn. Your property right will continue whether he remarries, fathers a new family, or enters a nursing home. If you were divorced after 1985, it may even continue as a survivor's benefit after his death.

Melissa and Tish, both divorced after long marriages, met in pre-nursing classes at the local community college. Melissa had $500-per-month spousal support; Tish had $500-per-month as her one-half share of her former husband's pension—marital property. Melissa's former husband had a stroke, entered a nursing home, and incurred medical expenses of $30,000 per year. Her spousal support was terminated because the judge decided her husband's need was greater; he suggested she get a job in a fast-food joint at minimum wage. Tish finished the program, became a nurse, and began at the local hospital at $20,000 per year. There she met and married a physician. Their annual income is $150,000 per year—plus $500 per month from her former husband's pension, which she uses to fund her youngest daughter's college education.

On the other hand, it could work out like this: Melissa

slips in her bathtub, incurring head injuries which keep her hospitalized and in physical therapy for months. She cannot complete the pre-nursing program. Her husband, meanwhile, has been promoted to CEO of his large company. Her $500 spousal support *might* be increased because of her increased need and his increased ability to pay. Under the same circumstances, Tish's property award would stay the same.

In other words, it can work out either way.

Be very clear in distinguishing between support and property when talking with your attorney. You understand your circumstances better than your attorney does, so you must be the one to decide which road to take. Be sure you understand the different income tax, capital gains, and property tax implications of property and income. One strategy is to secure property rights to as much as you can, while *not* giving up permanent rights to spousal support. Some attorneys like to secure at least one dollar per year, so that modifications upward remain a possibility.

▶ *Rethinking spousal support.*
One of the problems with spousal support is the myth of the "alimony drone." There she sits in her convertible, spending her days shopping on Rodeo Drive, or tripping the light fantastic with her fancy new beau, while her ex, sweat pouring off his brow, is unable to buy so much as a jello salad as a small treat at the end of his eighteen-hour workday. Hollywood created her, and divorced women have had to live with her ever since. According to Lenore Weitzman, the vast majority of divorced women are not awarded alimony in the first place, and most of those who are receive a time-limited award, often less than two years.

One reason that awards are inconsistent is that the rationale for alimony has become out of date since the resurgence of the women's movement in the early 1970s. The old idea was that women were, and always would be, economically dependent upon their husbands. The husband's marital support obligation, although terminated upon divorce, could be extended through court order for the rest of his wife's days. Because she could not earn a living, and as "used goods" would probably not remarry, the alternative was welfare, and public policy decreed that it was better that he pay for his mistakes than the taxpayer. No need to emphasize how demeaning this scenario is for women—and how economically precarious.

Nevertheless, equity demands that some method be devised to compensate both partners fairly. Weitzman proposes three more sophisticated premises for alimony than the provider/dependent model:

• *Delayed compensation.* Alimony pays the wife back for what her marriage cost her career.

• *Unemployment insurance.* Like other American workers, homemakers qualify for benefits upon their "unemployment."

• *Opportunity cost.* If the wife started her marriage as a mid-level bank clerk, she is compensated to recognize that absent the marriage, she would now be a senior clerk.

WHOSE PROPERTY IS WHOSE?

Three aspects of marital property are important upon divorce:

• The type of asset

• Its value

• How it is divided between the parties

While the attention of the parties usually focuses on the second and third, in fact the real inequities and controversy swirl around the first. Weitzman found that women and children are much worse off after divorce than men (older women fare the worst), largely because of the failure of the law to recognize certain intangible assets. Her finding that, a year after divorce, women and children face a 73 percent decline in their standard of living while men enjoy a rise of 42 percent generated enormous controversy. Divorce lawyers seemed to take her findings personally. The divorce bar refused to admit that the 42–73 percent gap could exist.

But Weitzman's critics missed her whole point: that the unrecognized property that formed the bulk of the assets of middle-class marriages usually left those marriages with the husband, including professional training, education, and business goodwill, and the earning power of the spouses, all of which remain unrecognized as marital property in virtually all states. Pensions are still not even recognized in every state as marital property. These, Weitzman found, usually comprise the bulk of the marital wealth, yet because few courts recognize them as such, they remain with the partner who controls the asset, generally the husband. Weitzman found that, for all income levels, net worth was typically lower than the annual income of the couple, indicating that the real marital asset is the earning power of the partners. In most states, these assets are as unrecognized now as when Weitzman identified them.

To understand Weitzman's thesis, let's look at Jessie and Barney. They married while students at Berkeley. Jessie was working toward a law degree but dropped out, because Barney was accepted to medical school and they needed her salary. Because of her support, Barney was able to complete his training without having to take on extra work, which put him at the top of his class and enabled him to qualify for a prestigious fellowship, during which Jessie continued to support them. At the end of his training, Jessie had ten years' experience as a secretary; Barney had a medical degree, with a specialty in cardiology. Within months of going into practice, Barney divorced Jessie. The couple owned nothing tangible, because all of their economic efforts had gone into Barney's education. Jessie was now 32 years old, with a dead-end job and no way of getting her law degree. In other words, because of their marriage, the two partners, who had started out in the same position ended up in very different ones. Barney had everything he hoped to obtain when they married, and Jessie had nothing.

Nor was Jessie starting over at square one. Square one was when she was 22. She has lost those ten years, not only from her life, but from her career path as well. Employment counselors agree that to attain the highest levels professionally, you must start your career in your twenties; those who enter after 30 seldom catch up. Still, Jessie's deferral of her career in favor of Barney's was not necessarily a stupid thing to do. Had Barney kept his end of the deal, her decision could be seen as a reasonable investment. They would both have enjoyed the fruits of the medical degree over time, and after Barney put her through law school, they would both have benefited from her training as well. But in almost all states, the court will not see the medical education as a joint investment of the marriage. They will see it as Barney's alone. Tough luck for Jessie. There's a slim possibility she can argue for support from Barney while she completes her education, although if she's young and childless it is more likely no support will be awarded at all.

Whether it's doctoring or plumbing, valuable trades walk out of the marriage with their "owner" regardless of whose efforts were involved in obtaining them. It is not because these intangibles are too intangible to measure. Courts put values on future careers all the time in negligence actions, where the value of lost future earnings is routinely included as part of the damages. Although small headway has been made in some states in recognizing career assets as marital assets, it will be a long time before such recognition is universal.

In the meantime, be realistic. Place your hopes and dreams in the long future of your marriage; but recognize that the state won't back you in the gamble. When you forego your own career opportunities in the expectation of joint future returns, you place yourself

at serious risk; and no amount of bitterness and recrimination will finance you if things don't work out in the end. I can advise you to make a pre-nuptial contract, in which post-divorce expectations are clarified, but I know you won't do it. This device has simply not caught on outside of legal circles, probably because no one really wants to raise these issues before the marriage. Absent a contract, you should take responsibility for building your own career status, and by all means see to it your sons and daughters understand that under today's marital laws, putting all their eggs in one spouse's basket may very well mean that, in the end, only that spouse will enjoy the omelette.

▶ *The vagaries of marital property laws.*
Assume you and your two sisters all married businessmen. All three of you are in the same economic circumstances when you all divorce after fifteen years of marriage. None of you has professional training; all of you have college degrees now two decades old; all of you moved in and out of the paid labor market and now earn about $14,000 per year at clerical jobs. Your husbands all earn about $60,000, and your children are all grown. Equity would demand that your post-divorce circumstances be relatively equal, no matter where you live. But that won't happen. The Californian may get support through a professional education; the New Yorker may also get part of the value of her husband's professional education. The Texan will get no support at all. In terms of marital property and support, the states are all over the map. In some, all of the property of either spouse can be divided upon the divorce, in others, only the property acquired during the marriage. A handful will divide property one partner inherited. Not all will divide pensions; even fewer will divide business goodwill, professional educations, insurance benefits, and other intangibles. In other words, where you divorce has everything to do with your economic well-being after the divorce.

If American courts can't agree as to what is to be divided after a marriage, then it should be left to the parties to set their own definitions in negotiations. Instead of having one court dividing the pension, another the business, yet another limiting itself to the bank account, they should open all forms of property to negotiation. When states recognized the harm of differing state commerce laws, all states adopted the Uniform Commercial Code. Uniform laws on divorce and marital property have been proposed, and even adopted, by a few states, but not the majority. And the uniform laws themselves are not perfect. They are drafted by the Uniform Law Commissioners, a privately funded body of legal scholars who offer their model bills to state legislatures to enact. Although public input is invited by the commissioners during the drafting process, controversial provisions can remain in the final draft and thus become law.

What can you do if your divorce happened before your state recognized pensions as marital property? Your husband will have a $3,000-per-month pension, and you will have only your Social Security of $500 per month. In some cases, courts have reopened the property aspect of even a final divorce, on the theory that, if the asset wasn't recognized by the earlier court as marital property, then it hasn't been finally adjudicated and is open to division at a later time. This is an unusual situation, and your attorney may not know if your state does this. It's worth finding out about on your own.

▶ *Selling the family home.*
You and your husband are headed for divorce. You've been married twenty years; your three children are now 16, 13, and 10. You have joint bank accounts and other financial assets worth $20,000, consumer debts of $8,000—and a four-bedroom house. You've had the house fifteen years, and your equity is $100,000. Your mortgage payments are $165 per month, homeowner's insurance another $100.

Your housing costs, in other words, are only $265 per month. Obviously, the sensible thing would be for you and the kids to keep the house. They avoid the substantial trauma of being moved from their neighborhood, schools, and friends—as well as the almost certain downward mobility of apartment living in a significantly poorer part of town.

Is this best possible arrangement going to happen? Almost certainly not. Most states subscribe to "equitable-division" when it comes to marital property, under which the court, often with legislative or judicial guidelines, looks at the totality of circumstances and decides what's fair. A few states hold to "equal-division"—if the couple cannot arrange a suitable division between them, the court will order the property split down the middle. In some states the marital debt will also be split evenly; in others it will be awarded to the party best able to retire it. Whether the state is "equal" or "equitable," the unfortunate fact is the house will usually be ordered sold. One reason the sale of the house is popular among divorce practitioners is that legal fees are payable out of the proceeds. Very often, only by selling the house can the lawyers be paid.

Sometimes the house can be swapped for the pension. You get the house and give up all claims to his future pension. If you've been married at least ten years, you will still get your 50 percent share of his Social Security, which stays constant no matter how many times he remarries. Your Social Security claim will not reduce his benefit in any way. Any number of things could reduce his future pension: he could die before it vests, or switch jobs. Still, think very hard before trading future income for the house. The appreciation in the house's value might provide a nest egg for future retirement income; on the other hand, it might not.

For the mother and children, the sale of the home can be devastating. A few courts have awarded the home to both parties, but delayed the sale until the children reached majority. For the midlife homemaker, for whom the home may be her entire life's effort and environment, the delayed sale may merely defer the catastrophe. But very few, if any, courts will delay the sale for her lifetime.

☑ **Sometimes a delayed sale can be negotiated. The other partner, on the deed as a tenant-in-common, has an appreciable asset. He has a real estate investment, and perhaps his child and spousal support payments will be lower because of the lower housing cost. In addition, his interest in the house is a guarantor of his support payments. The resident partner, in effect, has a lien upon his support, because his delinquent payments can be deducted from his equity when the home is finally sold.**

ATTORNEYS: A FACT OF LIFE

Your divorce is no time to indulge in false economies. If your instinct is to preserve the marital assets by cutting attorney's fees, do it intelligently. Midlife and older women are the most likely of all persons to be disadvantaged by an "economy" proceeding, because recent trends in the law favor sophisticated handling of property division, and longer marriages generally result in more assets to divide. There are good ways to keep attorney fees under control, and there are terrible ways.

☑ **Do not use your attorney as a therapist. The fee meter runs by the minute, and attorneys are not trained for it. It's an expensive way to vent your anger, and a good way to ensure your attorney will become "unavailable" when you call. Lean on family friends instead, or seek out support groups.**

You have numerous choices in divorce representation. Here they are, from the least expensive to the most expensive. Neither extreme is recommended.

- **Do-It-Yourself.** You buy a book, and go from there. Women should be very wary of this approach, unless the marriage was short and childless, and property and income very low. You may not recognize intangible property you have rights to, and sign it away.

- **Divorce clinics.** A bargain price for little more than filling out the forms for you. Same problems as the do-it-yourself approach.

- **Summary divorce.** Some states provide for a short, simple, inexpensive procedure for short, childless, low-asset marriages. A good thing if appropriate. But be careful, because support is not usually possible.

- **Mutual lawyer.** One lawyer represents both parties. A bad idea, because to fulfill his duty to both clients the attorney will have to compromise. You and your husband's interests, even if entirely in accord emotionally, are not in concert legally. You are necessarily opposed to each other economically, in that what one gains, the other loses.

- **Mediation.** The goal of the mediator is to achieve agreement. Appropriate for child custody disputes, but not so good for property decisions. Many divorce experts feel that in mediation the power structure of the marriage continues, usually to the woman's detriment. You will live with the economics for the rest of your life, so don't underestimate the value of the adversarial system in recognizing and fighting for your rights.

- **Default divorce.** This is the best method for most people after a lengthy marriage. Through independent attorneys, the parties work out their differences out of court, commit their property and support decisions to paper, and submit their agreement to the court, uncontested by either. You get your money's worth from the attorneys' negotiating skills, rather than wasting it on useless courtroom appearances.

- **Divorce trial.** Divorce at its worst. Costs are highest, emotions run hot, and bitterness is almost guaranteed. Sometimes a trial is necessary, but don't be the one to push for a trial on "principle." This is not the way to spend your money.

It's not easy finding the right lawyer, but here are some ideas.

- **Asking friends** and women's organizations is one way, but not foolproof. You can also consult women's bar associations, divorce specialist bar associations, and state and local bar associations. There's always the Yellow Pages. Ask about fees in your first phone call.

- Generally, do not retain a lawyer who is a *family friend.* The lawyer will inevitably feel personal conflict in opposing the other spouse.

- Think twice before you retain your *family lawyer,* if he or she has dealt primarily with your husband. They may speak the same language, to the detriment of your interests.

- You can't presume all *women lawyers* will represent you better than men. Don't select attorneys by gender.

- Retain an *experienced family* (or matrimonial, or divorce) *law practitioner,* but think twice about spending your money on the local "hot shot" if the lawyer actually handling your case will be an inexperienced associate.

- Examine the *attorney's track record* on representing women divorcing after a lengthy marriage. The child custody specialist may not be the best for dividing the pension and other intangibles.

- Remember that, in the attorney-client relationship, *you are the employer.* While you can't direct the lawyer's legal decisions, you can demand clear, written fee arrangements up front and demand that your attorney communicate with you. You can always fire your attorney, complain to the bar association, or sue for malpractice.

• Interview at least *three attorneys* before you settle on one. You'd get three estimates for car repair or a roof job; this is more important.

• You and your attorney will go through a lot together. Be sure the relationship "fits." Look for an attorney who is willing to explain things to you (but remember the running meter). Don't accept a patronizing attitude ("Don't worry, I'll take care of everything") because unknowns create extra anxieties, the last thing you need.

▶ *Attorney fees.*
In 1987, the California Senate Task Force on Family Equity heard testimony from divorce attorneys who either had stopped taking women clients or did so reluctantly, because women generally did not have the financial resources to pay legal fees. In one poll, twice as many divorce lawyers preferred male clients to female, among other things because men were "in a better position to pay legal fees." Attorneys who do represent women often have to wait until property is divided and distributed to get their fees. This means that money is not available to prepare exhibits, or properly research, investigate, negotiate, or develop the case. Although the wife's attorney's fees may be ordered paid by the husband, such orders usually come too late in the case to affect her presentation.

☑ **Beg or borrow a lump sum to be used for a retainer up front. The property and support decisions from your long marriage will be with you for the rest of your life. Consider your divorce a major investment in your future, and do it right. The average cost of divorce in this country is over $10,000. You would spend that** amount on a car; do not hesitate to make it available for your case.

CONCLUSION

The California Senate Task Force found a direct relationship between inadequate and poorly enforced support and property awards and poverty among women. At least some of the economic hardships faced by women can be ascribed to the divorce system.

This knowledge won't help you much, but it is worth something to know that, because of the system, you will have to work harder and plan cleverly to come out even. And if you're happily celebrating your twentieth wedding anniversary, congratulations! Let your gift to yourself be a financial assessment of your *own* net worth and economic prospects, lest the unthinkable happen and you end up among the one in five women over 65 expected to be divorced in the next century (a 400 percent increase over today).

And lest your long marriage make you complacent, American laws are full of unpleasant surprises for married women who will never face divorce. We'll look at those in the next chapter.

CHECKING UP ON YOUR DIVORCE

If too many of your answers to these questions are the "wrong" ones, go ahead and get angry. Blame the attorneys, your ex, the system—but use your anger as the tool to move you to action. Throwing up your hands in despair will get you exactly nowhere, and that's not why you bought this book. Study chapters 3, 4, and 5 for strategies which may bail you out of some of your economic dilemmas.

✔ **Does your divorce attorney communicate with you?**

✔ **Are you misusing your attorney as a therapist?**

✔ **Are you giving up too much in mediation in order to "get him back"?**

✔ **Has the attorney secured a pension survivor's benefit for you?**

✔ **Has he or she secured life insurance on your husband?**

✔ **If the pension will be divided later, will it be paid directly to you?**

✔ **Do you have your former husband's Social Security number?**

✔ **Were you married at least ten years (for Social Security purposes)?**

✔ **Do you understand your attorney's fee arrangement?**

✔ Have you secured your health insurance rights?

✔ Do you have a court order securing your children's college costs?

✔ Have you preserved your right to future alimony?

✔ Are you attempting to economize inappropriately on your divorce?

✔ Would delaying the sale of the family home be wise economically?

2

FACTS OF LIFE
AND LAW FOR
MARRIED WOMEN

The wedding march swells, the bride approaches the smiling groom. She wipes a tear from her eye, hands her bouquet to her attendant, and the familiar rite begins. She is right to cry, he to smile. Rights are being protected here, and they aren't hers.

Lorna earns $500 a month in a part-time job. James earns $4,000 a month as an airline mechanic. They live in a small, rented apartment with two bedrooms. Two of their three kids share a bedroom, and the other sleeps on a fold-out couch in the living room. Lorna and the kids want to buy a house, with four bedrooms and a large backyard. They can afford it on their joint earnings.

But James prefers to spend the money on very expensive cars. Among his peers, cars confer status, and besides, he enjoys tinkering on them in his free time. James rationalizes the car collection as his "retirement investment." He is convinced they will increase in value far beyond ordinary investments, including real estate. James, in other words, feels he has a right to spend "his" money as he wishes, so long as he keeps his family in "necessities." And the law in most states agrees with him. Lorna can do nothing to force James to spend more on the family's housing needs, so long as he is providing basic support. He can spend "his" money as he sees fit.

Or how about Adele? Had she divorced Edward a year

before his death, she would have received her "equitable" share of the marital assets, in her county a little less than half. But as his widow, she received only one-third of the real estate, and none of their personal property, such as savings and investments.

Lorna and Adele are in this fix primarily because they live in "common-law" states, although, as we shall see, even in most community-property states Lorna would have problems forcing James to share more of his earnings. Plainly put, married women in America do not have the law on their side. The American wife is shockingly disadvantaged when it comes to income and property rights.

This chapter explains the practical differences between common-law and community property, who owns what in a marriage, who has control over it, the legal and financial duties of spouses to each other, wives' credit rights, unmarried couples, inheriting, the right to will property, and what happens when husbands die without a will.

But before getting down to the details, a little background will help us see the jam we're in. Like many public policies gone awry, American marriage laws have evolved haphazardly.

Historically, only 41 of the states accepted the English common-law notion of unity when it came to marriage, while nine states (Arizona, California, Idaho, Louisiana, Nevada, New Mexico, Texas, Washington, and Wisconsin) adhere to community-property principles, which assume that a marriage is an economic partnership to which both spouses make equal contributions, regardless of their role.

In a community-property system, all the income, profits, real property, and personal property acquired during the marriage are owned equally by both partners, regardless of which spouse acquired them, or whose name they are in. The exceptions are gifts, inheritances, and property acquired prior to the marriage. These are the "separate" property of the acquiring spouse.

Common law sees things very differently. Until the middle of the last century, American married women were subject to the English common-law disability of "coverture," which meant that the wife ceased to exist as a legal person. The husband and wife were one, and that one was the husband. Unity. A union. The marital *unit* was spoken of, rather than the marital partnership.

The consequences of coverture were far more than semantic. Because the married woman no longer had legal existence, after her marriage she could no longer acquire property. Anything coming to her belonged to her husband. Of course, anything *he* earned or acquired was his alone. She had the right to support (necessities); he had the right to all her services (consortium). These were legally enforceable duties. After his death, if he was a member of the propertied classes, she had the right (dower) to retain the use of one-third of part of his land for her life. After *her* death if she had had land settled in her name before her marriage, he had the right (curtesy) to the use of 100 percent of it for his life. The husband had full management and control of all property she brought to the marriage. She did not own the dower estate, and because she did not inherit anything from him, she owned nothing to dispose of by will. He even owned her clothes and jewelry by "paraphernal right," the origin of the word *paraphernalia*.

Dower, curtesy, coverture, consortium—quaint terms from our English past with chilling meaning for the married American woman today. The common-law concept of marriage is very much with us now in most states. If you're married, it affects your rights in a very real way. It affects the way your property would be distributed upon divorce, and it affects your right to inherit, and your right to dispose of property by will.

The common law in its pure state no longer exists in any state or in England. But the changes have not been consistent, and if you're a wife today, you exist in a kind of legal limbo. Do you own property, or do you not? If you divorce, you might get one thing; if you're widowed, quite another. Does the law see your marriage as a partnership? A union? Both?

It all begins with the rites of marriage. The familiar words of the traditional ceremony were not words of poetry; they

were words of law. Each lilting phrase was chillingly pre-
cise—a limiting of responsibility here, a termination of obligation there, the transfer of ownership of a human being.

The beautiful words of promise were nothing more than a
property agreement, now encrusted with tradition and hal-
lowed by time. Marriage vows were a legal agreement in
which the husband undertook to provide the necessities for
his wife until he died—only the necessities and only until
he died. The old English said it more prettily, of course, but
to a lawyer's eye, there is nothing romantic or sentimental
in traditional marriage vows. Although the states, not
church recitations, now decide the property rights of married people, the concepts embodied in the old vows remain
very much alive.

TO HAVE AND TO HOLD

"To have and to hold, from this day forward . . . " So
romantic, so lovely. Maybe you heard these words at your
own wedding. But the "holding" referred to is not an embrace. It refers to a transfer of ownership—and the property
in question was the bride.

In old England, when land was sold, the buyer and the
seller went to the parcel, the seller picked up a handful of
dirt and handed it to the buyer, uttering the words "to have
and to hold," etc.). The new owner literally held a piece of
the land to complete the transfer. Thus, the father (who
owned his daughter) walked her to the altar, and placed her
hand in the hand of the groom. When the "to have and to
hold" formula was recited, ownership of the woman was
legally passed from one male to the other. Father to husband. To have and to hold. The words were not meant to be
sentiment.

American married women were given the right to own
property in the mid-nineteenth century by "married wom-
en's acts" enacted in all states, but not without a struggle. Radical though they seemed at the time, these acts did
not establish a partnership model for marriage. Even today,

if you're a married woman in a common-law state, you can acquire property only by gift, inheritance, or your own earnings.

Your sister in a community-property state can, in addition, acquire property through the efforts and acquisitions of her husband. The common-law states generally assume that the fruits of the marriage belong to the one whose name they are in. Earnings, pensions, inheritances, investment income—the title determines the owner, and in most marriages, that owner is the husband. And when it comes to inheritance, as we'll see, the shadow of dower and curtesy are still very much with us. Of course, as you'll recall from chapter 1, when it comes to divorce, marital property is treated differently from the intact marriage, in that the equitable division imposed by the court is without respect to who owned what by title in most states.

Do you know what system your state uses? If you've moved around during your marriage, you may have property under both systems. Make a list showing what property was acquired when. For example, during your six years in community-property Texas you purchased a summer home entirely with community-property earnings, and you still own it. And during your eight years in common-law Oregon you purchased a long-term bond with common-law earnings, held in your husband's name—and you still own that, too. You'll need an expert to sort it out, but tracing your marital property to its common-law or community-property origins is a good way to begin the process.

WITH ALL MY WORLDLY GOODS
I THEE ENDOW

Nicely said, but the groom's promise was worded very carefully. Endow, not bestow. A bestowal is a gift, a transfer of property. An endowment is quite different. The endowed bride owns nothing. She gets the benefit of certain attributes of property—perhaps some of the income from investments, perhaps the right to live on certain property for life. The "dowager" of old was a propertyless widow, with the right to live on property which now belonged to her son or another male relative. Her dower rights extended to the *use* of part of the land. Nothing more.

The heritage of dower is very much with us. It is reflected in the inheritance laws of common-law states (about which more later). The result is that many widows in common-law states find that they would have been better off financially had they divorced. Under the law in many states, the widow is limited to her "forced share" of one-third of the marital estate, absent a will leaving her more, while a divorced wife can theoretically receive one-half or even more. At divorce (or annulment, which voids a marriage rather than dissolving it), most states divide the marital property according to what the court finds is "equitable"; in practice, the wife often receives less than half, but it can mean, under compelling circumstances, that she receives more than half. In addition, in most states and under certain circumstances, the divorced wife from a long marriage can receive alimony. A disinherited widow can receive only her forced share—and no support.

▶ ### What you own in a common-law state.

The problem in common-law states is that their laws have developed inconsistently. The married women's acts of the nineteenth century stripped the "unity" theory of its central thesis that there was only one legal person: the husband. With two legal identities in the marriage, the idea of a union was necessarily lost; the two people were no longer one. The wife could now be sued independently of her husband, or pursue a lawsuit in her own name. She could sign a contract; she could convey land; she could own whatever property she could manage to acquire, including her own earnings. The legislatures, however, failed to recognize that with the loss of the union, a de facto partnership arose. Not understanding that the central philosophy of the common-law marriage had been abolished, lawmakers enacted some laws on the unity model, and others which seemingly recognized a partnership. The common-law states are now a hodgepodge of inconsistent marital property theories, which recognize the modern notion of a partnership in spirit, yet contradict the principle in fact.

In a common-law state, earnings and property belong to the spouse who earned it, who acquired it by gift or inheritance, or whose name appears on it. Remember, we are speaking here of the rights of the wife in an intact marriage—your property rights upon divorce can be quite different.

In the common-law states, the management and control of the marital property or income is solely vested in the titleholder—more likely than not, the husband. Management and control is enormously important, as the story of Lorna and James at the beginning of the chapter illustrates.

If you live in a common-law jurisdiction, consider changing all your bank, brokerage, and other financial accounts, as well as deeds, to joint holdings. "Tenancy by the entirety," for example, is a form of joint ownership available to spouses in common-law states. Do not do this without expert advice; a divorce lawyer is best. Ask especially about the inheritance and tax consequences.

▶ *Community property.*
The competing theory, community property, comes to us from a different tradition. Although community-property states are few in number, nearly one-third of the U.S. population lives in them. Ancient Europeans devised the community-property system—the Visigoths brought it to Spain, which was responsible for its spread to the United States. Far from being a radical trend, community property is older than the English common-law system.

Although the community-property states differ in important particulars, the general theory is that the fruits of the marriage belong to both partners equally. This means that Margaret and Richard, she a housewife and he an engineer earning $48,000 per year, both own his salary equally. The house they bought with a down payment saved from Richard's pay and a mortgage paid out of his monthly salary, is owned equally by both Margaret and Richard, even if the deed is in his name alone. Title, in other words, does not determine ownership.

☑ **Even in community property states, it is useful to get title in both names because often institutions will deal only with the named owner.**

▶ *Who is in charge?*
How would Lorna and James (the car collector) fare under community-property laws? Could Lorna force James to lighten up on the car collection and provide better housing for the family? As with the common-law states, it all depends on who has the right to "manage and control" the community assets. In some states that right is given to the husband, in others the titleholder, and in yet others it is joint. As a practical matter then, during the marriage there is little real difference between common-law and community property states, as long as management and control are vested unequally.

☑ **If you live in a community-property state, don't assume that separate property remains separate no matter what. Lots of things, such as mingling of community and separate funds, gifts from one spouse to the other, and expenditures for necessities, "transmute" separate property into community property, and vice versa. You need a specialist to sort things out.**

California gives joint management and control to both spouses regardless of title; other states give it to the title-holder, a definite disadvantage for women since men have the greater opportunity to establish title in their own names. Without equal decision-making authority over their marital assets, the wife is a partner in name only. Business partners don't give up their shared authority without an express agreement. The law should permit marriage partners the same right to work out between themselves the allocation of decision-making.

☑ **If you live in a community-property state, learn which rule applies (see Appendix I on how to research the law, or call a divorce lawyer from the Yellow Pages— you may get a free answer, since the question is short). If you are in a common-law state, the titleholder most likely has management and control.**

▶ *Pay attention to your credit.*
Since 1975, the federal Equal Credit Opportunity Act forbids creditors from considering your marital status when you apply for a loan. Nor can they discount your income because you are a woman, or married. You have the right to build credit in your own name, whether you use your husband's surname or your birth name. If you receive alimony or child support consistently, the creditor must consider it as part of your income. You do not have to disclose support income if you do not wish to. Many states have credit rights acts which exceed the federal standards. Under the federal act you have the right to:

• Get credit in your name if you meet the creditor's standard.

• Use a cosigner other than your husband, if one is needed.

• Refuse to reveal your plans for having or raising children.

• Keep your accounts after marriage, divorce, or widowhood.

• Have welfare, pension, and support considered as income.

• Know the specific reason you were denied credit.

• Know what information the credit bureau has in your file.

• Have a credit record in your name for spousal joint accounts.

• Demand that incorrect information in your file be changed.

Make sure your name appears on all credit cards, charge accounts, notes, and loans, either alone or jointly with your husband. This way you and your husband will each build a credit history. If your husband has a bad credit history, you have the right to present evidence to the bureau that, despite him, you have the ability and willingness to pay. Do this right now. Look in the Yellow Pages under "credit bureaus" for your local credit-reporting companies, and ask each of them for a copy of your credit record (TRW and Equifax are two large national agencies). They will charge a small fee, unless you were turned down for credit in the last thirty days because of their report, in which case they must issue the report free. If you dispute any entries, you can state your side of the issue in writing, to be included in your file.

▶ *The limits of trust.*
A fiduciary is one who has the legal duty to act in someone else's best interests. A real estate agent, for example, must act in the interests of the principal (the seller or buyer), not his or her own. A trustee must act in the interests of the beneficiary, and a business partner must act in the interests of his or her partner. These are fiduciary relationships, and fiduciary duties are enforceable in court.

Take the CPA partnership of Clyde, Dorothy, and Clare, for example. If Dorothy, without telling her partners, used half the partnership funds to speculate in penny stocks, Clyde and Clare could sue Dorothy for breach of her fiduciary duty, and recover the funds from her personally. This would be true even though Dorothy had no intentions of private gain (that would be embezzlement, a crime). Assume Dorothy had great faith in the stocks, and meant to place every dime of the gain back in the partnership account. In other words, she acted in good faith—but good faith is not enough in a fiduciary relationship. Dorothy had a duty to inform her partners and get their consent before she acted.

Most states do not hold the marital partners to fiduciary standards. The marital partners are generally held to a much lower standard, such as the "good faith" standard which would have permitted Dorothy's misuse of the partnership funds. If Rod, for example, married to Elizabeth, squandered their marital funds at the racetrack, it is unclear whether Elizabeth would have a "good faith" claim against him. It would depend upon Rod's record at the track, and the reasonableness of his belief in his horse-picking skills, and the ability of the marital unit to sustain the loss. But if Elizabeth and Rod had a fiduciary relationship like business partners have, then Elizabeth would have a very strong claim. Of course, even if Rod were found by a court to have acted in bad faith, or to have breached his fiduciary duties, it could well be a hollow victory for Elizabeth. All she might get would be her lawyer's bill, Rod's lawyer's bill, and at most a settlement to her own account from the remaining marital assets, or separate assets if Rod has any.

Or take the situation of Bill and Kate. They own a gas station, where they both work full-time. Bill takes out an unsecured loan based on the good record of the business, despite Kate's vehement objections. He invests in a land deal that flops, and they lose the gas station. The shock is too much for Bill, who dies two months later of a heart attack. Kate is left with the debt. She has a legal responsibility to make the payments and retire the loan—a loan she never wanted and certainly didn't benefit from.

There would be concrete benefits to both marital partners if a fiduciary standard required they keep "open books" with respect to each other. Because in many marriages, the man is still the "keeper of accounts," millions of widows have floundered helplessly, either in the dark about what they own or, unable to handle things if they do know. An enforceable duty for both partners at least to inform themselves of the ongoing affairs of the marital partnership would also benefit the partnership while both partners are alive, because two informed and responsible minds are better than one. In most states, spouses have no right to knowledge of, control over, or access to assets held in the other's name during the marriage, other than their own separate property. The result for most women is crippling ignorance of the partnership assets and accounts.

Legal standards such as "good faith," "best interests," and "fiduciary" duties may seem like remote technicalities which have no relevance whatsoever to a smoothly and competently run marital unit. But they are like fire insurance—you want the protection even if you hope you never need it.

Some states, like California, give each spouse the right to an accounting. Upon request, either spouse must disclose to the other the condition of all accounts and assets. Even in the majority of states which don't compel an accounting, it's a good idea to ask for one anyway. Be informed. Even the most trustworthy husband can suddenly die.

▶ *If you can't marry.*

Not everyone is legally free to marry. Brothers and sisters can't; neither can persons of the same sex. A status conferred by law (such as marriage) which carries such well-documented economic benefits should be available to all who wish to accept its responsibilities of mutual support along with its benefits. Women, most of whom are destined to be single in their later years, would especially benefit if the legal status we know as marriage were available to everyone, regardless of sex or blood relationship. The sexual (or asexual) aspects of the relationship would be up to the couple, as they are now, de facto. Registered domestic partners, such as they have in Denmark, could inherit from each other, make next-of-kin medical decisions, be the automatic beneficiary on fringe benefits, and qualify for certain tax breaks (but be penalized by others), and would enjoy the favored status conferred by many statutes on relatives (such as wrongful death actions, child custody, and others). Midlife and older women, the documented losers in the marriage sweepstakes, should not be shut out of this valuable legal status through no fault of their own. But it will be years before registered domestic partnerships become the law of the land.

✔️ **Couples unmarried, by law or by choice, can secure some of the benefits automatically conferred upon the married by the intelligent use of contracts, trusts, powers of attorney, wills, and joint holdings. Contracts can define how property will be divided if the relationship ends, as well as who owns what; wills and trusts can overcome the law's preference for blood relatives as heirs; durable powers of attorney for health care (or in some states, living wills or natural death acts) can give the companion more authority than the next of kin in medical decision-making; and joint tenancies and tenancies-in-common (these are very different) can assist in estate planning (although they have tax consequences you must investigate). NOLO Press (see Appendix II) has many books which cover these areas, including some directed particularly to unmarried couples. A lawyer who works with the lesbian/gay community might be a good one to consult, since gays and lesbians frequently encounter such legal problems and have devised creative solutions.**

UNTIL DEATH US DO PART

This phrase is seriously meant. The wife's support rights end with her husband's last breath. Under common law, her dower rights generally permitted her the lifetime use of one-third of certain of her husband's lands—but, of course, she didn't own them. Nor was she entitled to live in the same way she had while married. She moved from the main quarters, now her eldest son's, to a secondary room, or even a cottage on the property referred to as the "dower" or "grace and favor" (rent-free) cottage. She took her meals with the family or in her room, but she no longer had the status to preside at table. She lived out her life as a kind of hanger-on—kindly honored in some families, tolerated or ignored in others—but in all cases with only her dower rights standing between herself and starvation.

Echoes of the dower are still with us in modern America. Eight common-law states still give the wife only a one-third share of the real property for her lifetime (her "forced share") if her husband leaves her less than that in his will. In those states, she has no right to a share of the personal property, including bank accounts, furnishings, cars, stocks, and bonds. In fourteen common-law states, the survivor gets one-third of the estate, including both personal property and real estate; two states give less than one-third; and the remainder give one-third to one-half, depending on the presence of living children.

Forced share works like this: If Butch wills all of his property to his girlfriend Annelisa, in many states his widow Amy can force the executor to hand over one-third of the marital assets. But if Butch wills 40 percent of the property to Amy, and 60 percent to Annelisa, Amy takes the 40 percent, even though the lion's share of what Amy and Butch worked for together goes to someone who did not participate in the marriage. Furthermore, on Butch's death, Amy receives no support money from the estate. Had she divorced Butch when she learned of Annelisa, Amy might have received more than 40 percent of the marital assets, and she might have received alimony for a period of time, even until Butch's death. As the last chapter discussed, Amy probably would not have fared well at the divorce. But the point remains that in most common-law states, the divorcing wife can theoretically receive half or more of the marital assets plus alimony, while the widow has a claim on just one-third, with no support, unless her husband chooses to will her more. While most states use an "equitable distribution" concept for dividing the marital property at divorce, no state has adopted such a concept for marriages dissolved by death.

The viciousness of common-law marital property is never more evident than at the death of the husband. Studies have shown that about 15 percent of husbands leave their wives less than their forced share, thus activating the forced-share statutes. Since most wills are drawn by lawyers, it can be assumed that one reason many wills leave at least the forced share is because the drafter knows it is futile to leave less. Without the forced-share statute, the percentage of disinherited wives would no doubt be even higher.

In community-property states, because the wife *owns* half of the assets of the marriage regardless of title, she will retain her one-half share no matter how her husband chooses to will his half. Here's how forced share and community property work:

Dave and Roxie, residents of a common-law state, celebrated their fiftieth wedding anniversary three months before his sudden death. All their property was in his name, except for a $20,000 note Roxie inherited from her mother. In his will, Dave left Roxie a $5,000 savings account, and they were joint tenants on a $3,000 bond. Dave expressly disinherited Roxie from the rest of his estate, which included their $150,000 home, and $30,000 in savings, for a total of $185,000. Under forced-share laws in a typical state, Roxie keeps her $20,000 note, and in most states takes a forced share of one-third of the remaining assets. Some states would deduct from the forced share the $5,000 bequest from Dave, as well as the $3,000 joint-tenancy bond, and $1,000 for the necklace Dave gave Roxie on their anniversary, so Roxie's total share would be about $53,000. In other words, the forced share is something of a welfare scheme. The wife does not own the property under common-law theories, but, to keep her from being a burden on taxpayers, the state enacts forced-share statutes which keep her widow's mite at a minimum.

In a community-property state, Roxie would keep her $20,000 note (as her separate property), her half of the community property ($92,500), plus her necklace, the joint tenancy bond, and the $5,000 bequest from Dave's half of the community property, for a total of $101,500. In short, the widow Roxie is twice as well off in a community-property state.

☑ **Inter vivos, or "living," trusts are popular will substitutes. They avoid probate, with its high fees and tedious procedures. Used intelligently, they are much better than wills for many people, especially for those with large estates. Unfortunately, they have also been used to keep the widow from outright ownership of assets. If the family lawyer, bank, or a trusted relative is named trustee with the duty to pay interest to the widow, she is separated from her assets. If she chooses to indulge herself in her life's dream—perhaps an expensive cruise—the trustee may well not release the funds to her. Far better that she be named the trustee (she can still be the beneficiary) so that some control remains in her hands.**

The forced share has been criticized by some commentators because it can produce a windfall: Aldo and Bonnie were married only two months when he died. It was a second marriage for both of them; each had two grown children from earlier marriages. Aldo's will left Bonnie a $10,000 certificate of deposit from his total estate of $500,000. Bonnie had $400,000 from her first husband's estate. They lived in a common-law state, so Bonnie claimed $166,000 as her one-third forced share, less her $10,000 bequest. Since they had been married only two months, the $166,000 far exceeded the funds acquired during the short marriage, and Aldo's children were deprived of the funds Aldo meant for them.

Had Aldo and Bonnie lived in a community-property state, Bonnie would have received the $10,000 bequest, plus very little else (remember, property acquired before the marriage is separate property). If their income during their short marriage came from his pension, her Social Security, and interest from their separate holdings, then there was no community property to divide. In other words, the one-half share in a community property state can come out to less than the one-third forced share in a short marriage. Nevertheless, the one-half is a fairer distribution, and a more dignified one: unlike the forced share, it confirms to the wife her ownership rights to an equal share of the fruits of the marriage. Like a business partnership, if the efforts of the partners failed to yield a return, then there is nothing to divide. The forced share model, when it results in a windfall, reinforces the notion that if a woman "catches" a husband her future is insured—rather than the notion that the partners together build their economic future, and gain or lose accordingly.

Invite a probate lawyer to address your club or group of friends. The lawyer should be pleased to come for free in exchange for the exposure. Say you are especially interested in learning about your inheritance rights as wives, and the state's forced-share or community-property system.

Of course, not all husbands die first. If the wife wants to leave something in her will for her favorite charity, or she wants to leave something for the grandchildren, she cannot do so in a common-law state unless she has acquired title to some property. In a community-property state, she can will her one-half share to whomever she pleases. Art and CeCe, residents of a community-property state, owned $175,000 in community assets, held all in Art's name, and acquired entirely from his earnings. CeCe had volunteered for fifteen years at the local YWCA, and wished to leave it something to convert a storeroom into a playroom. In her will, she left $50,000 to the Y, and the rest to Art. CeCe could have left the Y $87,500 as her one-half share had she wanted to, and Art would have had to liquidate the community property held in his name to fulfill the bequest.

But if Art and CeCe had lived in a common-law state, CeCe could not have left anything to the Y. You can't will what you don't own. The common-law property states say that the owner of property is the one whose name is on it, and that only that person can dispose of it by will.

Brian and Kathleen lived in a common-law state for all the forty-five years of their marriage. Neither of them had any money before they were married, nor did either of them acquire anything during their marriage besides their own earnings. All their marital property was in Brian's name. Both worked, and their earnings went into their $112,000 home and a brokerage account worth $75,000. Kathleen willed all of her property to Brian, except for "her" one-half share of the brokerage account, which she willed to a favorite niece. The niece gets nothing, because Kathleen can't will what she doesn't own. Since her name was not on "their" property, she could not dispose of it by will. It was not hers.

✔️ **If possible, familiarize yourself with your husband's will, and let him see yours. Think through all the provisions of both wills against various scenarios, such as simultaneous deaths, one spouse preceding the other in death, children and other beneficiaries dying first, and consequences of second families. If his will confers a trust on you instead of outright ownership, be sure you think this through and agree with the reasons. A trust may limit you to the income from the assets—not much protection against inflation. Lawyers sometimes routinely recommend trusts for the wife on the theory she cannot handle the assets herself. This is arrant sexism, and bad financial planning as well.**

▶ *When your husband dies without a will.*

Forced-share rights exist only when the husband or wife has written a will that leaves the survivor with less than his or her statutory (forced) share. But two out of every three Americans die without any will at all. What happens to the surviving spouse?

When there is no will, the intestate laws of the state take over. In general, in both community-property and common-law states, the property is distributed to spouses, children, parents, siblings, in that order; then nieces, nephews, and remote relatives. If there are no relatives at all, the property escheats to the state—that is, the taxpayers get it. In a community-property state, the widow(er)'s intestate share can be all of her husband's community property, plus all or a share of his separate property.

Carl and Elva have lived in California for all thirty-five years of their married life. They hold $360,000 in community property, and Carl has separate property of $50,000 which he inherited from his mother. They have two grown children, four grandchildren, and each has two sisters. Carl dies without a will. Elva keeps her half of the community property, of course, plus Carl's half, plus one-third of Carl's separate property. The remaining two-thirds is divided equally between the two children. The other relatives get nothing. Elva, in other words, ends up with nearly $377,000 if Carl dies without a will. Had Carl willed all his property to his sister, Elva would have been left with her one-half share of the community property ($180,000), and nothing from the separate property.

In common-law states, the intestate share of the surviving spouse differs widely. In some, the separate property of the wife is deducted from her intestate share. In others, she gets use of the property for life, then it goes to their children. In general, the intestate share will depend upon the existence of children (including those from a prior marriage), parents, and, in some cases, remote kin. Sometimes, if the second wife is childless, she gets only a life estate—on her death it reverts to his children from his first marriage. In all states, if the spouse is the only surviving relative, she will receive 100 percent of the estate.

☑ **You *must* urge your husband to write a will or a trust. Under either the forced-share or community-property systems you have nothing to lose and everything to gain. Even 40-year-olds die unexpectedly. Don't delay. It needn't be expensive; you can even do it yourself, with the proper guidance. NOLO Press has several will- and estate-planning books and software programs, good in any state (see Appendix II).**

Many inheritance laws contain a hidden trap for wives. They require that each spouse must survive the other by 120 hours (five days) in order to be eligible to receive the intestate share. On the surface, this seems fine. If you're dead before five days, who needs an inheritance? Let's look at Suzanne and Wayne. They were married in a common-law state at age 45. Each had children from former marriages, and neither had any money when they married. For fifteen years they both worked full-time in their small antiques business. Everything they earned or acquired was held in Wayne's name, and it amounted to $100,000. They were too busy to make wills. When they were 60, they were in an auto accident. Wayne was killed instantly; Suzanne died three days later. Because the property was held in Wayne's name, it went to his children. Suzanne's children got nothing, despite her equal efforts in the business. If Suzanne had lived another three days, she would have inherited at least $50,000, which would have gone to her children upon her death. Because marital property is more likely to be held in the husband's name, this common provision has an unfavorable impact on wives—especially those with children from a former marriage or a parent or sibling whom they would like their estate to go to.

☑ **People in second marriages need special advice if they have children from the earlier marriage. Your divorce lawyer may not be the best person to draw up an** estate plan that will protect all interests. See a probate attorney, or one expert in elder law.

▶ *Why Congress is not a wife's best friend.*
Traditionally, marital property has been the business of the states. But the states' historic monopoly has recently been invaded by federal legislation, generally not with happy results. While the attention of marital property reformers has been focused on state legislatures, new federal laws have significantly undermined the marital property rights enjoyed by residents of community-property states. And in weakening the community-property laws, the federal acts and regulations pose a threat to marital property reform efforts generally.

The community-property concept is not generally understood outside the subscribing states, so Congress members have not adhered to notions of equality when drafting laws which affect marital property. These federal laws have conflicted with the more progressive community-property concept, and there have been numerous legal battles over whether or not the federal law preempts the state marital property laws. These conflicts have presented themselves in the context of Social Security and Medicaid laws, and the Employees' Retirement Income Security Act (ERISA). They have profoundly affected the economic interests of millions of midlife women.

For example, although ERISA permits the pension to be divided if a qualified divorce decree orders it split, nothing in ERISA states that the pension must be divided upon divorce, nor does ERISA declare that the pension is the joint or community property of both spouses even in an intact marriage. Community-property states declare that it is, but this is of little practical value without equal management and control of the pension. ERISA is not the only deficient pension law in this respect; the federal, state, and local public pensions also vest management and control in the hands of the wage-earner, even if the marital property law of the state decrees equal ownership.

Sam and Laura, both architects, are in their late forties. Sam has a good pension plan from his job as an urban planner with the state. Laura has only Social Security from her job with a local developer. They live in a community-property state, so they have equal ownership rights in the pension. Sam leaves his job at age 49, and decides to withdraw his contributions to the fund, rather than wait until he can draw a monthly benefit at age 55. Laura objects bitterly. Sam invests the funds in speculative stocks, losing almost all the retirement money. Although theoretically the owner of half the pension, Laura had no management and control rights over the state pension plan. She was unable to stop Sam's withdrawal, and her retirement income went down the drain along with his.

ERISA governs private pensions across the country. In addition to Social Security, federal government pensions such as Railroad Retirement, foreign service, civil service, and military pensions have all at one time or another been declared off-limits to community-property laws. The right to divide the pension upon divorce is a substantial right, but it does not confer equal ownership of the asset to both spouses in an intact marriage, nor does community-property ownership result in equal management and control.

To backwards federal policymakers, "management and control," and the discredited "title theory" (the owner is the title holder) of marital property ownership are very much alive, and both fly in the face of progressive trends in the states. The lack of sophistication of federal authorities when it comes to marital property rights probably derives from their lack of experience with domestic relations laws generally, and is a subject of increasing concern as deficient federal laws continue to preempt state marital property laws.

CONCLUSION

Our legal concept of marriage must adjust to meet the changes that have already taken place in our population. Just as the married women's acts of the nineteenth century recognized that women were no longer propertyless chattel, we in the twentieth century must abandon a legal status that no longer fits most of us. Married women and men must benefit equally from marriage; that goes without saying. Laws must be changed to accomplish that. State domestic relations laws, uniform laws, and federal laws must be scrutinized for the gender bias now rampant. Even community-property statutes need reform. Equal ownership, equal management and control, and equal benefit from all the acquisitions of a marriage due to the earnings, skill, or effort of either spouse can only benefit all of society, as this enormously successful economic unit we call marriage is strengthened and enriched.

CHECKLIST FOR WIVES

It's depressing discovering you have problems you never knew you had, but some marital property inequities can be cured by taking appropriate steps, like writing a will or creating a trust, taking care to establish credit, or securing joint title. Use this list as a reminder of what you need to do.

✔ Do you live in a community property or common-law state?

✔ What about all the states you've lived in since marriage?

✔ What will you get if your husband dies without a will?

✔ What will you get if he leaves everything to someone else?

✔ Whose name is on your house deed? Other real property?

✔ Whose name is on your accounts (bank, brokerage, etc.)?

✔ Have you confirmed the beneficiary on all insurance policies?

✔ Do you and your husband have wills or trusts?

✔ Do you review them at least annually?

✔ Have you read and understood your husband's will or trust?

✔ Have you urged him to get a will or trust if he hasn't yet?

✔ Do you and your spouse share all financial information?

✔ Do you understand each other's pension rights?

✔ What will your children from your former marriage inherit?

✔ Have you checked *your* credit rating with a credit bureau?

✔ Do you have your husband's Social Security number?

3

SEX, AGE,
AND YOUR JOB

Working women have problems that go beyond unequal pay for equal work. Even if equal pay were a fact for
every job in the land, women would still trail men, because
of family roles, sex-segregated occupations, and outright
discrimination.

But, of course, equal pay in America is not a fact. And lest
you think you are exempt from its effects because of your
high-level career, think again. The gap between men's pay
and women's widens as you go up the pay scale. Female
laborers are paid about 78 cents for every dollar paid men in
the same jobs. But women lawyers and judges earn only 71
percent of what their male counterparts do, and female managers only 61 percent. Ever was it thus, it seems. In Moses'
time, women's wages were 60 percent of men's (check it
out—Leviticus 27:1-4) and in the thousands of years since
then we've only managed to raise that to 68 percent.

Our aim in this chapter is to acquaint you with circumstances that point to illegal sex or age discrimination, and
what to do about them. We'll discuss sexual harassment,
forced retirement, sex-segregated occupations, the role of
unions, class actions, and ways to redress your grievance,
even if the federal discrimination laws seem not to apply.
Along the way we'll describe the laws, the enforcement
agencies, what attorneys can (and can't) do for you, and
illustrate the points with horrible little scenarios that too
many of you, I'm afraid, could top from your own experi-
ences. In this chapter we assume you already have a job.

Re-entering the job market, the special employment problems of homemakers, and part-time and self-employment are discussed in the next chapter.

To get started, let's look at what happened to Cecilia. This is a true story; it happened to a friend of mine. Cecilia (not her real name, of course) was a mid-level manager for one of the world's largest banks for eight years. As she got older, she began to notice signs that her career star was falling. One morning she was greeted by her boss, who said, "This is not going to be a good day for you." As her heart plummeted, she was told that her job had been eliminated, and she was being "redeployed."

Redeployed, it turns out, was just a fancy way of saying she was fired. A "redeployed" employee gets two weeks in which to find another job with the bank, in competition with all other applicants. If none is found, the employee is out on her ear. Cecilia, too stunned to say anything, was silent. Her boss then said someone was waiting to talk to her in the conference room. The someone was from personnel. She was kind, but straightforward. She took Cecilia's keys, business credit cards, employee ID, and parking-lot pass. Still reeling, and feeling very much set up, Cecilia was offered the opportunity to sign a waiver of all her rights under all employment discrimination laws, state and federal. The carrot for signing the waiver was an $8,000 "redeployment bonus" (in other words, they were offering to buy her right to sue for $8,000, but weren't so crass as to put it quite that way). The bonus offer was only good for seven days.

Cecilia's boss stayed with her while she cleaned out her office of eight years' accumulation of personal items. She was not given the courtesy of even a few minutes alone to compose herself. It was clear that he was there not to console her, but to make sure she didn't steal anything, or sabotage expensive equipment. The insult behind this by-the-book procedure was devastating to Cecilia. Her boss then escorted her down the elevator and out the front door, assuring that she could not say goodbye to colleagues of many years. In her presence, the doorman was informed that she no longer worked there, so no longer had access to the building. Cecilia's humiliation was complete.

The bank was slick. They had cornered Cecilia when she first came to the office and kept her either sequestered or escorted until she was out of the building. This way she couldn't elicit the sympathy or support of longtime work companions, thus harming morale or germinating discontent, which could blossom into a genuine grievance. The bank presented a waiver of all her discrimination rights which had to be signed (or lost) within a period of time so short that she would almost surely have to make the decision while in a state of panic, and without legal counsel. It would also be before she could possibly find a new job, and the offer of $8,000 would be extremely hard to turn down when faced with the possibility of months of unemployment. The bank could also claim they hadn't fired Cecilia: she had been "redeployed." If she failed to get another job with the bank, well, what could they say?

Cecilia wasted no time. She called employment law attorneys until she found one who could see her immediately. The attorney said she should be prepared to spend up to $40,000 if a sex- or age-discrimination case were to go to full trial. Cecilia negotiated, and finally hired the attorney to evaluate her case for $300. But in the end, she signed the waiver without full legal advice, because she couldn't risk facing unemployment without the $8,000 to live on.

Whatever your rung on the career ladder, chances are excellent that, before you retire, you too will suffer discrimination. At first it may be because you are a woman, but shockingly soon age will enter into it. Even a 28-year-old may be over the hill for "image" jobs such as cocktail waitress, receptionist, teller, and model.

JOB DISCRIMINATION IS A FEDERAL OFFENSE

When Congress was debating the Civil Rights Act in the early 1960s, one senator who opposed the racial equality sections of the bill thought he could kill it by amending it to prohibit sex discrimination. He figured that by adding sex, his fellow senators would vote the whole bill down as ludicrous.

And the rest, as they say, is history. A few years later, Congress passed the Age Discrimination in Employment Act (ADEA) prohibiting employment discrimination against people over 40. Since then the 1964 Civil Rights Act (we'll call it Title VII, because that's the section that addresses employment discrimination) and the ADEA have been the principal federal acts addressing job discrimination.

Title VII covers only workers in companies with fifteen or more employees, and the ADEA requires twenty— a major weakness for women, who constitute the majority of small-business employees. However, many state fair-employment statutes cover smaller businesses. There are other ways to make claims against your employer, so don't fail to check yours out with a qualified employment-law attorney, even for a business with only one employee. Your state or local fair-employment practices office can tell you if your employer is covered by state or local acts.

▶ *Why the ADEA doesn't fit women.*
The problem with the ADEA is that it does not protect workers under age 40, and women suffer age discrimination at much earlier ages than do men. The ADEA is about one decade out of step for women. Women in their thirties (and even earlier for some occupations) are frequently discriminated against because of age, but have no recourse to the law because they are too young. Sometimes age discrimination against women under 40 can be turned into a Title VII sex-discrimination case. For example, it was open speculation that Jane Pauley was shunted aside by her network for being too old at 39. Her co-anchor, Bryant Gumbel, was not too old at 41. If a woman is too old for her job at 39 but a man is not, then that is sex discrimination, redressable

under Title VII. Nevertheless, having to make a sex discrimination case out of something that is essentially age discrimination is a clumsy and unsatisfactory remedy for young "older" women. The ADEA should be amended to cover anyone discriminated against on the basis of age. Period.

☑ **Don't conclude that there is no chance for you because you are under 40. Some state discrimination statutes extend to younger years, and some policies and regulations for government jobs do the same. In addition, there are other statutes and laws which could protect you on other grounds. You need expert advice.**

Age and sex discrimination take many forms. Sometimes the victim is unaware it is happening; at other times, all too aware. Indeed, in many cases, even employers are unaware that their hiring practices or promotional policies foster illegal discrimination. Recognizing the illegal practice is the first step, so here are some of the ways illegal discrimination occurs:

▶ *The smoking gun.*
Of course, this is the easiest way. Perhaps your personnel record includes a memo—like one in an actual case decided by the U.S. Supreme Court—that suggests you "walk more femininely, talk more femininely, dress more femininely, wear makeup, have your hair styled, and wear jewelry." Television newswoman Christine Craft was told (in her thirties) that she was "too old, too ugly, and not deferential enough to men." (The experience, I'm happy to say, put Craft in law school.) Such outright discrimination is harder to find these days, as personnel officers become more sophisticated about what goes into the files.

☑ **Maybe you don't have access to your personnel file. Don't worry. Your lawyer, or the equal employment agency can get it, even if you can't.**

▶ *Indirect discrimination.*
Some application processes and promotion requirements inherently discriminate against groups protected by Title VII and the ADEA. For example, height requirements for firefighter and police jobs may have an unfavorable impact on women, as well as Asian and Hispanic males. Unless the departments can prove that height is a "bona fide occupational qualification," or a "business necessity," the requirement may be struck down as transgressing Title VII.

☑ **Both the ADEA and Title VII are supported by regulations, as are many state anti-discrimination statutes. Federal regulations are found in the Code of Federal Regulations (C.F.R.). You can find the C.F.R. in most law libraries (see Appendix I). The regulations are much more detailed than the statutes, and give examples of prohibited and permitted practices.**

Sometimes experience requirements have an unfavorable impact on women (lawyers call this "disparate impact"). Martha, for example, wanted to be a truck driver, but found that all employers required at least two years' experience. Far fewer women than men can show two years' experience driving trucks, so the court asked the employers to devise other ways to judge applicants' driving abilities that would not prove such a barrier to women. Experience barriers are particularly tough for women because so many of us have a checkered job record due to family responsibilities, following transferred husbands, and leaving dead-end jobs. Thus, most women hold many more low-experience jobs than men.

Vicki, a deputy sheriff, wanted to qualify for sergeant, but the position required four years as deputy. She was able to prove in court that 93 percent of male deputies, but only 50 percent of female deputies, could satisfy the four-year requirement, so the court ordered the department to find a way to equalize the applicant pool.

Just as the experience factor can shut out female jobseekers in traditionally male occupations (Title VII), the "inexperience factor" can have the same effect on older applicants (ADEA). Seeley, for example, had taught in one school district for twenty years. She moved, and applied to the new district, which said it only hired teachers with less than five years' experience, because it didn't want to pay the union scale for twenty-year teachers. This kind of discrimination against experienced teachers persists, despite rulings that it violates the age statutes because of its disparate impact on older teachers. Experience caps are why want ads which seek applicants with "up to two years' experience" may signal illegal age discrimination.

Robin was a victim of a seemingly gender-neutral practice which in fact discriminated against women. She was hired for a job loading pallets in a wholesale distribution center. New hires were given up to thirty days to establish their ability to load 150 pallets per hour. Robin was fired on the thirtieth day with an average of 140 pallets per hour. The company rehired her when her attorney proved that their standard for veteran pallet loaders was only 120 pallets per hour. The hiring policy discriminated against women because it required an entry-level challenge that well exceeded the actual working requirement. This practice is not prohibited in itself, but if it works against a protected class under Title VII, then it may be. Because women are, in general, less muscled than men, the requirement had a disparate impact on women applicants. And because the challenged standard was not required of veteran pallet loaders (in legalese, not a "bona fide occupational requirement") the hiring practice offended Title VII.

▶ *Code words.*

The 25-year-old woman composed her features, and carefully used the light to her best advantage.

"I'm sorry," said the modeling director, "but you're a little more sophisticated than what we were looking for."

Sophisticated. Another code word for "too old." Like the all-too-familiar "overqualified," it signals to every woman who hears it that her options are narrowing. For the elderly model, it means the end of a career. In the next chapter we discuss code words in want ads and employment agency referrals and what you can do about them. For now just realize that euphemisms or diplomacy that mask real discrimination are prohibited by the ADEA and Title VII.

▶ *Younger older women vs. older older women.*
What if a 55-year-old receptionist was replaced by a 41-year-old, and the older woman suspected age discrimination? Wouldn't this be okay, since the 41-year-old is also over 40? No. If age was a significant factor in the decision, then the decision was illegal, no matter how old the parties. In fact, if a 48-year-old man replaces a 42-year-old woman because 42 is too old for a woman but 48 is just right for a man, age discrimination has taken place, even though the older of the two got the job. For age discrimination, disparate-impact situations might include application or promotional tests of physical prowess that don't relate to the job's functions, and even, under some circumstances, training programs that emphasize classroom methods and testing skills, which disadvantage applicants who last saw a classroom twenty years ago.

This doesn't mean that experience, fitness, or size requirements are out the window. Still, the "patterns and practices" may be less obvious than a smoking gun, but just as illegal and just as redressable under the law. Learn to think through the hurdles standing between you and your dream job. Would women as a class have a tougher time qualifying because of the hurdle than men? How about people over 40? You may find discriminatory practices which can be remedied by simply bringing them to the attention of your boss.

Age and sex discrimination can take very subtle forms, and you should go to an experienced employment-law attorney to sort things out. The attorney can also help you form realistic expectations, because the U.S. Supreme Court has recently handed down some decisions which strongly favor employers in these kinds of lawsuits, and Congress has reacted with a number of bills.

The Equal Employment Opportunity Commission (EEOC) is the federal agency that enforces Title VII and the ADEA. Your local branch office is the first place to go if you suspect job discrimination. Look for it in the U.S. Government section of your phonebook, or call the EEOC headquarters in Washington, D.C. You can also file a complaint with your state's fair employment office.

Whichever agency you choose will coordinate your claim with the other. The EEOC or state agency will first try to mediate your dispute. If unsuccessful, they may (rarely) pursue it in court, or (more likely) close your file so you can pursue it in court on your own. You aren't required to have a lawyer during the agency process, but it's good to have one to keep the agency on the job and to help plan strategies. Try to get at least a legal consultation before you go it alone with the agency.

Sexual harassment.

Anytime your job is made more difficult because of the unwelcome or intrusive sexual behavior of your colleagues, you should think of Title VII. If your supervisor keeps asking you for a date despite repeated firm refusals, this can be illegal harassment even if he doesn't "harass" you in the popular sense of the word. If he persists after you've made clear that the advances are not welcome, get serious and complain to the EEOC. Their initial contact with him may be all that's necessary—and it will cost you nothing. Of course, obvious sexual harassment—such as unwelcome touching, suggestive comments, insulting references to women, or insinuating that sexual favors foster advancement—is also prohibited on the theory that it is more difficult for you to do the same job than the man working next to you because of the added burden of having to cope with unwanted sexual advances or innuendo.

▶ *Retaliation.*

If you need your fellow workers to help you prove your case, you may find them unwilling, out of fear of reprisals, however subtle. Retaliation against you, or anyone else who helps you secure your civil rights, is prohibited by both Title VII and the ADEA. If your colleagues agree to talk to the EEOC, or testify, or otherwise give evidence to support your claim, your employer may not retaliate against them in any way. A retaliation complaint can succeed even if the main claim fails.

Megan claimed age discrimination against her employer, Blue Sky School. The EEOC investigated, then notified her that they found no discrimination. In the meantime, Megan had quit her job and was making the rounds of employment agencies. When one agency called the school for a reference, the principal said she was competent for the position she had held. The agency asked if he would rehire her. He said no, because she had sued the school. Megan went back to the EEOC, filed a retaliation suit, and settled with the school for $1,000 damages. The principal, by admitting Megan was competent, but declining to reconsider her only because of her discrimination claim, had committed an actionable retaliation offense, even though cleared of the original discrimination charge.

▶ *Performance evaluations.*

Let's say that for years you've received rave reviews at evaluation time. Your supervisors have filled your file with glowing comments on your integrity, reliability, initiative, and competence. But suddenly things change. Your boss now calls you "minimally acceptable," or even "mediocre," "substandard," or "poor." If you know your work has not slipped and you've kept up with your colleagues in every way, maybe a little paranoia is in order. When an employer is sued for job discrimination, a personnel file filled with negative reports may be its best defense. It's entirely possible you're being targeted for a future negative job action. Even if not, it's obvious that poor evaluations will block promotional opportunities, raises, bonuses, and even good references if you apply for another job. You need to take a downward trend in evaluations seriously.

 If you feel illegal discrimination is the reason, or even part of the reason, for poor evaluations, a complaint to the EEOC or comparable state agency is in order.

▶ *Skills training.*
Some companies think that it is not cost-effective to train older workers because of impending retirement. Nevertheless, the ADEA demands that all persons, regardless of age, be entitled to company training programs that update or improve skills. Without this provision, older employees would be unable to compete with younger ones.

▶ *Retirement discrimination.*
Lynn worked thirty-two years for her company. She received steady promotions and excellent evaluations until she was 57. Then her upward path was mysteriously, but decisively blocked. She was moved from her corner office to a windowless, inside cubicle. Her important duties were reassigned. Soon she was left with little more than her title and a phone. She was left out of meetings, and soon the picture was crystal clear. No one said so, but they wanted her to resign. An employment-law attorney told her that she was probably a victim of illegal "pension" discrimination. In order to avoid paying her a pension based on the top salary, the company would prefer she'd move on. Nothing personal, you understand. Just business economics. Lynn was able to prove a pattern of such behavior, and she recovered damages.

 Look into your fringe benefits for hidden age or sex discrimination, especially when you are applying for jobs. If you find discrimination, check it out with the EEOC or buy a half-hour of an employment-law attorney's time. If it's legal, at least you know what's coming, and have a chance to prepare.

▶ *Mandatory retirement.*

Except in a few occupations, mandatory retirement at a set age is a thing of the past. No longer can they force you out at 65 or 70, or even 80. Of course, if you become unable to perform your duties, you can be removed for those reasons, but not because you have reached a certain birthday. This is a fortunate development for women, because so many spend their later years in the paid labor force, having raised their kids or having found themselves alone and poor.

But the end of mandatory retirement does not mean that employees are never coerced into retiring. If the company, in an effort to reduce its workforce without layoffs, offers generous retirement bonuses to induce eligible employees to move out, has the ADEA been transgressed? Probably not, at least if the company is careful that it merely offers the opportunity without leaning on you to accept it. But the line is a fine one.

▶ *Class actions.*

Title VII and ADEA complaints can be pursued by individuals, or by groups. Group suits, or "class actions," are usually the ones you read about with blockbuster awards. If an individual's damages are $18,000 in back pay, and there are 100 such individuals, the zeros in the damage award add up. This is another reason to buy a half-hour or so of an experienced employment-law attorney's time before you decide your problem isn't big enough to pursue on its own. Attorneys have a way of making a class action out of a situation you thought was only your problem.

The rules for ADEA class actions are different than those for Title VII. Under the ADEA, all members of the class must consent to their inclusion, often making for smaller classes—and smaller damages—than under Title VII. In Title VII class actions, you don't need to identify the other members of your class. If you were a job applicant, a class can be made out of all applicants "similarly situated" without anyone ever knowing precisely who these individuals are or exactly how many there are. The court and the attorneys work out a reasonable estimate based on population patterns and past hiring records. Under the ADEA, you're out of luck if you can't locate them and entice them to sign onto the suit. If your grievance is shared by your fellow employees, you have the considerable burden of persuading them to risk your employer's displeasure by signing onto a class action which may or may not succeed. Despite the law against retaliation, it's bound to be a tough sell. Still, whatever bad thing happened to you probably happened to someone else, too, so class actions should always be a consideration under either act.

Mary Liz, 44, had worked for Allgood Widget Company for twenty years as a technical editor. Soon after Allgood was bought by a larger company, Mary Liz and the nine other technical editors were demoted to the position of copy editor. All were women who had worked for Allgood for many years, and all were over 40. They were replaced by ten men, all under 30. Allgood said it was because the company was going into computer manufacturing, and the new technical editors knew more about computers. Mary Liz and one other victim, Sylvia, went to the EEOC and complained. As is so often the case with that understaffed agency, their cases were closed after mediation failed.

Mary Liz and Sylvia then went to different attorneys. Mary Liz's attorney looked at her case as one of age discrimination, and said it wasn't worth pursuing unless she could make it a class action. That was because the damages suffered by Mary Liz alone amounted to her pay differential—less than $7,000—and it would cost at least that much to bring it to trial. None of the remaining editors was willing to sign on to the ADEA class, because they were afraid they would be retaliated against in ways they could never prove in a complaint. Mary Liz, therefore, did not pursue her claim, because the potential damages under the ADEA for a single plaintiff were just not enough to make a lawsuit economically sound.

Sylvia, on the other hand, got an attorney who saw the case as a Title VII sex-discrimination action. That attorney, too, told Sylvia that her complaint was too small by itself.

However, she filed a class action alleging $7,000 damages for each of the ten demoted editors, for a total of $70,000. Since the editors could remain in the suit without being named or making an affirmative consent, the class remained at ten. This large "pot" made it possible for the attorney to take it on a contingency-fee of one-third of the final damages.

The difference between Mary Liz's claim and Sylvia's was the difference between the two statutes' class-action rules, and the differences between the way their attorneys saw their cases as age or sex discrimination.

☑ **Always discuss the possibility of a class action with your attorney. If you were an applicant, perhaps a pattern of discrimination against all women applicants can be uncovered, resulting in a nice class action with scores of plaintiffs. This has magical effects on the total damages, and makes attorneys much more interested in taking the case on contingency, which means you don't have to pay hourly fees or high retainers. If you lose, you'll owe the attorney nothing, except perhaps the costs of suit such as filing fees, deposition costs, and so forth.**

There are times when you might not want to be part of a class action. Nola was close to settling her individual claim against Smokeball, Inc. for discriminating against female clerks in promotions to supervisor. She learned of a class action on the same complaint initiated by twelve of her fellow clerks. Nola preferred to remain out of the class, because her $15,000 individual settlement would be more than her share of the class damages.

☑ **To opt out of a Title VII class action, you must notify the attorney representing the class in writing, and within the time period allowed by law. Don't fiddle around making up your mind, or you may find yourself in a situation you can't get out of. Because you have to** sign onto an **ADEA class action, opting out is not an issue.**

▶ *The age/sex nexus.*
Women over 40 have both Title VII and the ADEA to protect them, while white males, at least, have only the ADEA. The double protection sounds too good to be true—and in many ways, it is.

Ironically, the ADEA and Title VII work against each other for many midlife women. One reason is that attorneys tend to specialize in either Title VII or the ADEA but not both. If a 45-year-old woman shows up with a complaint, the Title VII attorney may see it as sex discrimination, and proceed accordingly. The ADEA attorney would see the age elements, and develop age theories. In fact, an attorney experienced in both statutes might easily see the advantages of one over the other, and choose to ignore or minimize the weaker claim. Many women over 40 end up pursuing an unsound claim because of biased professional advice. This is less likely to be a problem in firms which specialize in employment law generally.

☑ **If you're over 40, always ask your attorney or EEOC counselor about their qualifications in both Title VII and the ADEA. Make every effort to find advisors experienced in both—and preferably state statutory, tort, and contract claims as well. The local trial whiz kid with no employment-law experience may do you more harm than good if he or she can't analyze your situation against a variety of complex laws and come up with the strongest one to press forward with.**

Many midlife and older women are discriminated against because they are *both* older and female. Younger women would be acceptable for the position, as would midlife men. This age-sex nexus has proven very difficult for midlife women.

▶ *Never ignore technicalities.*

The ADEA is very different from Title VII in several important procedural ways. The statutes of limitation are not the same for the two statutes, and rights to a jury and damages differ. This is why you must, as soon as you suspect a problem, talk to one of the agencies or an experienced attorney. A significant number of claims fail for technical, procedural reasons alone.

 Title VII and the ADEA cover not only private employers, but federal, state, and local government jobs as well. The EEOC may not handle some government complaints but a phone call to them will tell you where to go.

▶ *Foreign employers.*

The EEOC has investigated complaints against Japanese and other foreign employers for blatant employment discrimination based on race, sex, age, and national origin. Cultural differences make this almost inevitable (although not excusable), at least until the foreign employer gains experience with the American work force and our laws. If you are working for a foreign employer in the United States, American laws protect you as much as they do anyone else. You have every right to pursue your claim in the EEOC, your state agency, and eventually in American courts.

BEYOND FEDERAL LAWS

▶ *State fair-employment statutes.*

Sometimes the federal laws can't help you. Perhaps your employer is too small, or the statute of limits has run, or you are too young. But don't assume federal laws are always stronger or more progressive than state laws. Many states have fair-employment (or civil rights) statutes which go beyond the federal ADEA and Title VII. California's Fair Employment Practices Act covers employers with as few as five employees, providing an alternative to the federal acts for employees of small businesses. If your state has such a law, there will be an appropriate agency enforcing it, and qualified employment law attorneys will know all about it.

For tactical reasons your attorney may choose to bring your action under the state statute rather than the federal one. Maybe your state's courts have been more generous to plaintiffs. Or perhaps the statutes of limitation are longer under the state statutes, or damages better, or proof easier. There may be good reasons for selecting one statute over another, even if you may have a case under both.

Other state remedies.

In some states, even if you do not have a discrimination case, you can recover for "wrongful discharge." Laurie was a salesperson for a weight loss center. When her center was bought by a large chain, the contracts were changed to conceal certain important facts. Deciding that the new contracts were fraudulent, Laurie refused to use them, and was summarily fired. The court agreed that the contract terms amounted to fraud. Because her refusal to violate the law caused her to lose her job, Laurie recovered damages from her employer for "wrongful termination."

Kelly worked ten years for an insurance company, gathering excellent evaluations all along. Two months after getting a new supervisor, and in a period when there were no layoffs or work slowdowns, Kelly was fired without explanation, and replaced by a woman about her age. No provable sex, race, or age discrimination—but Kelly recovered, because the court felt that, given her long and excellent record, her employer breached an implied contract to fire her only for "just cause."

Plaintiffs have recovered for emotional distress and fraud, and on the strength of oral employment agreements. But the boom days of these kinds of lawsuits have busted in recent times, and some courts have begun to retreat from promising trends favoring plaintiffs.

☑ **If you have lost your job and feel in your gut that they "done you wrong," but can't see where the federal statutes would apply, by all means get to an employment law attorney and talk it over. Do not waste time debating the merits of your claim in your own mind. Statutes of limitation can be quite short. If you have a good claim, the attorney may take it on contingency, which means it may cost you nothing up front and little or nothing if the case loses. Other attorneys will ask for a retainer and charge by the hour, but the fee for the initial consultation should be affordable or free. Always ask about fees when making your appointment.**

▶ *Sex-segregated occupations.*
Perhaps you're a registered nurse with five years of college, ten years of continuing professional education, and fifteen years on the job. You look at your $28,000 income, and wonder why the young doctor you're training will very soon make five times that amount. He doesn't have five times the training. Nor does he have nearly your experience. He did not spend five times more on his education. But you're in a "woman's" job, and all the equal pay in the world won't help you. The male nurse working next to you is also stuck in a profession that is low-paying because of its history as women's work.

Gender segregation in the workforce is a fact. And it is no coincidence that the female sector is paid far less than the male. Women make up 95 percent of registered nurses, 98 percent of dental hygienists, 99 percent of secretaries, and 83 percent of waiters. They comprise 2 percent of firefighters, 1 percent of auto mechanics, 5 percent of welders, and 2 percent of truck drivers. In fact, half of all women work in only twenty of the 427 occupations recognized by the federal government.

The legalese for this kind of sex discrimination is "comparable worth." Definitions of comparable worth vary, but its goal is to treat all similarly skilled workers equally, regardless of their job title. Education, experience, responsibility, risk and other job characteristics should be rewarded without respect to whether the occupation is primarily a "woman's" job or a "man's." If jobs are rated on a point system according to training, skill, risk, etc., then 10 points should be worth the same for a librarian as they are for a tree trimmer. If secretarial work requires the same degree of training, experience, and responsibility as carpentry, then the pay should be equivalent. In one study, registered nurses were rated as comparable to vocational educators. Yet nurses were paid 25 percent less than voc-ed teachers, mostly male.

Some important victories have been won by women working in government jobs, but there have also been some notable defeats. The Supreme Court has said this kind of sex discrimination is not prohibited by Title VII, so advocates have had to pursue other legal remedies. Your state's fair employment statute might require equal pay for jobs of comparable worth. If you are called a "seamstress," and work for $6 an hour, while the mostly male "tailors" at your company earn $8, you may want to look into it. Your union might be a good place to start.

☑ **Sometimes very little additional training will put you into the "male" side of the profession. Law school takes only three or four years, and often can be done at night, and many onetime legal secretaries are now lawyers. The difference in pay between lawyers and secretaries, doctors and nurses, CPAs and bookkeepers may well be worth your additional investment in training.**

Maybe you think this is someone else's problem, because you have a law or medical degree. But some experts report that as these professions demasculinize, they will either become lower-paying as a whole, or women's niches will be carved out within the profession which pay less than "men's" fields. Pediatricians, for example, are not as well paid as general surgeons. Probate lawyers, where women in large firms often work, make less than tax lawyers. CPAs serving the non-profit sector make less than partners in large firms. Women cluster in the lower-paid ranks of these professions, which as a whole are rapidly becoming 40 to 50 percent female.

If high income is your goal, learn which fields in your profession pay best. Don't waste time gaining experience as a first-grade teacher if, with a little more education, you can become a college professor. Don't be a paralegal if you can become a lawyer with one more year of training. However, be absolutely certain you know what your chances will be in getting a job before you take additional training. There are an awful lot of people with worthless master's degrees and doctorates out there.

▶ *If they tell you you're unfit.*

Under federal and many state laws employers cannot refuse to hire or promote someone because of a disability unrelated to bona fide job requirements. If you use a wheelchair and are refused a job as a computer operator for that reason alone, illegal discrimination has occurred. But many midlife women are trapped in the gray area of the law, where the situation is not that clear cut, and courts could easily rule either way.

Sophie was 42 years old and had ten years' experience as a social worker when the welfare agency refused to hire her because she was overweight. Even though Sophie had always been healthy, the agency was afraid that, if they hired her, their health insurance costs would go up. The lawyers blitzed each other with dozens of studies which proved that a) obesity was a factor in ill health; and b) it was no factor at all. Sophie's lawyer felt her chances in court were less than fifty-fifty, so recommended against pursuing the suit.

☑ If this has happened to you, don't conclude that you
have no case. Always see an experienced employment-
law attorney for an analysis, as it is a tricky and subtle
branch of law. One consultation should not cost you
too much, even if you decide not to proceed.

A big concern lately has been the burgeoning medical
data collection industry. Similar to credit reporting bureaus,
medical (or health) data bases gather information on your
age, health, fitness, and things such as your use of alcohol
and tobacco, your weight history, and even stress management. Even your ethnic or racial background could be considered statistically relevant to your health record. The
information is sold to health and life insurance companies
and employers. A University of Illinois survey found that in
1988 half of the Fortune 500 companies use employees'
medical records in making decisions about hiring and promotion. The data comes from your health insurer, school
and camp records, and a myriad of public and private reports.

☑ Congress has been looking at strengthening the Fair
Credit Reporting Act to clarify consumers' rights to
review and correct medical data records. If legislation
is approved, you will be able to demand access to your
medical data file and correct any misinformation.

That will not be enough. Access rights don't speak to the
massive invasion of privacy and opportunity to discriminate
these files represent. Information a company cannot legally
require you to disclose on an application (like race or age)
can come to it through a health data base. As medical costs
continue to escalate well beyond the inflation rate, employers are becoming alarmed at the rapidly increasing costs of
their employee health benefits. It has occurred to some of
them that employing certain types of individuals might
ensure a workforce that is cheaper to insure. If African-
Americans are more prone to sickle-cell disease and have
lower life expectancies than whites, does that permit an

employer to refuse to hire them? I assume not, because statistical data has been held, in other contexts, to violate the Civil Rights Act when used to discriminate against an individual job applicant or employee. But what if, because an applicant is a single male, a company searches a medical data bank for evidence of AIDS, and finds it? Can he be refused a job or promotion? What about a woman whose records reveal she once had a benign cervical lesion treated? Can she legally be refused the job? Maybe. It depends on the state of the law at the time. This is an evolving area, and state and federal laws are changing daily. But it is clear that statistical data applied to an individual to deny her a job is a violation of the state and federal civil rights acts, and the fact that employers are trying to get around these acts under the guise of health costs is bad news for all of us.

The probablies and maybes describe the problem. Lawyers like to say "for every wrong there is a remedy," but in the gray areas of employment discrimination the remedy is increasingly difficult to achieve.

▶ *Appearance discrimination.*
This is a touchy legal area. Title VII and the ADEA don't prohibit appearance discrimination in so many words. Of two women with identical qualifications (and matching characteristics, such as race, age, ethnicity, etc.), the employer can choose the one who most appeals to him physically. Of two equally qualified men, the employer is free to choose the tallest, and studies prove that many do. Everyone knows that appearance discrimination is a fact of life— cosmetics, plastic surgery, hairpieces, and fashion attest to everyone's anxiety about "looking their best." All women fear appearance discrimination as they move beyond their very early twenties. It hurts a lot more than feelings. Appearance discrimination costs jobs.

Earlier, Sophie couldn't get a social work job because employers equated being overweight with illness and feared their health insurance costs would go up. But what if the welfare agency didn't really care about their health costs and only used them as an excuse not to hire Sophie because they didn't care for her appearance?

What are the Sophies of this world to do? There's always the chance a case could be made under sex, handicap, or age discrimination statutes, or even a state statute which covers appearance. In 1989 Pan Am settled a $2.3 million Title VII lawsuit by 115 female flight attendants who had been suspended for being overweight. Male flight attendants could qualify under large- or medium-frame weight charts, but females could not exceed medium-frame standards. American Airlines flight attendants are suing their airline for sex and age discrimination because of the different weight standards applied to men and women, arguing that weight allowances should increase with age.

Women in the public eye are particularly vulnerable to appearance discrimination. Mary Lou Retton is suing the National Bowling Council for dumping her as spokeswoman because of "changes in her physical image caused by her maturing as a woman." Weight discrimination is particularly ominous for midlife women, because one out of four American women between 35 and 64 is at least 30 percent overweight.

▶ ### Professional discrimination.

The self-employed professional is not protected by job discrimination statutes. Potential clients legally *can* and do discriminate. Maybe you are an employee, and therefore technically protected by the discrimination statutes, but in your profession, you have to make your reputation early, or not at all. Your professional reputation might suffer because of your age, race, or gender and thus indirectly (but decidedly) affect your career. Jacob, a historian, became an assistant professor right out of grad school. He was content to start out at the state teachers' college, but his goal was a full tenured professorship at the university. When he was 50, his opus on thirteenth-century mysticism was published to rave reviews within his specialization. But no offers from the university came his way. He had missed the boat, professionally speaking. He peaked too late to be a rising star in academia, and he would never receive the prestigious invitations and consultations which the university expected from its faculty.

At Grace's law firm, partners are compensated according to the business they bring in. Because of client discrimination, the women and minority partners made less than the white males.

Professional discrimination poses special concerns for midlife women, because of interrupted career paths. Mona finished her Ph.D. in physics when she was 26, then worked part-time as a research assistant at a top university until her youngest child started school. She was hired as an assistant professor when she was 36. At 49, thirteen years into her career, she made a major contribution to the theoretical understanding of quarks. She was promoted to associate professor, but lucrative grants, invitational conclaves, membership in prestigious societies, and invitations to address professional groups did not come her way because her big work, although early in her career, came when she was too old to be a young trailblazer. The career fits and starts that are the hallmark of so many women's working lives have devastating effects on the reputation-building which is the lifeblood of a professional career. Because of family roles, this insidious form of age discrimination hits women hardest.

☑ **Don't let your reputation slide while you take time out to assume family duties. Keep your contacts up, continue to research and publish if possible, even part-time and for non-profit charities or foundations with little or no pay. Write a law review article, get your name on a scientific or medical publication—whatever it takes in your profession to keep your reputation. Consider pursuing anything that will fit on your resume when you go back to work. You'll lose pay, promotions, and pension credits when you take your family care break, but you can take steps to minimize the loss of your reputation.**

▶ *Unions.*

If you are a union woman, you may have an extra layer of protection. Through the bargaining process, you can fashion contracts which will close the loopholes in Title VII and the ADEA. And through your grievance procedure, you have a dispute-resolution remedy unavailable to non-union workers. Of course, even though unions are subject to Title VII and the ADEA (through EEOC complaints, just like employers), some are better than others when it comes to protecting the rights of their female and minority members. Your union is also subject to state and federal labor laws, something your employment-law attorney may not know a lot about, as labor law is a field in itself.

☑ **Get your union to write the protections covered in Title VII and the ADEA into the contract with your employer. Then the grievance procedure can handle a sex or age discrimination charge without the EEOC or attorneys. However, don't let the statutes of limitation run out while your grievance procedure lags on. File a claim with the EEOC to stop the statute from running. You can always drop it later if the union resolves the problem.**

If you can influence the negotiation package, do so. Help women applicants by requiring that the employer consider volunteer and home experience as well as recent, paid experience. Be sure the special problems of mobile or re-entry women are considered. Get pay equity and comparable worth issues into the contract. And keep an eye on the benefits package—are there hidden biases against women?

▶ *Private club discrimination.*

In many places, private clubs are where important business is done. Historically, most clubs excluded women and minorities, and some of the nation's most prestigious private clubs still do. If you are a woman CEO in many places, your male assistant can charge lunch with important clients to his account at the club, but you cannot because you can't be a member. In a day of women judges, supervisors, mayors, legislators, and chief executives, it is appalling that this stricture continues to exist in forums where business contacts are made and nurtured. There can be no doubt that this puts professional women at a disadvantage. Some places have outlawed this type of discrimination by city ordinance. In others, lawsuits have opened the doors to women and minorities on the grounds that state-granted liquor licenses (and other privileges) convert the private club into a public accommodation. The clubs continue to hide behind the constitutional guarantee of freedom of association, yet their use of public facilities and licenses makes them, according to some courts, at least, subject to civil rights actions.

☑ **Join those who question appointees to important office about their club affiliations. Force them to resign from their clubs as a condition of confirmation. This has proved effective across the country, and could turn the tide, as men begin to realize that membership in discriminatory clubs could prove disadvantageous to future ambition. When all the prestigious men resign, the clubs will stop discriminating on the basis of race, religion, and gender.**

CHANGE IS NEEDED

It's not all bad news. As the Baby Bust generation enters the labor force—the first of them, born in 1964, graduated from college in 1986—midlife workers will become, if not exactly cherished, at least appreciated. The number of 18- to 25-year-olds entering the workforce declined 44 percent between 1979 and 1990. This development, coupled with the trend among men to take early retirement, should open opportunities for midlife women.

Still, much needs to be done at the policy level if we Americans are to make the most efficient use of our workforce. This means ridding the workplace of all kinds of prejudices—race, age, disability, religion, nationality, and gender—and redesigning the options so that reproducing and nurturing the species no longer costs mothers in the marketplace. Here are some places to start:

- *Labor statistics.* Until statisticians break down every figure according to age, sex, and race, we will not be able to formulate policies which reflect the real world.

- *Lower age limit.* The protections of the ADEA should be extended to age 30 or abolished altogether. Why should it be okay to discriminate against a 28-year-old in favor of a 20-year-old?

- *The EEOC* and state enforcement agencies are dreadfully underfunded for the work they're asked to do. Budgets and training need to be greatly increased.

- *Medical databanks* need to be strictly regulated if they are to cease being the loophole which swallows the discrimination acts.

- *Appearance discrimination* needs to be recognized in the regulations for what it is—a variant of age and sex discrimination and a violation of Title VII and the ADEA.

- *Health insurance discrimination* in hiring should be prohibited as a violation of protections against age, sex, and disability discrimination.

CONCLUSION

Hidden discrimination makes a mockery of statutory reforms like Title VII and the ADEA. If it's illegal to discriminate against a woman because she's 45 but okay if she's 38, where is the justice? What have we accomplished with our fancy reforms if employers can get, through a medical data base, information they are not allowed to ask for on their applications? If you don't get the job, what does it matter whether it was because you were 51 or because you were overweight?

Life on the job at midlife is different for women than for men. Midlife women experience discrimination in different ways, and at a younger age. The legal remedies are different. Your strategies, therefore, must likewise be different if you are to make these years all they can be.

CHECKING OUT YOUR JOB

We aren't the free little birds we'd like to be—darting from one enticing opportunity to another, happily tasting the fruits of life. Five years at the wrong flower can be bad news, because you may have to start over, perhaps with lower pay and benefits; your retirement income will be very vulnerable; and you will more likely suffer age discrimination. Check out your job every year.

✔ **Can my present job lead to a promotion? When?**

✔ **Do I risk age discrimination in my job in ten years? Fifteen?**

✔ **What are men paid for my position?**

✔ **Did I start my career later than the usual age?**

✔ **Have I moved in and out of the paid labor market?**

✔ **Is my company too small to be covered by Title VII/ADEA?**

✔ **Am I protected by state law?**

✔ **Am I being shut out of a job or promotion because of size or fitness?**

✔ **Am I asked to run personal errands for my boss?**

✔ **Am I referred to as "broad," "chick," or "girl"?**

✔ **Am I afraid to be branded a troublemaker?**

✔ Do I feel I should lie about my age?

✔ Are my performance evaluations going downhill?

✔ Am I also burdened by race or disability discrimination?

✔ What happens to my health insurance if I work past 65?

✔ Are people pressured to retire at my company?

✔ Do I have a feeling my appearance stands in my way?

✔ Can I join any private club in town?

✔ Is "professional" age or sex discrimination a factor in my field?

4

HOMEMAKERS AND PAID WORK

We Americans are great on rhetoric when it comes to homemakers: "The most important job in the world," "Entrusted with our most precious resource," "The hand that rocks the cradle rules the world,"—and all that.

But homemaking doesn't cut the mustard when it comes to making bucks. Ten years of homemaking is ten years of nothing when it's resume time, and since half of American women are out of the paid labor force at any given time, the impact of the Big Nothing cannot be ignored. A 40-year-old woman returning to the job market after ten years at home raising two kids is in a very different position than the 22-year-old competing for the same position. Nor can she compete with the 40-year-old man with ten more years' experience than she.

She'll have to sell herself creatively. In this chapter we'll talk about the homemaker who wants a paycheck, whether it be part-time work, work at home, or self-employment. We'll also review resume strategies, want ads, job interviews, and dealing with lawyers—all with the special problems of homemakers in mind.

▶ *Working at home.*
This is the era of "telecommuting." Never has it been easier for homemakers to combine home responsibilities with paid work. Although most home workers are self-employed, modern technology and changing attitudes about home offices have made it possible for many women to work as

employees in their own homes, either part- or full-time. Telecommuters communicate with their offices over the telephone wires. With faxes, modems, computers, laser printers, answering machines, call forwarding, accessible data banks, computer network services, on-line research, home copiers, and overnight deliveries to your front door, it is easy to see why this option is so popular. Even the federal government has gotten into the act, with a "flexiplace" program designed to let certain public employees work from their homes up to three days a week.

For women with family responsibilities, telecommuting is a dream come true, but some employment counselors recommend caution before embracing the opportunity to work at home. They worry that lack of visibility, office contacts, and not being in the right place at the right time can stall a career. Out of sight, out of mind.

Warning: Some employers try to turn their telecommuters into self-employed independent contractors, with loss of fringe and statutory benefits (such as worker's compensation, unemployment insurance, and Social Security contributions), as well as promotional opportunities. Usually it's a better deal economically for you to stay on the payroll rather than become an independent contractor.

▶ *Part-time work.*
This is an increasingly attractive option for millions of women balancing multiple roles and responsibilities. Women (not teenagers) dominate the long-term part-time labor market. According to the Commerce Clearing House, 44 percent of employers now use part-time help of some kind; three out of four of them only began the practice in the last eight years. But the ballooning part-time sector is a double-edged sword. On the one hand, it's an opportunity; on the other, it has all the drawbacks of self-employment. Fringe benefits are seldom offered, promotions are scarce, respect isn't as forthcoming, and job security is nil.

☑ **Don't work "off the books" to save taxes—it's illegal. Even if you don't qualify for the company pension as a part-timer, you will accumulate Social Security. Don't miss the opportunity to build your Social Security record. You may also get worker's compensation, unemployment benefits, and other state-mandated benefits even as a part-timer. And the company can cover you in their group health insurance and pension plan if they want to. Such coverage may be more important than the dollars in your paycheck. Consider negotiating for fringe benefits in lieu of a raise.**

▶ *Temporary work.*

Temporary workers are in high demand. Often the temporary job leads to full-time employment. Most temporary agencies welcome re-entry applicants, even "mature" ones. Kelly Services, for example, has a program for workers over 55. Even executive-level temporary agencies exist in some areas, catering primarily to women caring for a child or an elderly person, or who want a phased retirement.

▶ *Self-employment.*

Countless discouraged homemakers in effect hire themselves. They become self-employed. Because of pressure by the women's movement, the Small Business Administration began focusing on women's start-up businesses; now this is their area of highest growth.

But you have to separate golden self-employment opportunities from marginal work that leads nowhere. Of course, if you're juggling family responsibilities with flexible jobs, then a patchwork quilt of consultancies and part-time work represents a triumph of planning. Just don't confuse it with a career path. Nobody else will.

Think these things through before you go the consultant-independent contractor route:

- Loss of fringe benefits such as group health, pensions

- Cash-flow problems

- Risk of bankruptcy

- Loss of state benefits such as worker's compensation

- Tax hassles, such as estimated tax and Social Security

- Loss of fair labor practice protections

- Loss of unemployment benefits

You can buy some of these benefits yourself, such as health insurance (if you can qualify). Others, such as unemployment benefits, you cannot.

The biggest loss will probably be your retirement savings. If you are self-employed, pay special attention to setting up a Keogh or similar plan. And resist the temptation to take cash "under the table" to avoid taxes, because cash doesn't build your Social Security account. Even a minimal Social Security check carries with it hundreds of dollars' worth of Medicare premium reductions. You want Social Security. (For more about retirement savings and Social Security, see chapters 5 and 6.)

☑ **For the self-employed, Social Security taxes are paid when you file your income tax return, and are reported on Schedule SE.**

Many women-owned small businesses find it distressingly hard to buy liability insurance. If you are self-employed, you will probably find it very difficult to obtain disability insurance, especially if you work at home. In addition, you may pay more than twice as much as a man doing the same work.

Health insurance may be impossible for you to obtain— women over age 40 find it much harder to qualify medically than men, and pay almost twice as much in premiums. Even if you have a few employees, you may find it impossible or prohibitively expensive to obtain group coverage. Many insurers require medical examinations for members of small groups, and the entire group is charged if just one employee (or her dependent) has a serious disease. In addition, exclusions for pre-existing medical conditions are common in small groups, whereas large groups usually cover every employee without a medical examination or excluded conditions. Many happily self-employed people chuck it in and go to work for a large employer simply to obtain the health insurance. (See chapter 7.)

Look into group policies. Some health insurance groups, for example, are as small as three members. Perhaps your professional association (a bar or medical association, for example) offers group health, disability, and life insurance. Or your occupational association (a child care center association, for example) may offer liability protection. If you can get into a group which includes both sexes, you may find your costs much more affordable.

Another problem for the self-employed midlife woman is age and sex discrimination. The employment discrimination statutes were written to protect employees, not the self-employed. Thanks to a strong insurance lobby, for example, your retirement savings may end up in a gender-biased annuity which will pay you lower monthly benefits than a man, or cost you a higher premium. These discriminations, illegal for employees, are business as usual for the self-employed woman.

It's a fact that many midlife women turn to self-employment when they find no one will hire them. They become consultants, sell real estate, try freelance writing. Age (or sex, race, etc.) discrimination can go unremedied under these circumstances. You can't sue clients who won't sign on with you because of your age (or race, sex, etc.). One New York literary agent said he would hesitate before accepting a new author over age 50 on the basis of age alone. He reasoned that there were fewer years left for the writer to produce books, and that editors didn't like older writers.

There is very little the would-be author can do about this, except find a more enlightened agent. This kind of blatant discrimination is beyond the reach of the law, because employment, technically, is not at issue.

Women professionals are in a similar situation. A former president of the Los Angeles Bar Association was quoted as saying that law firms' partners' pay is increasingly linked to the ability to bring in clients. Because male businessmen tend to seek out male lawyers, women partners are falling behind in pay because, through client discrimination, they don't bring in new business. This kind of discrimination may or may not be redressable by law. Until it is challenged, highly able and trained women will continue to lose out because of prejudices beyond their ability to combat.

▶ *Family caregiving.*
Patty worked hard all her life. She completed two years of college before marrying Don. She worked three years as a clerk while Don finished his B.A. and master's degrees. For three more years she worked part-time while their two kids were babies. She returned to her full-time job in a small office while taking night classes to complete her B.A. and teaching credential. After six more years, at age 32, she was ready to teach. She earned the entry-level salary of $22,000 per year, although others her age were earning $32,000 because they had 10 years on the job. Patty, despite equal pay all along, lost 10 years' job experience because of family responsibilities, and she will never recover it.

Page, on the other hand, began working at 20 and never let up. To pursue her career, she chose not to have children. When she was 48, her mother began to require full-time care. Page's two brothers were "unavailable" to help, so Page arranged to continue work on a part-time consulting basis while she took care of her mother. When Page was eligible for early retirement, she took it. She lived the remaining 30 years of her life with half the income she would have had if she had remained on her career track, taken promotions, and accumulated high-pay pension credits until retirement at age 65.

Family responsibilities cannot be underestimated when it comes to explaining the continuing gap between women's and men's earnings. According to the Census Bureau, nearly three out of four women had career interruptions of six months or more, compared to only one out of four men. The Bureau further found that job interruptions for family reasons tend to be longer than for other reasons, such as unemployment. While 95 percent of top male executives have children, only 40 percent of women executives do, probably because women understand only too well what parenthood will do to their careers. University of California (Berkeley) sociologist Arlie Hochschild, author of *The Second Shift*, found that married women work about 15 hours more per week than married men. These hours are put in on "the second shift" at home. Today, two-thirds of all mothers work full-time, including half of all mothers with infants under the age of one.

In many respects, parenting roles and their impacts on careers are beyond the reach of the law. The school system was not required to equalize Patty's salary with that of others her age. Nor was Page's employer required to come up with a full-time, full-benefit alternative to part-time consulting. Job experience and tenure continue to influence pay, and women workers continue to lose income because of their mobility (the average man stays on the job about one-third longer than the average woman) and family responsibilities.

But there are legal limits to caregiving's penalties. For example, certain pension rights are retained when you return to the same employer after an absence of up to five years (or the period of time equaling your prior employment, whichever is greater). There is a right to parental or family care leave in some states, and a strong movement to establish family leave in federal law. For midlife women, it is critical that family-leave acts include all family caregiving, not just child care.

▶ ### Phased retirement.
When mandatory retirement went out the door, creative retirement walked in. Phased retirement is simply part-time

work at the end of your career. A man with forty years of work behind him is more likely to welcome—and be able to afford—a slowdown near retirement than a woman of the same age with only twenty years behind her. Still, this is an attractive option for many women who need to combine work with caring for an elder relative or spouse.

▶ ### Back to school.

Many midlife women, newly re-entering the paid labor force think first of completing their deferred education. And many midlife and older women today look at their B.A. framed on the wall, and wonder if it was worth it. They universally agree that it enriched them immensely. But college and graduate degrees have proved disappointing as door-openers to good jobs for many midlife or older women without prior paid experience.

Midlife women are a big business in the college circuit today, as institutions try to fill the spaces left by the departed Baby Boomers. Some schools have come up with imaginative programs to assist the returning student. In others, only the midlifer's tuition is welcome. No effort is made to accommodate her special needs. These include:

- Placement services with midlife resumers in mind.

- Employment counseling aimed at midlife women.

- Age/sex discrimination workshops and seminars.

- Free or low-cost employment-law consultations.

Before you go back to school, think about it. Are you counting on a liberal arts B.A. to open employment doors? Might it be more realistic to aim for a license or credential, such as nursing or teaching (both professions have shortages)? A law degree takes only three years, and is one of the very few top professions which can be reached via part-time or night school.

If employment is the goal, consider the investment

against the pay-off. Some paths point toward greater rewards. For example, in 1989 it would have cost you $31,300 to get a degree at Harvard Business School, and in your first year as a financial consultant, you could expect to earn $65,100. That's a terrific return on your investment. A J.D. from Georgetown Law School cost $37,800 against first-year earnings of $52,000. A nonresident student at UCLA in social work would pay a mere $6,486 for a B.A., and earn $26,000 her first year. But a University of Pennsylvania degree in media planning cost $51,000 against a first-year income of only $18,000; and an Illinois State University teaching credential cost $28,000 for a starting salary of $17,000. Invest in the right education. By the year 2000, it is projected that dental hygienists will earn $39,800, dentists $120,480. Think hard about being the dentist.

☑ **If you think the extra training will take too long, and that you'll be "too old" after the seven years it will take, how old do you think you'll be in seven years if you don't take the training?**

▶ *The resume problem.*
A mother who orchestrates a birthday party for twenty 5-year-olds has demonstrated her executive ability. She has coordinated the bakery, the invitations, the guest of honor, the entertainment, the games, the gifts, and the setting—all to come together at precisely 2:00 P.M. on Saturday at the park. She has made a sophisticated judgment in human psychology by considering all the elements of the day within the limits of 5-year-olds. She has kept the competition in mind by not duplicating Jerry's party last month, or Dick's last year. She has exercised cost control, and handled the procurement from a variety of suppliers. Very likely she has manufactured some of the goods herself, in her oven or at the sewing machine. She took pains to ensure that no element of the party would be missing or late.

Yet very few employers will recognize what she's pulled off. They gripe about their poorly attended meetings, with latecomers and no-shows and equipment that doesn't arrive and rooms that are double-booked; and when this woman comes knocking at their door, she's brushed off with barely an acknowledgment.

Advice abounds on how best to show off a homemaker's considerable skills. Organized homemakers have succeeded in getting some companies to recognize volunteer work as "experience" for hiring purposes. This isn't the same as recognizing family work like birthday parties, but it's a start. Years running the 200-member PTA, or coordinating cookie sales for the Girl Scouts, or lobbying city hall for safer streets confer real skills, cognizable in the paid labor market *if* you can get around employers' blind prejudice against unpaid work. The challenge is to describe these activities on your resume and in interviews in ways employers recognize as business-related. There are "creative" resume books you can read. They'll tell you not to say "no job experience"; or, little better, "President of PTA, five years"; but to relate how you organized meetings, lined up speakers, recruited members, and resolved disputes. If you were in charge of the books, say so. If you raised funds, tell about it. Did you edit the newsletter? Let's hear it.

Some resume counselors recommend concision to the point of starkness. "CEO, Chrysler Corporation" is probably all you need to say—if you can say it. Few homemakers re-entering the paid labor force have such a heavy hitting job in their background, so a descriptive approach will probably be more helpful. Do not pad your work history, because if you are competing with hundreds of applicants for one position, the screeners are not going to take time to digest your three pages of narrative. There are very few job records that cannot be edited to fit onto two single-spaced pages. More than two pages tells the reader that either the applicant was a major job-hopper or is using narrative to pad unimpressive credentials. Put your background under a microscope. Think of everything you know how to do, from using a copy machine, to programming a VCR. Then translate those skills into appropriate experience on an application for office manager, for example. You cannot say you have "no experience" when you're 40 years old. You have 40 years of experience and skills. Just learn to identify your skills and translate them into business needs.

You do not have to put your age on your resume, nor is your prospective employer supposed to ask it (other than if you are at least 18). Many people omit the dates of their degrees as well, although this may flag your application as coming from someone age-sensitive. Leave out personal data such as height, weight, marital status, children, and gender—it's amateurish. Some people omit their work experience of a generation ago, but if it is your only paid experience, you should make reference to it, including a line or two describing your responsibilities.

✔ **For heaven's sake, don't lie on your resume. Under the Immigration Reform and Control Act of 1986 employers must see proof of your legal residency or citizenship, which means you must produce a birth certificate, passport, or a similar document loaded with personal information that may conflict with your more imaginative resume entries. If you *have* fudged your age on your resume or application, and your employer later finds out, you still cannot be fired for being too old. Nevertheless, if you say you're 43 when you're really 48, you may risk detection when you're really 65 and want to start receiving Social Security and Medicare. You can ask Social Security not to contact your employer for proof of age, but if you use Medicare, your employment group health insurer could find out and tell your employer. Better to be clean from the beginning.**

▶ *Getting paid experience.*
I once worked with a dynamite lobbyist in Texas who agreed to work for our poor non-profit for $1 for the full legislative session. Why? This enabled her to register as a paid lobbyist, which she then translated into paid experience on her resume. We won our legislation over almost impossible

opposition by the well-funded insurance lobby partly because she parked herself in front of the only men's restroom
and, in time, cornered every legislator as he came out. Yet
her brilliant work would have been labeled "volunteer" and
therefore as good as nonexistent had she not registered and
been paid.

This route is open to you, too, if you have the time to
work for token wages in order to build a paid record. Every
non-profit I've ever known hungers for fundraisers—and
professional fundraising commands a nice fee when you've
established a good track record. Lobbying is another skill
which is highly paid on a professional level. Even if you
have to start at city or county level, reputations are made
breathtakingly fast in state or local legislatures. Many
women have gone from unpaid, to token paid, to well-paid
legislative consultants by starting out with the right non-
profit. In fact, I've met dozens of women legislators who
first ran for office after age 50, and did it from a background
of the right volunteer work. Think of non-profits as step-
ping stones to paid work, not just as time-fillers or places to
"keep busy."

This priceless experience-building through non-profit
volunteer work is not just available to homemakers or retired people. If you are stuck in a dead-end job without a
marketable skill, and you feel experience rather than education is the route for you, then meet with a likely group and
talk about weekend work, evenings, or vacation stints. You
can probably work something out that will pay off in time.

To build experience through volunteer work, interview
several organizations, with skill training in mind. Of course
you want a group which is in accord with your beliefs, but
make your needs the priority here. In other words, if the
dearest thing to your heart is saving the African elephants
but the local wildlife organization is merely a mail-drop for
the real work being done in their headquarters in Washington, don't waste your time opening envelopes and answering phones. If another group is very active in the state and
local legislatures, and in the middle of every network and
coalition—*and they don't restrict responsible activities to their*

paid staff only—they may be just the place for you, even though they are concerned with preserving school music programs, something well down on your priority list.

Be up-front with the group. Explain that you will trade your time and talent in a professional manner in return for volunteer tasks which carry some responsibility. Tell them you are willing to do menial work (envelope stuffing, door-to-door collecting) for a limited period of time to establish your reliability, but that you must have their commitment to either advance you (with no pay at first, and token pay in time), or to tell you plainly that they cannot do so. Then commit to as many hours per week as you can, and treat the obligation as seriously as you would a paid position. If you work dependably for six months without getting the kind of responsibilities that people get paid for in the business world, look around for another group.

Look for these training possibilities in the non-profit world:

- Development (fundraising, grant writing, direct mail)

- Legislative representation (lobbying)

- Policy analysis (analyzing and drafting legislation)

- Editing (newsletters, position papers)

- Writing (technical, promotional, creative, expository)

- Public speaking (workshops, seminars, meetings)

- Bookkeeping (budget control, collection, payroll)

- Supervisory (overseeing other volunteers)

- Public relations (press relations, media events)

- Office management (computers and other technology)

Some savvy non-profits offer "permanent" volunteers a chance to join the paid staff's group health insurance—even for unpaid work.

▶ *Job interviews.*

You respond to a want ad by phone. Your conversations go very well, and you come in for an interview. The warm voice on the phone becomes distant in person. The job you were sure you'd get goes to someone "more qualified." You are a 48-year-old woman.

Midlife women experience this scenario with regularity. If the reason for the big chill is age, that's illegal. Proving it is another matter. Extensive investigation by your lawyer or a private investigator could possibly turn up a pattern of discrimination, but it won't come cheap. The EEOC might investigate at no cost to you, but full-bore investigations by the EEOC are not an everyday event. Still, you might get lucky and uncover a smoking gun, like the codes recently found being used by one employment agency: "Talk to Maria" meant the client preferred Hispanics. "Mary" meant Caucasians, "Mariko" meant Japanese, "MaryAnne" meant African-Americans, "Adam" meant men, and "suite 20 to 30" meant age 20–30. Or the subtle code turned up by CBS's *60 Minutes,* where the employment counselor reversed his or her initials if the employer did not want African-American referrals. Richie Smith would initial his report "SR" in that event. It is against the law for employment agencies to discriminate in their referrals. If an employer tells the agency it only wants young white males, the agency must refuse.

An employer cannot hide behind the prejudices of its customers. "We have no prejudice against anyone, but if we hired 45-year-old women in sales, our customers would all go to the competition." Nor can it say having older employees in the front office will conflict with the energetic, go-getter image it is trying to project. That kind of attitude is the very reason the ADEA came into being.

▶ *Make the best use of your lawyer.*

Re-entering homemakers who encounter age or sex discrimination in employment service referrals, applications, personnel interviews, or any other phase of the job search have the same Title VII and ADEA rights the paid worker does. (See chapter 3 for more on these federal acts, and the EEOC, which enforces them.) If, after you complain, the EEOC lets you down, you need an employment-law specialist. The field is just too complex, with its overlay of state and federal statutes, regulations, and common-law torts and contracts. Also, the law is rapidly changing at every level. Call the state bar association to see if there is a specialized bar association, such as the California Employment Lawyers Association. Your family lawyer can make a referral, but know that often this will be a friend of his or hers. It's not that the attorney necessarily wants to drum up a friend's business; it's more that we lawyers often don't know who *is* the best outside of our own area of practice. Even asking friends or women's groups for referrals is not foolproof. It should get you to a lawyer with good client relations (not a small consideration), but it's no guarantee of the best legal mind. For that, you'll have to rely on credentials, reputation, experience, and your gut.

When you've decided on a lawyer, call for an interview. Before you make the appointment, ask about the fee for an initial consultation. It should be affordable, or even free. Keep fees at the forefront of your conversations when you meet for the first time. You don't want surprises—and neither does the lawyer.

If you decide to proceed, ask the lawyer to be very realistic with you. Don't be dazzled by the lofty amount of damages in the formal demand or complaint. They are set high for negotiating purposes. If you let your expectations get unduly raised, you may not recognize a good settlement when it comes along.

In the last couple of years, the U.S. Supreme Court and some state courts have retreated from earlier pro-employee directions. The highest employment-law awards have been in California, where in 1987, juries awarded an average of $250,000 to wrongful dismissal plaintiffs, and employees won 67 percent of jury verdicts. It's early yet, but such awards are likely to come less easily under recent precedents. California often leads the nation in evolving areas of the law, so watch for more pro-employer decisions across the country. Also, understand that very few cases go all the way to trial. The overwhelming majority are settled out of court for far less cost and with far less fuss.

Your strategy should be to:

- Start with the EEOC.

- Disregard the EEOC closure of your case.

- Find a qualified employment law attorney.

- Decide whether you and the lawyer are compatible.

- Ask questions to avoid unrealistic expectations.

- Trust your attorney when she recommends settlement.

LET'S SEE SOME CHANGES

Some employment problems are unique to midlife women. They are shared neither by younger women, nor midlife men. Take the "re-entry" woman in her thirties, forties, or fifties, for example. Out of the paid labor market for ten or fifteen years, her education and training far behind her, the returning 38-year-old homemaker finds herself competing with 22-year-olds for entry-level jobs. Midlife men don't usually find themselves in this position. It's bad for them when they lose their jobs—no mistake about it. But when they apply for new jobs they aren't at the entry level, so their competition is closer to their own age.

▶ *Job training legislation.*

From time to time, Congress and state and local legislators pass job training or rehabilitation legislation which targets certain groups for special attention. For example, employers can take tax credits for employing certain disadvantaged groups, training programs can receive funding if they concentrate on certain groups, and so forth. Teenagers, minorities, the poor, the disabled, displaced homemakers, workers displaced from obsolete industries—all have received special attention in this way. It is important that re-entry women (not just the displaced homemaker) be included in these programs, and that vestiges of age discrimination such as age limits for apprenticeship training, be removed. When money for entry-level training is targeted at teenagers, the re-entry woman of 40, who may need skills training at the same level, cannot participate. Likewise, when money is targeted for re-training workers in obsolete industries, this leaves out women, who were never welcome in those industries in the first place. The Jobs Partnership Training Act of 1982 is the principal federal legislation in the field, but not the only one.

▶ *Regulatory reform.*

The Department of Labor should promulgate regulations under Title VII and the ADEA to establish an age/sex subclass so that employers can no longer follow a policy of discriminating against midlife and older women while maintaining defensible records of hiring young women and older (management) men. If a bank hires only young women (tellers) and men (management), it can show the EEOC statistics indicating that half its workforce is female, and that half is over 40 (male). Regulations should make clear that women over 40 are a protected subclass and that discrimination against them violates the federal statutes. This reform would greatly assist midlife homemakers re-entering the paid labor market in their competition with younger women for entry-level positions.

CONCLUSION

The employment problems of homemakers are fundamentally different from those of other women or midlife men. Protective legislation enacted with the male work pattern in mind simply doesn't do the job for women, who by age 35 or 40 have already accumulated the burdens of job mobility, home responsibilities, and subtle forms of discrimination not recognized by law.

It's also clear that America's productivity (and therefore our individual and collective wealth) will never be all it can be until the workforce makes the most efficient use possible of its raw material. As long as the biological realities of childbearing, and the social realities of care for children and the elderly fall mainly upon women, then an efficient job marketplace should accommodate the work patterns brought about by these different roles.

HOMEMAKERS' CHECKLIST

Give each question a little thought—you can only gain by it. Taking on a paid job will radically change your life, and you should think through every aspect of that change.

✔ Will a little more formal training pay dividends?

✔ If so, are night or weekend classes available?

✔ Do I risk age discrimination by staying at home longer?

✔ Will I start my career later than the usual age?

✔ Have I moved in and out of the paid labor market?

✔ Have I worked part-time, shared a job, or consulted?

✔ Will I use sick leave or vacation to care for kids or elders?

✔ Have I been told I'm "overqualified"?

✔ Do I feel I should lie about my age?

✔ Does my resume "translate" volunteer work into job skills?

✔ Do I also suffer race/ethnic/disability discrimination?

✔ Do I have a feeling my appearance stands in my way?

✔ Is "professional" age/sex discrimination a factor in my field?

5

WHAT WOMEN NEED TO KNOW ABOUT PENSIONS AND SOCIAL SECURITY

Let's suppose you're in your forties, have been working since you were 25, and now earn $65,000 per year. Or perhaps you're a contented homemaker, expecting to retire with your husband on his ample pension. Either way, your life is on track, and you like it that way. You don't want your golden years to be anything less than golden, so you decide to get practical and take a hard look at what your life will be like after retirement.

Perhaps you're aware that three out of four poor people over age 65 are women. That's unsettling, but it's just a statistic. This, after all, is the post-feminist era. You figure the women's movement took care of the economic issues more than a decade ago—if you make as much money as a man, you'll retire on the same pension, right? Your goals are realistic—you want the same life after retirement as you have now. So is there a problem?

You bet there is. Unless you are just starting out, most of your earnings are not protected by recent pension law reforms, and your retirement, whether as a worker or a homemaker or both, is going to be tougher to fund than you thought. In this chapter, working women will learn how to recognize the nasty surprises in their pension and Social

Security portfolios; and homemakers, widows, and divorced women will take a hard look at their husbands'. Then we'll spend chapter 6 learning how all women can beef up those portfolios through intelligent savings strategies, or desperation measures if saving is out of the question. You *can* beat the odds. You don't want to be like Susan, Kat, or Magdalena.

Susan arrived at her sixty-fifth birthday with her dreams intact. She had made it a point to work in her pension-covered clerical position for forty years, even when that meant she had to accept a lower salary. Over time, she was sure it would pay off. Susan was stunned, then, to learn that her pension checks would be about one-half of what she had expected. "Integration," the plan administrator told her. "Your pension has been integrated with your Social Security benefit—that's how we do it here. It's perfectly legal, and quite customary."

Kat and her husband Ray were happily retired on his generous pension. But when Ray died suddenly, Kat learned at his funeral that his pension died with him.

Magdalena's husband Howard urged her to stay home and take care of the kids, reminding her that his pension and Social Security would fund their retirement. When he divorced her after nine years of marriage, Magdalena learned that she hadn't been married long enough to qualify for a former wife's Social Security benefit, and that in her state, divorce courts considered the pension to be entirely the property of the wage-earner.

Susan, Kat, and Magdalena were not stupid women. Each had thought through her retirement and made what seemed to be appropriate plans. But each was tripped up in ways that are typical for women: low wages subject to "integration" (which we'll discuss later), and the problems of being dependent on a husband's retirement benefits. In this chapter we'll pay special attention to pensions and Social Security. If you're depending on your husband's retirement benefits, read the sections addressed to working women with him in mind. They are just as relevant to your plans as they are to career women. Along the way, we'll also point out the special retirement concerns of homemakers, widows, and divorced women.

How much is enough?

Do this right now: Take the salary you (or your husband) expect to be earning at the end of your career (be conservative), and multiply it by 60 percent, 70 percent, and 80 percent. Even the 80 percent looks awfully low, doesn't it?

Yet retirement planners routinely recommend that retirement income be 60 to 80 percent of pre-retirement income—and it's here that women begin to lose out because of assumptions about men. Women, who statistically live one-third longer than men after age 65, have a much greater exposure to the ravages of inflation on fixed incomes. And as a group, women begin their retirements with only about two-thirds the income of men, so need to maintain far more of it just to meet necessities. This is just as true of wives, because, like it or not, you are overwhelmingly likely to die unmarried. Four out of five women do.

So don't apply the 60–80 percent figure to yourself unless you *know* your expenses will drop accordingly. Try for 100 percent.

The three-legged stool.

Think of your retirement as policymakers do, as a three-legged stool resting on pension, Social Security, and private savings. All three legs should be strong and sound if your retirement dreams are to become reality.

Now your task appears simple. Put together a package of pension benefits, Social Security, and investments to equal 100 percent of your pre-retirement income, or whatever level you feel comfortable with, and you're home free.

Unfortunately, because you're a woman, the hidden gender biases in important laws and practices can cause your legs of the stool to be short or missing. But there are ways to manipulate your priorities so that you can enjoy security—and understanding the system is the first step.

PENSIONS: GETTING IT RIGHT

Behold the deadly, womanly Rule of Halves:

- Only half as many women get pensions as men;

- Those that do get half as much;

- Retired men have half the poverty rate as retired women.

Blame the Rule of Halves on the forfeitures built into every pension plan—they have a different impact on women than on men. Although technically complex, the principles which guide pensions are almost elegant in their simplicity:

(1) The more people who pay into the fund, the bigger it gets.

(2) The fewer the people who take out of the fund, the more there is for those few.

(3) To keep the people in (2) few, obstacles are placed in the way of the people in (1).

At the beginning of the pension sweepstakes, the workers line up in droves. Over the course of their working lifetimes, some trip and some drop out, while others run a full race, but on the wrong racecourse. Far fewer remain at the end—and for those that do, the prizes vary. There are grand prizes, lesser prizes—and even booby prizes which look like the genuine article but are as illusory as the wind. There are over a trillion dollars in American pension funds, and the real winners are few.

The game is designed that way, of course. The obstacles cause forfeitures, and forfeitures are the dirty little secret of the pension game. When lots of people pay in and fewer people take out, it is a very desirable situation for the few. And forfeitures are a big reason why you, as a woman, are more likely to lose the pension race, since the hurdles are not the same for all runners. They are erected to reward the long-term, steady, well-paid worker, and that worker's name is Man. If you don't lose, the winners can't win. You are losing even if you think your pension is a "free" fringe benefit. You are paying for it in two ways: your salary is lower to pay for your fringe benefits, and you are losing irreplaceable time to build a sound pension.

Women stumble over these hurdles because they are more likely than men to be:

- In a job without pension coverage

- Poorly paid

- Mobile workers

- Long-lived

Your first big hurdle is to get a job which includes pension coverage. Your second is to qualify for it. Before we get to how you do that, let's take a look at some of the laws that can either help or hinder your hopes for retirement.

▶ ### ERISA: the friend with two faces.

The Employees Retirement Income Security Act (ERISA) was enacted by Congress in 1976 to protect workers in the private sector from certain pension practices that amounted to little more than fraud. ERISA also contains protections for widows, but offers scant protection for former wives. ERISA does not regulate the thousands of government plans, whether local, state, or federal, nor does it affect military pensions, railroad pensions, or Social Security. But if you or your husband works for a movie studio in California, an oil company in Louisiana, or a brokerage in New York, the company's pension, if there is one, is subject to ERISA.

ERISA does not require that your employer offer a pension as a fringe benefit, nor indeed, any fringe benefits at all. One reason why retired women have less to live on than retired men is that women's jobs are more likely than men's to offer no pension benefits at all. Women workers are clustered in the service sector and in small businesses—exactly the jobs least likely to provide pensions.

☑ **Here is your first task in getting your retirement right: ERISA gives you the right to get information about your pension plan from its "plan administrator." Ask your personnel or payroll department how to reach your plan administrator, likely a fund manager such as an insurance company or a financial management service. Ask the plan administrator for your pension's "summary plan description" (SPD). In addition to the summary, you also have a right to a copy of the actual plan agreement itself. Compare your SPD with the provisions described in the checklist at the end of the chapter. If parts of it puzzle you, ask your plan administrator for an explanation. The administrator owes you an explanation you can understand.**

With your SPD at hand, and your plan administrator's phone number within reach, scrutinize your plan for typical problems for women:

☑ **If your job does not include a pension, don't despair. You will have to do it yourself one way or another—probably by doubling your savings leg to replace the missing pension leg. You can do it, too, even if you are in your fifties. (See chapter 6.)**

▶ *Part-time exclusions.*
Part-time workers are predominantly women, and are severely disadvantaged in the pension race. If you work part-time, you almost certainly have a pension problem. Maybe one like Lou's. She did books for the local pediatrician every Tuesday and Thursday for forty years. Or Gabrielle, who worked for three months every spring for a tax preparer. Lillian worked full-time the year round by juggling three part-time jobs to support herself and her daughter. And Donna worked as a consultant for several local insurance agencies, spending about ten hours per week at each agency, for a

sixty-hour week. Long-term workers all, but part-timers under the law, not required to be included in the company pension. ERISA defines part-timers as those working no more than nineteen hours a week, or seasonal employees working no more than 999 hours per year for any one employer. And that's the rub, of course, for women who hold down two or three part-time jobs in order to juggle family responsibilities or to get ahead.

To avoid paying fringe benefits, some employers will structure a job so that it does not exceed the nineteen-hour-per week limit, even if they have to hire two part-timers for the job instead of one full-timer. If you are in a job that limits your hours to nineteen per week, even though it is obvious that the job requires more hours than that, ERISA is probably the reason why. Talk it over with your employer. You may be able to increase your hours and gain coverage.

Integration with Social Security.

We opened this chapter with the story of Susan, and how she arrived at her sixty-fifth birthday only to learn that the pension she had been counting on would be half of what she expected. The plan administrator told her it was because of "integration" with Social Security. He told her the practice was quite usual.

Usual indeed, even common. This unfortunate practice lays its burden heaviest upon the lowest-paid workers, with women and minorities disproportionately among them. Integration works like this: your monthly pension benefit will probably be calculated by taking into consideration such variables as:

- The number of years you were on the job.

- Your wage history.

- Your age.

• Whether you will leave a survivor's benefit for your spouse.

Which of these elements are factored in, and how much weight is given each one is, of course, up to each plan. A plan which is integrated with Social Security might promise its participants that their retirement income will be (for example) 60 percent of their average wage over their last three years. So if Sandra earned $26,000, $28,000, and $30,000 annually over her last three years, she would expect an annual pension of 60 percent of $28,000 (the average of the three years), or $16,800. She expects her Social Security to be $6,000 per year, for a total retirement income of $22,800. Sandra is satisfied with this projection, so makes no effort to save for her retirement. Imagine Sandra's shock when she learns her pension will be only $10,800, which, with her Social Security, will only yield an income of $16,800.

What Sandra missed in the fine print is that the term "retirement income" does not refer just to the pension. It means that the pension and Social Security will *together* replace 60 percent of Sandra's wage base. Even so, Sandra is better off than many. She lost less than half of her pension to integration. Pension credits earned prior to January 1, 1989, could be completely obliterated, and often were.

☑ **Warning: If you have pension credits earned before January 1, 1989, those credits are still subject to the old formulas allowing 100-percent integration. Only your post-1989 earnings will be shielded from the 100-percent integration formula. If you are 40, with one half of your work life behind you, your pension can be substantially reduced. It will be decades before workers' retirement incomes are fully benefited by the change to 50-percent integration—around 2025.**

Even 50-percent integration is not satisfactory, of course. It is designed to the disadvantage of lower-paid workers, and because women as a class still earn about two-thirds what men do, any integration formula harms women after retirement.

☑ **Check the plan summary you got from your plan administrator. The integration feature may be hard to find, because the summary may not use the word "integration." Look for any mention of Social Security, especially in the part of the document that describes how your pension benefit will be calculated. Make a "ballpark" projection of what your Social Security will be (see the Social Security discussion below), then deduct it from your projected pension using the formula(s) your plan will apply to both pre- and post-1989 income.**

▶ **Vesting.**
You have a vested right to a pension when you have participated in the plan for the required number of years. Even if you leave your job long before retirement age, as a vested worker you will be entitled to a pension when you reach the plan's retirement age—although for the reasons discussed in this chapter, the benefit may approach zero. Of course, workers who make their own contributions to the plan through payroll deductions or otherwise are always 100 percent vested to the extent of their own investment.

☑ **You are entitled to a statement describing your vesting status. Ask your plan administrator.**

The American worker is a mobile worker, and women as a class are more mobile than men. The average man stays on the job about one-third longer than the average woman. The reasons women change jobs so often are obvious: family responsibilities, following transferred husbands, and leaving dead-end jobs.

Women's job mobility is due not to irresponsibility—it is rather to do with *great* responsibility. Sacrificing career goals to fulfill family demands, or leaving the security of dead-end jobs to advance oneself are tough decisions, often bitterly made. Younger women, of course, may change jobs without thinking about their retirement income, and midlife and older women often do so despite pension consequences because they feel it's too late to matter. Both are wrong.

In recent years, some employers have offered an alternative to the fast track for career women who are mothers. Reduced hours or flex-time are the hallmarks of this slow, or "mommy" track. If the "mommy track" survives questions about its legality and becomes a substantial part of American employment, Mom's first sacrifice will be her paycheck, her second will be promotion opportunities, and her third will be her pension. Career interruptions, part-time hours, contract work—all are deadly to building a pension. Mom's decision to devote time to her family will have lifetime effects on her income.

Since 1984, small companies have been subject to a three-year vesting rule, but for most private plans, ERISA permits several vesting formulas. The most popular one until 1989 was ten-year vesting. In 1989 the maximum vesting time was lowered to five years (or, as an alternative, a graded vesting schedule over three to seven years), an enormous improvement for women and other mobile workers, but still an insurmountable obstacle for millions of American women who cannot spend five consecutive years in the paid labor market or with any one employer.

Carol worked full-time for forty-five years in jobs which always included pension coverage, with no integration. Yet she had not a dime in benefits when she retired at age 65 in 1985. Carol failed to vest in a pension because she moved from employer to employer, never working at one job for the number of years required for pension entitlement. Twice Carol changed jobs because her husband was relocated and she moved with him; once she stopped working for a year because her youngest daughter had a lengthy illness; and twice she changed jobs to get out of a dead-end situation where upward mobility was impossible. Carol, in other words, was a typical woman worker.

Your big problem if you're a woman in middle years is that

the lower vesting requirements only recently took effect. If you worked on a job for fifteen years but left it before ERISA's enactment in 1976, you may well have lost all rights to a pension because of a twenty-year (or longer) vesting period. Or perhaps you worked eight years, leaving in 1988—not long enough under the old ten-year vesting rule. For pension purposes, much of your work history may well have gone down the drain. If you're counting on your husband's pension, work through his vesting requirements, too.

Remember, if you met the vesting and other requirements on a job held long ago, you may still be entitled to a pension, however small, when you reach retirement age. There is nothing to prevent you from collecting on several vested pensions when you retire. Explore your rights at all your former jobs— remember, the plan administrators must respond to your written inquiry. Even a $25-per-month benefit could brighten your second lifetime by funding a monthly lunch with friends.

Break-in-service.

Unlike Carol, Doris never changed employers. She worked on an assembly line at a major computer company for twenty-five years, always under pension coverage. Nevertheless, her pension came to nothing when she retired in 1982 at the age of 72. Doris's problem is a common one among women—her twenty-five years on the job were not consecutive. She worked eight years until she had children. She returned to her old job ten years later, leaving again after six years to take care of her elderly aunt. Seven years later she returned once again for three years, only to leave once more when her husband required care for three years after a stroke. And so it went, each break in service sending her back to the starting line in the vesting game. Instead of having only two more years to vest, Doris had to start over with ten. Because she always stayed away longer than her prior period of service, and never stayed with the job the required ten years (remember, she retired before 1989, so the 5-year vesting rule was not in effect for any of her work years), her pension did not vest.

Amendments to ERISA effective in 1985 are helpful. If you are an unvested worker, you can lose all the years you have accumulated toward vesting if you leave the plan for five years, or the number of years you worked prior to leaving, whichever is greater. Today, if you work three years, then take time off for five years to raise your kids, you can return to the same job and vest in the pension in two more years, instead of starting over with five. Unfortunately, work interruptions to assume family responsibilities average almost ten years for women—the Census Bureau estimates that women spend an average of 31 percent of their potential work years out of the labor force, compared with only 3 percent for men. The Bureau further estimates that 90 percent of women's career interruptions—against only 2 percent of men's—are for family reasons, so break-in-service sanctions have a dramatic gender bias against women.

ERISA did not change the break-in-service rules retroactively—a big problem for midlife and older women workers. Any break you had before 1976 is unprotected by ERISA; you could have been one day away from vesting, and still have lost it all by leaving your job even for a short time. Between 1976 and 1985, a break in service equaling the amount of time you worked prior to the break would be enough for you to lose all credits earned toward vesting. In other words, if you worked three years, then were away four, you would lose your pension credits. This standard still applies to work done during that decade, as does the "anything goes" standard for pre-1976 employment.

☑ **If you are a participant in a pension plan but not yet vested, see if you can work at least 501 hours per year (about three months) in your job, rather than leaving it entirely. That way, you can prevent the year from being included in the break-in-service calculation. You can stay away longer, and still not lose your credits toward vesting when you return full-time. Moreover, if** you expect to leave your job temporarily because of pregnancy, or to care for a newly born or adopted child, you will be entitled to up to 501 hours of pension credits in that year—enough to keep it out of the break-in-service calculation as well.

▶ The fractional rule.

If a fully vested worker leaves the job before the plan's retirement age, even if she had decades of employment, her pension will be greatly reduced by a complicated formula known as the "fractional rule." Suppose Eleanor starts work at 25 and leaves at age 40, making $50,000 per year. She expects her annual pension to be 1 percent of her final salary per year of service ($500 × 15), so she expects $7,500 per year in benefits when she begins to draw the pension at age 65. But when the plan administrator applies the fractional rule, Eleanor's benefit is reduced to a mere $2,813 per year. The rationale for the rule is to reward the lifetime employee, but in reality the fractional rule often catches midlife career women who are forced to leave their jobs to assume the care of an elderly family relative. This responsibility falls far more often on women than men.

 If you are being pressured by other family members to step away from your job to take on the care of an elderly relative, be sure you calculate the damage to your retirement income accurately. Perhaps other family members who consider themselves unavailable to help with the care would be willing to make good the lost pension income through regular donations to your retirement fund. Or perhaps you can be made the beneficiary on the older person's life insurance policy, or can be compensated through a provision in the will.

▶ Backloading.

In a practice known as backloading, the pension plan can skew the accumulation of pension credits so that the long-term worker is favored over the newer worker. In other words, the first ten years of work on your job can be worth less than the last ten years, in terms of pension credits. Brenda, for example, spent ten years apiece on three jobs, all with comparable pensions. When she retired, she had three pensions totaling far less than they would have had she stayed all thirty years on one job. Under backloading, ten "new" years are worth less than ten "old" years, and Brenda's retirement portfolio consisted entirely of light-weight "new" years. Prior to ERISA, backloading was uncontrolled. ERISA placed some limits on it, and required partial adjustment for credits earned before 1976. Of course, mobile women workers are disadvantaged by this feature, which has the effect of rewarding the lifetime employee, very often the owner of the business.

☑ **If you are thinking about changing jobs, consider backloading's effect on your retirement income. Look at your Summary Plan Description's section on pension calculation, and see if a higher value is assigned to later years on the job.**

▶ *Inflation and mobile workers.*
Like the "fractional rule," inflation is especially hard on long-time workers who are forced to leave their jobs before retirement age. Here's why: Pension benefits are often computed according to the worker's final wages or salary. If a 45- or 50-year-old vested woman leaves her job, her pension fifteen or twenty years later will be calculated according to wages which have been left behind by inflation. For example, if Kathy put in forty years by working ten years on each of four jobs, her four pensions at age 65 would total less than if she had stayed on one job for forty years, even without backloading, because three of the pensions are being calculated according to old, inflation-eroded wages. The Department of Labor estimates that a worker like Kathy would get only one-half the benefits of a worker who stayed with one job for forty years, assuming identical pensions and an inflation rate of 6 percent.

☑️ If you are vested in a pension and will be leaving your job long before retirement age, ask your plan administrator for a projection of what your benefits will be, assuming you quit now and begin drawing benefits when you are 65. You are entitled to this information once a year—ask for the "Individual Benefit Statement." Then reduce the annual projected benefit by 5 percent for each year remaining between your current age and age 65. Although inflation varies widely, 5 percent gives you some idea of what your future pension would look like in today's dollars. Then you can plan your savings leg of the stool more realistically.

▶ *Erosion of fixed benefits.*
JoAnn and Jim each retired at age 65 with $1,000 per month for life in pension benefits. Yet JoAnn was much poorer at her death than Jim was at his. This is because private pensions are rarely protected from inflation by in-dexing or guaranteed cost-of-living adjustments (COLAs). Although this misfortune appears "gender-neutral," in real-ity inflation poses a bigger problem for women than men, because of women's statistically longer lifespans.

At an inflation rate of 7 percent, Jim and JoAnn's pen-sions will each buy $500 worth of goods when they reach age 75, at which point Jim dies. JoAnn lives on another eight years, dying at 83 with a purchasing power of a little over $300 per month. JoAnn lives longer but dies poorer, because of the virtual nonexistence of COLAs in the pri-vate pension world. Women over age eighty are the poorest of America's poor, and the exposure of private pensions to the erosions of inflation are a part of the problem.

▶ *The longevity penalty.*
Here's a practice which could well reduce any pension cred-its you earned before 1978, and it's aimed directly at women. In an attempt to compensate for the longer payout period for women's statistically longer lives, many plans for-merly penalized women workers in either of two ways:

- A larger pension payroll deduction than a man's

- A lower retirement check than a man's

The United States Supreme Court outlawed the practice for employment-based pensions in a series of decisions beginning in 1978, reasoning that the Civil Rights Act of 1964 prohibited the application of a statistic, even a true one, to disfavor women if the condition did not apply to all women. If statistics were a proper way to discriminate against workers, then no men could be jockeys, since men as a statistical class are too large. But a few men *are* small enough, and of course, they dominate the sport. Likewise, if all women outlived all men, perhaps a pension adjustment would be equitable.

But all women do not outlive all men. Far from it, in fact. Eight percent of women live longer, and eight percent of men die younger. In other words, all women are made to pay, and all men are given the benefit, so that the eight percent of men and women on either end of the life-expectancy charts can be equalized. And this, in the context of employment, means unequal compensation, and that is illegal.

Pension plans do not have to correct credits earned prior to 1978, which means that millions of women now in mid-career have earned pension credits against which this discriminatory formula will apply. Because the change was not made retroactive, women's pension income will continue to suffer for decades from gender-based life-expectancy tables.

▶ *Holes in the safety net.*
Congress set up the Pension Benefit Guaranty Corporation (PBGC) to protect against the insolvency of most plans. Unfortunately, if you are like millions of women who are support staff (clerks, secretaries, paralegals, dental assistants, bookkeepers, receptionists) in small offices, the PBGC will not protect even your vested benefits in the event your employer mishandles your plan, or goes into

bankruptcy. Professional offices with fewer than twenty-five employees are not covered under this fund.

The PBGC offers important protection, not only from business bankruptcies and abuse, but also from investment losses which lead to insolvency. Nearly 40 percent of aggregate pension portfolios are in common stocks, which makes many plans very vulnerable to stock-market fluctuations. The crash of October 1987, resulted in net capital losses to pension funds of $152 billion.

The Department of Labor estimates that $4 billion in pension funds are being misused, but no one really knows how deep the problem is. And enforcement is biased against the very plans that cover most women. The department investigates the largest plans; those which cover fewer than 100 workers—the small workplaces where women predominate—are rarely reviewed.

And remember—just as employers do not have to set up a pension plan in the first place, neither do they have to keep one going. An employer can terminate any plan at any time. The vested benefits, and even some unvested ones, must be paid as owed, of course, but nothing accrues after the termination date.

If you have questions about your plan's investments, you have a right to a financial report. This is called the "Summary Annual Report" (SAR), or "form 5500," issued annually by large plans, or every three years by small ones. Ask the administrator. If, after reviewing the SAR, you feel your pension funds are being mishandled, you have the right to sue the plan administrators for breach of their fiduciary duty. ERISA protects you against financial losses caused by mismanagement and misuse of pension assets. At minimum, your plan's administrators must act solely for the plan beneficiaries' benefit, invest prudently, diversify investments, and operate in accordance with the plan document and the law.

If all else fails.

If your claim has been denied, or your benefit is not what you think it should be, don't assume your union representative, employee representative, personnel department, or plan administrator is the final word. If your gut tells you an injustice was done, appeal. ERISA gives you the right to get a second decision from the plan within sixty days of the first decision. It is critical to observe the time limits for each step. The plan administrator must tell you how to qualify for a benefit ("perfect" your claim), and how to appeal if the decision goes against you.

If you are still unsatisfied after the second decision, you can sue the plan in state or federal court. You should choose your lawyer carefully, being sure that he or she is well versed in pension litigation, as it is complex. Start by calling the National Pension Referral Service run by the Pension Rights Center in Washington, D.C. (see Appendix II), and learning if their national network of pension litigators includes a lawyer near you. These lawyers have been trained to represent workers' and retirees' rights. Your local bar association's legal referral service may also be able to refer you to a pension specialist. If they can't, look further before agreeing to be represented by a lawyer without this expertise. Look in the Yellow Pages under "employee benefits," "retirement rights," "pension rights," or similar descriptions of the attorney's area of practice.

Any retaliation against you for exercising your pension rights, including the right of inquiry, is itself unlawful. This includes letting you go because you are about to qualify for a pension, or coercing or intimidating you when you exercise your rights, or discriminating against your fellow employees for supporting you or testifying on your behalf. You can win a retaliation lawsuit even if you lose your main pension claim.

 The cost of a wife.

Homemakers comprise the single largest occupational class in this country. Nearly half the women in America are homemakers, yet because it is unpaid work, it does not count as a "real" job. Real jobs open the door to pensions, Social Security, and retirement savings. Homemaking does not.

Oh sure, you'll ride in on the coat-tails of your husband—maybe. You'll get a wife's Social Security benefit equaling half of his; share in his pension if he has one, and your joint retirement savings if he's thought ahead. But what if he dies? Or you divorce? Where are your benefits then? The average age of widowhood in this country is only 56, and some researchers say that of women now 25, more than one in five will be divorced from their last marriage by the time they are 65. An unmarried future is a fact of life for the overwhelming majority of women—fewer than one woman in five is married when she dies.

In technical language, a pension which ends at death is a "single-life" annuity. If the pension continues in some (usually reduced) amount until the death of the widow(er), it is a "joint-life" annuity. The pension plan, in other words, is insuring two lives. As a woman, you have a longer life expectancy (statistically), and are perhaps younger than your husband, so the pension benefit, in stretching to cover your life, reduces the monthly income for both of you from the beginning. If your husband took a pension benefit that would end when he died, he might get $600 per month. But he will have to make do with (for example) $500 per month if the benefit will continue after his death for your life, and it will probably drop to $250 for you after he dies. Plainly put, your pension may be lower if you are married than if you are single.

▶ **The widow's mite.**
Widows outnumber widowers six to one, so the survivor's benefit is a widow's benefit most of the time, although only one in four widows actually has one. One reason so few widows get survivor's benefits is that pensions were not required to offer them until 1976. ERISA changed this, but with a loophole that trapped thousands of women. From 1976 until 1985 the worker could make a secret decision to waive the survivor's benefit in favor of a higher pension

check during his lifetime, and countless husbands did just that. Many men gambled that their wives would die first—or assumed that "things would take care of themselves" after his death, so a little more in the pot while he was alive was worth the sacrifice of his wife's future.

Impoverished widows were heard by Congress. ERISA was amended in 1984 to recognize "the status of marriage as a economic partnership, and the substantial contribution to that partnership of spouses who work both in and outside the home." As a result, people who retired or will retire after 1985 are subject to different rules. Now, both husband and wife must consent in writing before the survivor's benefit is waived. But millions of women are still unprotected: those whose husbands retired before 1985, and those whose husbands work for local and state governments.

If you are the wife, widow, or former wife of the covered worker or retiree, you have the legal right to check your status with the plan administrator. You can find out who this is by calling your husband's union, personnel office, or employee association. This is one time when you should not rely on your husband's recollection. Retirement applications can be confusing, and memories can be faulty; and, sadly, some husbands willfully conceal the fact that they waived the widow's benefit. Forewarned is forearmed, and although you probably can't change things if your husband is already retired, at least you'll know what to expect, and perhaps take some of the steps outlined in the next chapter to protect your future.

Another of the 1984 amendments provides protection to workers who die before they reach early retirement age (often 55).

Alice and Zak had been married thirty years when he died suddenly at age 58 in 1983. All their retirement plans depended upon his pension—a sound one, with a survivor's benefit. Zak had stayed with the company despite tempting offers to go elsewhere because of the pension. Alice had done volunteer work without pay rather than earn Social Security and a pension on her own, because she expected Zak's pension. But on his death, there was nothing. He had not retired, the company said—even though he had been eligible to retire at 55. "The pension is not an insurance policy," they told Alice. "There is nothing whatsoever for you."

Thousands of women like Alice are now among the elderly poor. If Zak had died in 1985 things would have been different, provided Alice and Zak had not waived the early-death benefit. Now, early widows will get a survivor's benefit, but only when the husband would have reached retirement age, and only if he was entitled to a pension in the first place.

☑ **The early-death feature will not automatically apply to jobs your husband left before 1985. Make sure he contacts the plan administrator wherever he has vested benefits and secures this protection for you. After he has done so, exercise your rights as beneficiary and doublecheck with the plan.**

ERISA does not protect your survivor's benefits if you are one of the millions of women married to state and local government retirees, or the wives of federal government retirees who retired before federal retirement systems required spousal consent. These include teachers, police officers, motor vehicle clerks, bus drivers, highway workers, and so on. Each plan is a creature of a state or local legislative body, so provisions differ widely. In many, the worker still has the right to secretly waive the survivor's benefit; in others, the benefit ends if the widow remarries. Whether you have the right to learn your status on your husband's government plan is up to the particular plan.

☑ **If your husband will have a government pension, your pressure point is your legislature. Public pensions are creatures of statute, and your county board of supervisors, district supervisors, state legislators, or** congress members are the ones to work with to effect change. ERISA does not affect these plans, so to learn what rights to information and appeal you may have, contact your union or employees' association representative, or plan administrator.

If your husband's retirement benefit is a "profit-sharing" plan, you'll get what's left in his account when he dies. But if he decides to withdraw or spend all the money before he dies, ERISA does not protect you from a zero balance at his death.

And finally, ERISA does not protect you if you are not married to the worker. If you are his lover, friend, sister, or child, nothing in the law provides a survivor's benefit for you unless your interests were protected in a divorce decree. ERISA, like many American laws, is biased toward marriage.

A word of warning: do not waive your survivor's benefit in favor of taking out an insurance policy on your husband's life, unless you have very good, very objective advice. An insurance salesperson's charts and figures do not constitute objective advice. Your survivor's benefit is a right, backed by the government. An insurance policy is not. It can be canceled, the company can go broke, or your husband can change the beneficiary. You may well want to supplement the pension with insurance—but think long and hard before you replace it.

Assuming you leap over the hurdles and qualify for a survivor's benefit, how much will be your prize? It must be at least half of the benefit you and your husband received while he was alive—and in fact it is usually no more than that.

Some plans offer the retiree a choice. Plan A might be equal to the full amount you received while your husband was alive. Plan B might be three-quarters of that amount; and Plan C one-half. Plan D, the booby-prize, is the waiver:

no survivor's benefit for you at all. You must consent in writing only to Plan D: The others can be selected by your husband alone—and in secret. Nobody notifies you of his choice, so if your husband is already retired, there could be an unpleasant surprise waiting for you after his death in the form of a drastically reduced benefit.

Write the plan administrator and ask which plan your husband selected when he retired. It is very unlikely you can do anything to change his choice, even with his consent, but at least you will know what is ahead and make necessary arrangements to bolster your future income. If you learn your husband selected the lowest survivor's benefit, or if he wants you to consent to no survivor's benefit, the reason is this: he will have more money while he lives if you have less, or none, after he dies. It all goes back to the single-life/joint-life annuities described earlier. If your husband is like most people approaching retirement, he has a lot of anxiety about his future income. So when he is presented with the options, along with illustrations in dollars of their consequences, the temptation to ensure a comfortable retirement for himself at the expense of a full (or any) survivor's benefit for you is great. It is easy for him to rationalize that you will die first, or that the kids will take care of you, or that you will remarry or get a part-time job. Again, since 1985, he can't leave you with no survivor's benefit unless you consent to it in writing, but he *can* select the lowest-paying benefit without telling you, assuming he has a choice of options in the first place.

☑ **Take the trouble to inform yourself of the plan's benefits, and in particular its survivor benefits. The plan administrator must send you a summary of the plan's benefits if you ask for it in writing. If the plan offers two or three levels of survivor's benefits, have a candid talk with your husband about what you will both need during the period he is alive, and your own needs after he's gone, which could extend for decades. Settle upon a choice which takes your extended needs into consideration. Don't forget inflation; guaranteed** cost-of-living increases are rare. Under some circumstances you may both decide that no survivor's benefit should be selected; perhaps because you will have a substantial pension, or you have a terminal illness and the extent of your lifetime is known. In any case, after the retirement choices are made, you should exercise your right to inquire about your status with the plan administrator, just to make double-sure that what was agreed upon was what, in fact, was selected.

▶ *The remarriage penalty.*

If you receive a survivor's benefit from a private pension, you may well lose it if you remarry. Although Social Security and a few government plans permit remarriage after a certain age, ERISA does not require that plans offer that protection, so they rarely do. Of course, if you die before your husband, he can remarry at any time and keep the full pension. This is a holdover from the days when pensions were considered the sole property of the worker, and the survivor's benefit a mere gratuity to a grateful widow. Now, as the recent amendments to ERISA attest, and many state marital property laws across the country confirm, pensions are properly considered the property of both members of the economic partnership—the marital unit. A benefit that extinguishes upon the remarriage of one partner but not the other reflects archaic notions about the dependent role of women. (Also, if you married your husband after he retired, most plans will not permit him to amend his single-life annuity to leave you a survivor's benefit.)

Paltry or missing survivor's benefits are a principal reason why the pension leg of the retirement income stool is short or missing for American women, and a major reason why older women are so much poorer than older men. With three out of four widows receiving no survivor's benefit at all, and the few that do generally receiving only one-half of the joint-life benefit, it is no wonder that three out of four elderly poor are women.

☑ If you think there might be something coming to you, ask how to make a claim, or send a letter asserting your status as a widow, wife, or former wife, and spelling out your claim. The administrator must respond to *a written claim* within ninety days, also in writing. If your claim is denied, he or she must tell you how to appeal, or what you need to do to qualify for a benefit.

▶ *The divorced woman's plight.*

Divorce is now common even after long marriages. With one in four divorces involving a marriage of longer than fifteen years, it is no surprise that a lucrative asset such as a pension has taken center stage in the property negotiations of many divorces. The pension is likely to be one of the principal assets of the marriage for an older couple. It wasn't until the 1970s, though, that courts began to look at the pension as an asset of the marriage, and not merely as income available for spousal support.

While not all states recognize the pension as a marital asset, those that do place a value on the pension, and that value is divided between the couple as part of the property award. Except for some government plans which have their own formulas, the pension asset is generally split according to either of two ways: a "cash-out," or a deferred pay-out. The cash-out estimates the future value of the pension, then awards the wife immediately with an offsetting share of other marital assets. Very often the wife swaps her pension rights for the house, which, depending on a lot of things, including real estate appreciation and her former husband's longevity, may or may not be a sound decision from a retirement income point of view. The deferred pay-out splits the pension as it begins to be paid, according to whatever formula was decided upon at the time of the divorce. Until 1985, when ERISA directed plan administrators to pay the pension according to a qualified domestic court order, the deferred method often meant the wife had a collection problem with her former husband. Now the court will order the administrator to pay out two checks, allowing the former wife to receive her share directly.

Betty and Bob are divorcing after a marriage of thirty years. They are both 53. Betty was a homemaker and has no pension credits of her own. However, Bob worked for a large company with pension coverage for all thirty years of their marriage. He will be eligible to retire when he reaches 65. The pension is valued at $100,000, the house (paid up) at $110,000. They decide that Betty will get the house and Bob the pension, plus their $5,000 car to make up the difference in value. It isn't long before Betty learns that she is unwanted in the paid-labor market, so she is forced to sell the house, as she cannot afford the taxes and insurance on it. Although she intends to invest the proceeds and live off the interest, one way or another the fund is down to $20,000 by the time Betty is 65. She has no house, little income, and probably no right to any of Bob's $10,000 per year pension, other than a possible claim for alimony. If Betty had deferred her claim, she would at least have had her share of the pension when she reached age 65.

On the other hand, the deferred method also has its risks. Let's say that Betty agreed to take her share of the pension upon Bob's retirement, but Bob dies six months after he retires. Presuming Betty's lawyer protected her interest in a survivor's benefit, she will at least have that, but it will be very small, probably only half of the already reduced joint benefit. The house was sold at the divorce, and Bob's share of the proceeds, which he invested, will go not to Betty, but to his heirs—perhaps to their kids, or Bob's new wife. Betty has no house, almost no pension, and only her share of the proceeds from the sale of the house. Had she taken the cash-out, she might at least have all of the house.

Unfortunately, if you are a divorced woman, your retirement income may depend upon which state you live in. ERISA does not compel a state to divide the pension equally, or even at all. The law does not require your state to give you any share in the pension you and your husband both worked so hard to earn (after all, you *both* endured the lower salary he earned in order for his employer to provide a pension). ERISA confirms that the pension can be divided between you and your husband according to the terms of a qualified domestic court order (generally, a divorce decree). The specifics of that order, or whether there will be any order at all, are up to the state and the court in question.

☑ **If you were divorced before 1985, and your decree orders the plan to pay you a share of the pension, but the plan refuses, it may be possible to get the plan to pay you your share voluntarily by showing them the decree and how it conforms to the current law.**

Suppose you've been awarded a portion of the pension when your former husband retires—and then he refuses to retire. He loves his work, and intends to die in harness. But what about you? Since 1985, ERISA says your part of the pension must be available to you when your former husband reaches his plan's earliest retirement age, whether he chooses to retire then or not. But remember, the earlier you draw it, the smaller it will be. By waiting, you may increase your monthly benefit. On the other hand, by waiting you may only get the reduced survivor's benefit, because your former husband could die. Your choice should consider all the circumstances, including his health, your need for present benefits, and so forth. You can draw your share out in any way he can: as a lump sum, an annuity for a fixed term of years, or as a lifetime monthly annuity.

Then there is the whole question of the second wife. Suppose Bob and Betty agree that her share of the pension will be one-half of the benefit when he retires at age 65. Soon Bob marries a 38-year-old woman, Natasha. At 65 Bob retires, choosing a joint-life annuity to protect Natasha in the event of his death. But Natasha is only 38, and her long life expectancy causes the joint-life annuity to be very low. As the divorced wife, is Betty's one-half share reduced because of Natasha? No. Betty's share will be whatever was awarded her by the court, regardless of Ed's remarriage. Natasha's survivor's benefit will be based on Ed's one-half share of the pension.

☑ If you were divorced before your state began dividing pensions at divorce, then you may have no rights to any of your former husband's pension, other than a possible claim for alimony. In some states, courts will re-open even a final divorce proceeding to reconsider the property settlement in light of later changes in the law, under the theory that property not before the court at the time of the divorce was not subject to its final decree. It's a long shot, but worth a consultation with a divorce attorney who is *very* expert on pension division.

▶ *Divorce and survivor's benefits.*
Prior to 1985, *survivor's* benefits for the former wife were rarely ordered by courts. If you're divorcing now, he sure your final decree includes a survivor's benefit for you—if it does, the plan must honor it. ERISA requires the court order to meet certain technical qualifications, so be very sure your attorney fashions the court order accordingly (attorneys usually write the court order; the judge then signs it). Remember, ERISA's protection does not extend to public pensions, so former wives of government workers are at risk if their former husbands die before they do.

☑ There is always the possibility of a malpractice suit against your divorce attorney if he or she neglected to secure this valuable asset for you in the first place, whether cash-out, divided benefit, or survivor's benefit. This important recourse should not be overlooked, but try to avoid it by choosing your lawyer carefully in the first place.

THE WOMEN'S LEG OF THE STOOL: SOCIAL SECURITY

If you're under 50, you've probably written Social Security out of your expectations. An entire generation is convinced that Social Security will not be there for them when they retire. And they couldn't be more wrong. Although actuaries argue endlessly over the "solvency" question, the issue in the end is not actuarial at all. It is political. There is no chance—zero—that future politicians will permit the collapse, or even any major cutbacks to Social Security. You can count on it.

Social Security is currently more than healthy, and we must work to keep it that way. It is a lifesaver for women. Literally.

One out of five women over 65 has only Social Security income. The majority of Social Security beneficiaries are women. Social Security is *by far* the most important women's program in America today. It will need adjusting from time to time. After 2030, when everyone born before 1966 (the Baby Boom) is retired, Social Security may deplete its surplus, and need some adjusting.

▶ ### Social Security in a nutshell.

Social Security is earned on the job, and is paid for with a payroll tax shared equally by you and your employer (the FICA deduction you see on your paycheck), or income taxes paid by the self-employed. Simply put, your Social Security benefit will depend on how much you earned, and how long you worked.

You need 40 "credits" to be fully covered by Social Security if you were born after 1929, and you can earn up to four credits a year, depending on your earnings. This means that you can build Social Security credits with part-time and seasonal work. If you take a year to earn one credit, that is okay with Social Security. It is also fully portable—wherever you work, and however long you work there, Social Security will continue crediting your account.

You may hear, from time to time, that you could do better taking your Social Security taxes and investing them on your own for retirement. This ignores the insurance factor—while you work, even if you don't yet have all your credits, you are insured and so is your family. If you die or become disabled, your spouse and minor children may be paid Social Security benefits. You can't match the insurance aspect with a savings account or a mutual fund. Nor can you pay for your parents' retirement with your own retirement savings—yet their parents' Social Security checks make it possible for millions of midlifers to concentrate on college costs for their kids rather than putting food on the table for their parents. Nevertheless, you should not rely upon Social Security as 100 percent of your retirement plan; it is but *one* of the three legs.

☑ **If you don't have 40 Social Security credits, get them. One way to do this is to develop a sideline business— perhaps a consultancy, or if you're a teacher, a summer job. Document your earnings, report them on Schedules C and SE when you do your income tax (or form 1065 if you have a partner) and your Social Security credits will build.**

Social Security was enacted in the heart of the Depression, when the typical American family consisted of one (male) wage-earner, his lifelong homemaker wife, and their four or more children. The wage-earner earned Social Security credits on the job, which were paid for by him and his employer equally. His dependent wife and children did not earn credits on their own unless they were wage-earners, too, since credits were employment-related. His benefit included an insurance feature, so that if he died or became disabled before retirement, his family received an allowance based on his earnings record.

This structure was not set up to cope with divorce, multiple marriages, wage-earning wives, and non-traditional families. Neither did it reflect the notion of marriage as a partnership in which each spouse's contributions, whether in the home or in the paid labor force, were valued equally. Unlike some countries, no American Social Security credits are given for the care of children, disabled adults, or elderly people in the home.

Here are some special problems for working women:

"Zero years."

Your Social Security benefit is calculated according to a complex formula, which takes into account up to 35 years of employment. Unlike many pensions, it is not based on your most recent wages or your highest wages. It calculates all but the five lowest years, even if you had *no* earnings in some years. These "zero-earnings years" hit women far harder than men, and are a big reason why women's Social Security income is only about two-thirds of men's.

Anne earned $50,000 per year as soon as she left graduate school. She stayed on the same job five years, then left to care for her children for ten years, then returned to work. When her retirement benefit is calculated, Anne will be able to "throw out" five of her zero years, but the other five will stay in the formula to reduce her final benefit, even though Anne paid maximum Social Security taxes while she worked, because of her high income.

While you're building your account, you should check every two or three years to make sure Social Security is crediting your account correctly. This is especially important for women, because name changes are an opportunity for records to get mixed up. Call Social Security and ask for the "Personal Earnings and Benefit Estimate Statement," and fill out the form they will send you. It will give you loads of good information, including the amount credited to your account by year, and an estimate of your retirement, disability and dependent's benefits, based on their records and your projections of future income. Early and late retirement estimates are included. It's an essential tool for planning your retirement package. And it's free!

 Retirement age.

Social Security's "normal" retirement age for those born in 1937 or earlier is 65. If you fall into that category, you will receive 100 percent of your Primary Insurance Account

(PIA) if you apply at age 65 (the PIA is your full benefit, and is the benchmark upon which all your other benefits, such as spousal, are calculated). If you can't wait until then, you may apply as early as age 62. At present, the early benefit is about 80 percent of the PIA—and it remains at that level for life.

However, to cushion the shock of the retiring Baby Boom, Congress instituted a phased-in increase in the retirement age. If you were born after 1959, you will have to wait until you are 67 before you can draw your PIA. The measure was justified on the basis of the jump in life-expectancy for persons over 65, as well as the elimination of mandatory retirement. After the full phase-in, you will still be able to retire early at 62, but your lifetime benefit will be only 70 percent of your PIA, rather than the 80 percent as now. This reduction is phased in, so that if you were born in 1947, for example, you can apply at age 62 and receive a benefit of 75 percent of your PIA.

It's tempting to get annoyed at this point. Today's workers are paying a far larger proportion of their pay into Social Security than did today's retirees, yet they will have their benefits delayed. Obviously, despite the rhetoric about increases in life expectancy, the real reason is financial—the system needs these adjustments if the increase in Baby Boom retirees starting in 2011 is to be accommodated. Nevertheless, women must resist the temptation to join those who would dismantle Social Security by making it voluntary. When the cards are down, Social Security is the mainstay of women's retirement. You will almost certainly not be able to meet your retirement goals without it.

If you can delay your retirement past 65, you can increase your monthly benefit. If you delay drawing Social Security until you are 68, your benefit will be higher than if you begin at 65, and will include any COLA increases in the interim.

Secrets, secrets.

If, in an effort to mitigate job discrimination, you have been less than truthful about your age to your employer, you may find yourself in a quandary when you actually become old enough to draw Social Security or Medicare benefits.

Consider Emily. She told her employer she was 38 when she began work—although she was actually 43. She still works at the same place, but would like to begin getting Medicare and Social Security now that she is 65. Her boss thinks she's 60, and she doesn't want him to know otherwise. She is aware he can't fire or penalize her because of age, but she still wants to keep her secret.

Social Security will keep your application for retirement benefits and Medicare confidential from your employer if you request it. You will have to provide Social Security with the data it needs to prove your claim—data it would otherwise get from your employer. They will accept your birth certificate as proof of your real age. It is possible, however, that a Medicare claim could become known to your group health insurer from work, and in this way get back to your employer, and other inadvertent leaks could occur. Might be better to come clean.

Social Security is a lifesaver for millions of women who never worked for pay, or whose lifetime wages were so low only minimal Social Security was earned. If you are among them, you will (probably) be entitled to Social Security as either a wife, widow, or former wife of a retiree or deceased retiree.

Even though you may have zero credits in your own Social Security account, you can receive a check, in your own name if you prefer, reflecting your interest in your husband's account. Generally, a wife or former wife receives an amount equal to half the husband's benefit; a widow or surviving former wife receives 100 percent of the decedent's benefit.

▶ ## Wives and widows.

Remember how pensions are decreased for the married worker? Social Security does the opposite, increasing the married worker's benefit by 50 percent if the spouse does not have enough Social Security on his or her own work record to exceed the spouse benefit. With some exceptions for government workers, the couple gets 150 percent of what the worker would have received if unmarried. Social Security will pay this out in two checks or one, your choice. When the worker dies, the monthly benefit drops from 150 percent to 100 percent, which means the survivor will have to get along on only 67 percent of the joint benefit received while both were alive. Because many expenses, such as home upkeep, taxes, and insurance do not drop when one spouse dies, the drop in Social Security income leaves many widows in difficult circumstances.

▶ ## The widow's gap.

Widow(er)s receive 100 percent of their spouse's benefit after his or her death (subject to the "dual entitlement" rule, about which more later), can remarry after age 60 and keep the benefits, and can begin receiving (reduced) benefits as early as age 60, or 50 if disabled. But for the early widow(er), there is a gap in Social Security's family-protection scheme.

Louella's husband died when she was 41, and their daughter was 12. Louella received a parent's benefit until her daughter was 16 (and Louella was 45). Her daughter continued to receive her own benefit until she was 18. Louella had no Social Security protection for 15 years until she reached 60—the "widow's gap." This gap can leave the middle-aged widow destitute. If she is not wanted in the paid labor market, or can only get fast-food jobs at the minimum wage, she will learn that she would have been far better off blind or severely disabled—economically, anyway. There is no federal welfare program for her unless she has minor children, or is blind, chronically disabled, or over 65. Nor is she entitled to unemployment for her homemaking efforts, worker's compensation if she injured herself working in the home, or employment-based disability benefits. In short, she is up the proverbial creek. If you are a homemaker, you are a member of the only occupational class in America whose efforts are so disregarded by policymakers that not one strand of a safety net has been woven for you. When you fall through the net, you fall all the way down.

▶ ### *Homemakers who have earnings.*

Millions of women combine homemaking with sporadic, or part-time forays into the paid-labor market. Of course, unlike pensions, Social Security builds in your account whether or not you are a full- or part-time worker, and whether or not you move in and out of the workforce. So millions of women end up with a Social Security record which would entitle them to a (very) modest benefit. Since these women (and some men) have worked as homemakers and in the paid workforce, they are entitled to Social Security both on their own accounts, and on their spouse's account as wives, husbands, ex-spouses, or widow(er)s. Under the dual entitlement rule, you can draw the highest benefit you are entitled to, but not both.

Rosamond worked here and there during her twenty-year marriage to Ivan. They divorced when she was 45, and at 48 she married Haven. After eleven years, they were divorced. At 65 Rosamond found she was entitled to:

- $88 per month on her own account as a worker.

- $400 per month as Ivan's former wife.

- $350 per month as Haven's former wife.

Rosamond could not receive all three benefits. She drew $400 per month off Ivan's record because it was the largest.

☑ **Social Security pays a reduced (lifetime) benefit if you begin drawing it before "normal" retirement age of 65, or a lifetime bonus if you wait longer. Since you**

have a choice of which entitlement to draw if you are
dually or triply entitled, you may choose to draw on
your own work record at your earliest age, then switch
to your entitlement as a wife at 65 or older (or vice
versa). The benefit drawn before 65 will be reduced;
the one taken after will not.

Zero years.
Of course, many women are paid enough on the jobs they
rotate with homemaking that when it's time to retire, their
own work record gives them the highest entitlement. But
their benefits are crippled by the zero years discussed earlier.
A thirty-five-year record with 10 zeros will inevitably devas-
tate the earnings record of even well-paid workers.

**Stay out of the paid labor market for no more than five
years, if you can swing it. That way you can exclude all
five zero years from the benefits calculation when you
retire.**

Divorce and Social Security.
Divorce, an increasing phenomenon among the long-mar-
ried, leaves thousands of older women in desperate financial
straits. Social Security is helpful in this situation, but not
perfect.

If your marriage lasted ten years or longer, you are entitled to a benefit equaling 50 percent of your former spouse's
benefit while he or she is alive, or 100 percent after he or
she dies, a dramatic example of how you're better off with
your "ex" dead than alive (but then, of course, you knew
that!). This benefit, like the others, is subject to the dual-
entitlement rule. With the average marriage lasting less
than seven years, the ten-year requirement disqualifies
countless divorced spouses from a benefit. This affects more
women than men, because more women qualify for spousal
benefits since they don't earn enough on their own records.
During the years of your marriage, however long that may
have been, you were subject to the reduction in income due

to the Social Security payroll tax, so you should share equally in the benefits it purchased. In other words, you shared equally the burden, and should share equally in the benefit.

In addition, the divorced wife's benefit is inadequate. A married couple gets 150 percent of the worker's PIA (100 percent of the PIA for him, 50 percent for her—although they can ask Social Security to divide this in half and issue a check to each of them in the same amount). A widow gets 100 percent; a divorced spouse gets 50 percent. In other words, her benefits are calculated like a wife's, rather than a widow's. In reality, her economic situation is the same as a widow's, not a wife's, and her benefits should be increased accordingly. A wife, after all, has a theoretical one-half share of 150 percent, or 75 percent of her husband's benefit. One-half of a Social Security benefit is simply not enough to support anyone, and in this era of easy divorce, countless women are put into a situation they didn't ask for, and impoverished thereby. Social Security benefits for the divorced woman should parallel the widow's (100 percent), not the wife's (50 percent), benefit.

Widows and divorced widows can begin to draw benefits when they reach age 60. Wives and divorced wives have to wait until the *husband* reaches age 62. This is fine for wives, who have their husband's income to support them. For divorced wives, it is a hardship, especially if they are older than their former husbands. They may be in their upper sixties before they can draw a benefit.

RIGHTING THE WRONGS IN PENSIONS AND SOCIAL SECURITY

▶ *Pensions.*

For women the pension agenda is pretty clear: eliminate the penalties for interrupted careers and part-time work; weight pension credits in favor of the lower-paid rather than the higher-paid; index pensions to the cost of living, and eliminate integration. State and local government pensions must be reformed so as to meet minimum levels imposed by ERISA on private plans.

Mandatory pensions are a must. How policymakers expect Americans to achieve the three legs of the stool without mandated pensions is a mystery. If lawmakers continue to bow to the notion that businesses must be free to make these decisions on their own, then they have an obligation to build Social Security up so that the stool is stable on two legs. They simply cannot enunciate a policy of a triple-funded retirement, then tolerate a situation where one out of three Americans works in a job where the essential pension leg is missing. Furthermore, the percentage of American workers covered by private pensions shrank during the 1980s after rising in earlier decades, with losses concentrated among younger workers.

The controversial "mommy-track" spoken of earlier is a reality in the numbers of women sharing full-time jobs in order to juggle family responsibilities. Relegated to the status of part-time workers, many lose all rights to the fringe benefits. To be responsive to changing American work patterns, mandatory pension coverage must include part-timers as well.

If you could take your pension credits with you when you change employers, or move in and out of the paid labor market (as you can with Social Security), you would end up with more in your pocket on retirement day. "Portability" has gained currency because of the recent spate of mergers and acquisitions, which have resulted in massive losses of pension credits among unvested workers who have found their plans merged out of existence. Full portability would knock down many of the steepest pension hurdles for women. It would solve the problem of mobility, vesting, and breaks in service. But full portability is a dream at present. More than likely, portability will first include only vested pension credits, leaving unresolved the mobility problem of women workers.

▶ *Social Security.*

Social Security needs major surgery if it is to keep up with the changes in American lives. The old model of a working man married to a lifetime homemaker wife no longer reflects reality. As the underpinning of the country's entire retirement system, Social Security, more than any other program, must fit real lives.

The *homemaking penalty* can be mitigated in several ways. For women who combine homemaking and paid work, an increase in the number of years (now five) which can be excluded from the benefit calculation would certainly help, but this is still not the same as earning credits for the homemaking years. A precedent exists in this country for granting Social Security credits for "uncovered" work: gratuitous credits have been given for military service, and to Japanese-Americans interned during World War II. If policymakers agree that homemaking is a worthwhile activity, from which American society in general benefits, then crediting homemaking years (perhaps at minimum wage levels at the start) makes a lot of sense.

The *widow's gap* could be closed somewhat by the institution of a one- to three-year transition benefit for widow(ers) under age 60, to help the new widow pull herself together, get training perhaps, and find a job.

In recent years, a notion known as *"earnings sharing"* has been bandied about Washington. It has been introduced in bill form before Congress several times, and has duly failed each time. Commissions have studied it and proposed it, and advocacy organizations have supported it. Its day is coming, but it's taking a long time getting here. Earnings sharing works like this:

Dennis and Kay were nurses at a large hospital when they met. Each had ten years' work experience when they married, thus, ten years of Social Security credits on each of their records. They had a baby after one year of marriage. Kay quit her job and remained home ten years, as they had three children. She then returned to work for two years, whereupon she and Dennis divorced. Under today's rules,

Kay's Social Security record would credit her with twelve years, and force her to include her zero years in her computation when she retired. Dennis would have a full Social Security record reflecting his twenty-two years as a nurse. Since they had been married more than ten years, Kay could draw a divorced wife's benefit from Dennis's account if her own didn't provide benefits at least equal to half of his.

This system perpetuates their ties to each other, at a time when both would prefer to get on with their lives without reference to each other. Simply put, earnings sharing would add up the credits earned during the marriage (Dennis's twelve years plus Kay's three) and divide them down the middle. Each account would be credited with six-and-a-half years, plus the ten years each worked prior to the marriage, which would not be shared.

CONCLUSION

A retirement system which works against more than half the American citizenry is not worthy of us. A woman of 65 who has worked fifteen years in the home and twenty-five years in the paid labor force has contributed forty years of productive work. The fact that part was uncompensated and the rest poorly paid does not reduce her equal need for an adequate retirement income. Whether she is married, widowed, divorced, or never married, she will probably be a loser under the American retirement system.

Despite improvements in pension law and Social Security, if you're a woman worker or full-time homemaker, your financial future is a risky one. In the next chapter we will look at some ways to improve your outlook.

CHECKING UP ON PENSIONS AND SOCIAL SECURITY

You could say that pensions and Social Security are a woman's best friend. But even your best relationships need evaluating now and then, and never more so than when your second life depends on it. Use these questions as a starting point for some realistic assessments of pensions, Social Security, and you.

✔ Are you covered by a pension at work?

✔ What is your Plan Administrator's (PA's) phone and address?

✔ Are you vested? Have you checked with the PA to make sure?

✔ Do you have your Summary Plan Description?

✔ How much will your final earnings be?

✔ Have you asked your PA to estimate your monthly pension?

✔ Will your pension be integrated with Social Security?

✔ Have you checked former jobs for a possible vested pension?

✔ Did you leave your job before retirement age?

✔ Have you projected the effects of inflation?

✔ Is your pension protected by the PBGC?

✔ Has the PA confirmed you'll get a survivor's benefit?

✔ How much of his pension will you lose when your husband dies?

✔ Have you phoned Social Security for your estimated benefits?

✔ Do you have forty Social Security credits?

✔ Are there "zero years" in your Social Security record?

✔ What is "normal" Social Security retirement for your age?

✔ Have you had Social Security estimate your (and his) benefit?

✔ Has the PA estimated your husband's pension benefit?

✔ If divorced, were you married ten years (for Social Security)?

✔ Will you get a survivor benefit from your ex-spouse's pension?

6

STRAW INTO GOLD
FOR THAT
SECOND LIFE

All right. So your pension and Social Security legs are a little short—or worse, they're missing altogether. Worry, but don't despair. Most American women are in the same boat. In this chapter we'll look at ways all women—working women, homemakers, divorced, single, widows—can pull rabbits out of hats and turn straw into gold. There are many ways to strengthen the legs on your stool, including desperation measures if saving for retirement is out of the question.

The private-savings leg of the three-legged stool is your opportunity to make up for shortfalls in the other two. It usually is anything you have left after you put your kids through college, paid your mortgage, cleared your medical bills, and paid your father's nursing home bill. In other words, all too often it's nothing!

As a woman facing formidable problems in the other two legs, you must take advantage of the opportunities of the private savings leg. These could be individual retirement accounts (IRAs), certificates of deposit, rents, treasury notes, stocks—anything to fund your retirement. Congress encourages retirement savings, so some savings vehicles are tax-favored. In addition, you might be able to set up a simple retirement plan at work, which will be easy to administer and cost your employer little. Remember, because you will probably have more retirement years to fund than a man, you should be aiming at replacing as close to 100 percent of your pre-retirement income as you can.

First we'll talk about some alternative plans for working women (and women who depend on working men), then IRAs for both workers and homemakers, and finally some savings and funding options, including desperation measures as a last resort. After that, we'll address the public agenda—how to reform our retirement income laws so that they fit women as well as men—something that will benefit all Americans because a prosperous, efficient workforce, equally rewarded for like contributions, would enrich us all.

Judy was 47 when she realized her Social Security check of about $8,000 per year was not going to support the retirement lifestyle she wanted. She talked her boss into setting up a deferred-compensation plan (she was in the 28 percent bracket), and she faithfully directed $4,000 per year into it for eighteen years at 8 percent. At age 65, she began drawing it out—a nice $16,000-per-year reward for her advance planning. In other words, $4,000 per year paid in quadrupled in value to $16,000 dollars per year paid out in just eighteen years, tripling her retirement income.

For twenty years, Ben and Jane got along fine on Ben's $35,000 income, yet they had not really saved for retirement. He received only Social Security coverage where he worked, and the $2,250 they put into their joint IRA annually was not enough for what they would want from retirement. When the kids left home, they decided Jane (age 45) would return to teaching, and defer the maximum allowed amount of her salary to a 403(b) annuity. Now that Jane was working, they could open another IRA, so in addition they were putting $4,000 per year into the two IRAs. In this way, Ben and Jane sheltered the legal maximum on their retirement savings for twenty years before they both retired at 65—and Jane earned a teacher's pension as well.

There are many other ways to prepare for your retirement. In this chapter we will look at tax-favored savings, "do-it-yourself" pensions, annuities, life insurance, ordering priorities, intelligent use of windfalls, home equity, and turning straw into gold when straw is all you've got. Let's get to work.

Your retirement savings can be either tax-favored or tax-exposed.

The first type is better, but the second is more available. For women, most of whom are not in the higher tax brackets, the enticements of tax-sheltered investments are less compelling than they are for the more highly paid. Nevertheless, it is worthwhile to take advantage of all tax shelters available to you. Generally, tax shelters save you income taxes in one (or more) of four ways:

• *Tax-exempt* income is free of income tax—either state or both federal and state. Treasury bills, notes, and bonds, for example, are partially tax-exempt—the interest earned is subject to federal, but not state, income tax. Obviously, the value of this kind of investment increases if you live in a state with a high income tax.

• *Tax-deductible* vehicles, like some IRAs and the 401(k)s, 403(b)s, and Keoghs discussed on page 163, allow you to deduct the amount you put into the program from your gross income, therefore lowering your income taxes.

• *Tax-deferred* investments permit you to invest in a program, accumulate the interest over the years without including it in your annual taxable income until you draw the money out in retirement. Some programs are both tax-deductible and tax-deferred.

• *Tax credits* let you subtract the credit directly from your income-tax bill.

All other things being equal, the tax-protected investment is always better than the exposed one.

Since most women have few options—little or no pension, and modest Social Security—the fancier tax-directed devices (ESOPs, stock options, bonus plans, profit-sharing) are beyond the scope of this crash course. The purpose of this discussion is to introduce some readily available retirement savings vehicles which can easily be put in place at work. Whether you play out your options in mutual funds, treasury notes, certificates of deposit, or Ginnie Maes is up to you and, I hope, a qualified and objective advisor. Presented here are the "plain vanilla" options—the relatively simple, straightforward mechanisms appropriate for the average worker and homemaker.

MAKING SOMETHING OUT OF NOTHING

▶ *A do-it-yourself pension.*
Maybe the only reason your workplace doesn't have a pension plan is because your boss just hasn't gotten around to it. This is often the case with very small businesses, including marginal employers like non-profit organizations and churches. Of course, these small enterprises are overwhelmingly staffed by women.

But there is a way you can help your boss over the hurdle, and help yourself to a better retirement. Call your local office of the I.R.S. and ask them to send you Form 5305-SEP. Once the form has been completed and filed, contributions can be made to you for inclusion in your IRA (see discussion below). This is known as a Simplified Employee Pension, or SEP, and an amount equaling up to 15 percent of your compensation can be contributed to the SEP (over and above your own $2,000 IRA contributions). This is tax-deductible to your employer.

SEPs can also be set up to complement an existing pension plan, and are especially nice for mobile women workers since you can participate in a SEP after only one year of employment, and the contributions to the SEP cannot be lost because of failure to vest. You can go from job to job, or in and out of the paid labor market, and keep the contributions flowing to your SEP, as long as each employer is willing to set one up.

☑ **Don't agree to a salary raise so your employer can avoid the "hassle" of putting together a fringe benefit package. The salary raise is taxable; the fringe benefits are not, except in the case of retirement benefits, which are not taxed until you withdraw them. In addition, group benefits (health, life insurance) are usually cheaper than individual ones. In other words, a $200-per-month raise will not buy as much as $200 in group benefits, and you have to pay income tax on it to boot.**

▶ *Deferred compensation.*

If you can't get your employer to contribute to an SEP or pension plan, perhaps he or she would agree to a plan where you make the contributions by a reduction in your pay. But why is having your employer reduce your pay by $200 per month any better than doing it yourself by putting $200 into a savings account on payday?

Because of taxes, that's why. When your pay is reduced, you save some income taxes. And unlike ordinary savings accounts, deferred-compensation plans accumulate savings tax-free until you withdraw them, generally as early as age 59½. And, like all tax shelters, the higher your tax bracket, the nicer the gain.

Two programs, called 401(k) and 403(b) for the sections of the tax code that authorize them, are readily available deferred-compensation mechanisms. Generally, 401(k)s are for the private, for-profit sector; 403(b)s are for state and local governments, churches, charities, and schools. They are tax-deductible and tax-deferred. Some advisors feel these programs have lost some of their luster in the wake of tax reform; others love them still. When there were numerous tax brackets separated by only a couple of thousand dollars, you could divert sufficient income into a 401(k) or 403(b) to drop you into a lower tax bracket. In that way, often magnificent income-tax savings were turned like magic into retirement savings.

Now, with many thousands of dollars between the high bracket and the low one, it is not so easy to drop a bracket but tax deferred is generally better than tax now, so even lower-paid workers will benefit from taking advantage of one of these programs. If you find your income creeping toward the higher bracket, deferring income until retirement can be wise.

Franny earned $20,000 per year, and paid an income tax of $3,000. She asked her employer to divert $1,500 per year of her salary into a 401(k). At the end of the year, she owed only $2,775 in income tax, because her 401(k) was deducted before tax, making her taxable income only $18,500. In effect, she has recaptured $225 from Uncle Sam and added it to her retirement savings—a free gift from Uncle Sam to Franny! Her 401(k) funds are not taxed until she takes them out after she is 59½ (earlier withdrawals are penalized, unless there is a qualified hardship). The employer has paid nothing except the administrative costs, because all of the contributions came from Franny's pay. Franny is ahead $225 plus tax-free earnings.

If you are in the 15-percent income-tax bracket like Franny, you will have to decide for yourself whether the relatively modest income-tax protection afforded by a 401(k) or 403(b) is worth putting your funds out of reach until you are 59½. Someone taxed at 28 percent benefits much more. Ideally, 401(k)s and 403(b)s should supplement a regular pension plan or an SEP. Still, where the employer refuses to set up anything better, it's nice knowing they are available.

Your employer can partially or fully match your contribution to a deferred compensation plan if it chooses. Because "matching" contributions inspire savings (a dollar-for-dollar match, after all, gives you a 100-percent rate of return before the first dollar of interest is earned), many employers like to encourage this. Even a 10-percent match when added to (for example) 7 percent interest, is a return to you of 17 percent—a fabulous return on your money!

▶ *How to shelter windfalls.*

Deferred compensation plans are useful if you get an unexpected windfall, through a lottery, inheritance, or divorce or injury settlement, for example. Consider deferring an equal amount of your salary (up to the limit) into your 401(k) or 403(b), and using the windfall to replace the deferred funds. Your annual income remains the same, but you have put the "found" money into tax-deferred savings—something you can't do by simply opening up a savings account or investing in most securities.

☑ **Do you want to know how much your windfall will be when you retire? Here's the Rule of 72: divide 72 by the rate of return on the investment, and you will have the number of years it will be before it doubles. In other words, $40,000 at 9 percent will be $80,000 in eight years (72 divided by 9 equals 8), and $160,000 in sixteen. This rule assumes that the interest is compounded and tax-deferred.**

▶ *How to convert ordinary savings
to tax-sheltered savings.*

You can convert existing savings to a 401(k) or 403(b) tax-sheltered account. Find out what the current annual contribution limit is (it changes with inflation—call the I.R.S. or an employee-benefit specialist), and have your employer reduce your paycheck accordingly. But remember: If you are in the lowest tax bracket, balance the modest increase to your savings against the penalty you'd have to pay to withdraw them from the deferred plan before you are 59½. If you decide you have ways to meet emergencies without making penalized withdrawals from the sheltered savings, and the extra retirement income is worth it to you, then draw out the ordinary savings as you need them to meet your ordinary living expenses, and watch your retirement savings grow tax-deferred. Depending upon the size of your account, it may take a few years to transfer it all over, because of the annual contribution limit. You should fund your IRA to the maximum as well.

Gretchen used tax strategies with her $9,000 ordinary savings to build her retirement savings. Since she was getting a raise which would put her into the 28-percent income-tax bracket, she decided it was time to get serious about taxes and retirement savings. She instructed her employer to reduce her salary by $7,000 and divert it to a 401(k). She then put $2,000 into her IRA, and drew down her savings account as needed during the year to replace the $7,000 she lost from her paycheck. Gretchen turned her savings into a nice tax-sheltered nest-egg, made larger because of two tax savings: her lower bracket and the tax-deferred accumulation of earnings.

▶ ### Shelter a second paycheck.

Sometimes deferred compensation plans are used to shelter a second salary as part of a married couple's retirement plan. The story of Ben and Jane at the beginning of this chapter illustrates this point. By funding their 401(k), 403(b), and IRA opportunities to the maximum, they essentially converted all of Jane's salary into tax-favored savings. They continued to live on Ben's salary as they had always done, wisely resisting the temptation to increase their standard of living by spending all of Jane's as well.

403(b)s are usually annuity contracts with life insurance companies, although mutual-fund 403(b)s are also available. To set one up, just look in your Yellow Pages and call several insurance agents. Point out to your employer that this is a retirement-savings vehicle which will cost virtually nothing, yet will increase the fringe benefit package. If you can talk your employer into matching employee contributions—even 25 cents on the dollar—so much the better! A 25 percent guaranteed return on your investment, even 15 percent, is unbeatable in today's investment market.

401(k)s offer the same opportunities for employer matching, but can include a larger array of investment options. It is not unusual for a 401(k) program to offer two, three, or more options—perhaps an equity fund, a government fund, and a bond fund—for you to split your contributions be-tween. The Yellow Pages are full of employee-benefit (or retirement, or fringe, or pension) consultants who would be delighted to talk to you. The fuss to your employer will be a mere adjustment to the payroll, since the insurer or admin-istrator takes care of signing you up and keeping you up to date on the status of your plan.

▶ Sheltering Social Security.

If you plan a late retirement, you can draw Social Security even though you're working. A certain amount is exempt from penalty, after which the Social Security benefit is re-duced $1 for every $2 earned under age 65, and $1 for every $3 earned over 65. (Call Social Security for the current exempt amount—it is subject to change.) If you work and draw Social Security, you should reduce your earnings by the amount of your Social Security benefit and put that amount into a deferred compensation plan. This way you save taxes *three* ways:

- By lowering your income subject to income tax.

- By deferring the tax on the interest you earn.

- By swapping fully taxable income for Social Security (tax-reduced).

▶ Manipulating cafeteria plans.

Maybe you have double coverage. For example, if you are covered on your husband's group health insurance as well as one at work, either you or your husband is losing out on full fringe benefits. Talk to your employer about setting up a "cafeteria plan," where you can choose among a variety of fringe benefits, thus avoiding duplication of coverage. This way, the money going into your duplicate health coverage could instead go into a SEP, even if you already have pen-sion coverage. SEPs and 401(k)s or 403(b)s often exist in tandem with ordinary pensions, although there are limits to the total amount of income you can shelter. With a cafeteria plan, you can recapture your duplicated benefits and make them work for your retirement. You need an employee-benefits consultant to put a cafeteria plan together. It is important that the plan be devised with employee input—otherwise its parts may not fit the needs of the workforce. One place might need a dependent-care component, another might be better off with beefed-up retirement plans.

☑ **Your pension plan might permit you to make voluntary contributions. This is a way to save up to an additional 10 percent of your compensation, free from taxes until after you retire. Consider negotiating with your employer to have the plan amended to include this feature if it doesn't already. Of course, you are always 100 percent vested in any contributions you make, voluntary or otherwise. In other words, you will get your money back if you leave the job before you vest.**

▶ *Getting smart.*
Invite a retirement-benefits consultant to your workplace to address your fellow workers. Be sure he or she understands that you want basic information on alternative retirement income savings; you don't need to hear about esoterica just yet. You want to know about cafeteria plans, SEPs, 401(k)s (or 403[b]s if you work at a non-profit, church, or school, or for state or local government), employer contributions to IRAs, and basic pensions. Your company can make more than one kind of retirement plan available to you, but there are complex rules about maximum contributions. You need the help of an expert unless you are putting in a single plan like a SEP. Save health and life insurance for another day. You have enough to absorb just in retirement income. If you're depending on your husband's retirement benefits, get a group of friends together for a short series of "experts and coffee."

▶ *Tax shelters for the self-employed.*

If you own your own business, whether incorporated, unincorporated, or a partnership, you should investigate setting up a Keogh plan with a retirement specialist, but be careful—many such consultants are really selling a product, rather than giving you objective advice. A Keogh is like an IRA or 401(k) with higher maximum donations. You might ask three or four agents to provide you with their materials, then in consultation with an attorney or a CPA specializing in employee benefits, decide which plan would be best. Attorneys and CPAs won't sell you a product, but they will sell you their time—expect a fee. With a Keogh plan, you can shelter up to $30,000 of your personal service income (up to 25 percent) by deducting it as a business expense. Keoghs grow tax-deferred, as well.

▶ *Borrowing from yourself.*

Many women entering midlife had their children later than those of the preceding generation. College costs and retirement concerns collide rather than passing in convenient sequence. If you have a well-funded 401(k) and can defer your own retirement needs for a while, consider borrowing against the 401(k) to help out on college costs. You can borrow up to half your vested funds (up to $50,000), and the interest you pay will be to yourself. That's right. The interest goes to your own account, since it's your money you're borrowing. You generally do not need a credit check, because the money is your own. If you fail to repay the loan, however, the unpaid balance will be treated as a premature withdrawal, with a 10-percent penalty if you are under 59½.

About two-thirds of employers permit 401(k) loans. Many allow convenient repayment through payroll deductions. Then, when your college kid gets her fancy new job, she can pay you back as well.

▶ *The good and bad about IRAs.*

Individual Retirement Accounts (IRAs) are available to any worker, and to a minimal extent, homemakers as well. More than $200 billion is stashed away in IRA accounts, so this aspect of the private-savings leg of the retirement income stool has proved popular.

IRAs are savings or investment accounts set up to receive your retirement savings. There they accumulate tax-deferred, until you withdraw them beginning at age 59½ (or later, if you prefer). Banks, stock brokerages, investment funds—all would love to tell you about their IRA opportunities. You need only call.

Workers can put away 100 percent of their earnings up to a maximum of $2,000 per year in an IRA. If you are a married homemaker, you and your husband can put away a total of $2,250 per year into an IRA instead of the $2,000 limit per person. If you have any earnings at all, you can fund an IRA with 100 percent of them up to $2,000 for yourself. These must be employment earnings or alimony—you cannot put interest or investment income into an IRA.

Unfortunately, IRAs have a gender bias which works against millions of married women. Generally, active participants in qualified pension plans cannot deduct their IRA contribution from their taxable income if their adjusted gross income (AGI) is over $50,000 (married couple filing jointly). The problem is that even a married worker who is not covered by a pension is considered to be an active participant if his or her spouse is.

Christy is married to Lee, a high-school principal. Christy works as a computer consultant, and their joint income is $55,000 per year. Lee is covered by the state teacher retirement system, and Christy has no pension. They can each contribute $2,000 per year to their IRAs, but neither can deduct their contribution from their taxable income, because Lee's pension and their joint income disqualifies them both. Because it is twice as likely that husbands have pensions than do wives, this provision of the IRA statute has an unfavorable impact upon women, because greater numbers of them have neither a pension nor a deductible IRA under this rule. With the divorce rate among midlife and older couples at an all-time high, it is shortsighted for policymakers to assume that Lee's pension will be there for both to enjoy upon retirement. It is all-too-possible that

Christy will not be in the picture when Lee collects, so the better policy would be to recognize the fragility of the modern marriage and allow each working spouse to qualify for a deductible IRA on his or her own record.

☑ **Call the I.R.S. and ask them to send you Publication 590, *Tax Information on Individual Retirement Arrangements*. The formulas for determining if your IRA is deductible or not can be complicated, and this publication will bring you up to date.**

As with the working couple, the provision limiting a homemaker's IRA rather than permitting both members of the couple to prepare for their retirement with maximum contributions to separate accounts, unjustifiably assumes that the marriage will remain intact until and through retirement.

Whether married or single, "active participation" in a pension plan is determined without regard for whether the worker has vested in the plan. Since women are more mobile workers and have a lower vesting rate than men, a disproportionate number of women workers will not qualify for deductible IRAs despite the fact that they will never qualify for a pension.

All IRAs accumulate tax-deferred, whether or not you can deduct them from your taxable income. If you are at the 28-percent tax level, a $2,000 annual contribution to an IRA account earning 9 percent over a period of thirty years will amount to about $300,000. The same funds invested at the same rate but subject to income tax will earn about $100,000 less—not small potatoes.

Studies consistently report that IRAs are more common among highly paid workers. Like all tax-sheltered programs, IRAs discriminate in favor of the highly paid. It is worth more to shelter income from a 28-percent tax bite than a 15-percent one. Lower-paid workers can't put away the extra money anyway. Of course, this makes IRAs generally less attractive to women as a class than men—but until reforms in our retirement system are made to equalize benefits to the lower-paid populace (who, after all, need to eat after retirement too), women are stuck playing catch-up with a loaded ball. Still, because IRAs are readily available and easy to set up, every woman should consider a fully funded IRA her minimum investment in the private-savings leg of her stool.

☑ **Although you pay a penalty (10 percent of the amount withdrawn) for withdrawing IRA or 401(k)/403(b) money before age 59¹/₂ (there are hardship exceptions), there is a loophole you can make use of in an emergency. You can withdraw your IRA penalty-free, as long as you put it back in a different IRA account within sixty days (you must change trustees). So if you know (be sure) you will get $60,000 in one month from an inheritance, but you need $50,000 right now for a down-payment on your dream house, withdraw the IRA, use it for the down-payment, and replace it with the inheritance in a new IRA account within 60 days. There will be no penalty.**

▶ *Maximizing unsheltered savings.*
If a tax-protected program is not available to you, or if you have funded those vehicles and your IRA to the maximum, you still want to save for your retirement if you have the opportunity. Some investment vehicles carry tax advantages, such as treasury securities which are free of state income taxes, but whether they are the best option depends on your tax bracket, the earnings offered, and the earnings on competing investments. Municipal bonds are free of both federal and state taxes, but lost their glamour in recent times due to lower tax brackets and questions about their safety. A financial advisor can help you plan, but make sure he or she is advising, not just selling a product.

☑ **If you will be using income from retirement savings as part of your retirement income, you should plan to put aside enough so that you can draw out only the** amount which exceeds that year's inflation rate. In other words, if inflation is 5 percent and the fund is earning 8 percent, plan to draw out only 3 percent. This strategy will protect your fund from inflation. Needless to say, in years in which inflation outpaces interest, you'd have no income, and in other years the disposable income might be slight. Still, unpalatable as the prospect may be, it is the only way you can protect your fund from the ravages of inflation, and as a woman, you have a greater chance of facing long years of inflation than a man.

▶ ### Understanding annuities.

An annuity is a stream of income. It can be for life, or for a period of years (say, ten), or it can end upon a stated event (a widow's remarriage is a common example). Pension plans must offer to pay you an annuity—you will get a monthly check at least for your lifetime—unless there is less than $3,500 in your pension account, in which case a lump sum may be offered. Some also offer the option of a lump sum at retirement—then it's up to you to invest it wisely so it can do the same job as an annuity would. If you take a lump sum, be sure to roll it into an IRA (even if it's more than $2,000) within sixty days of getting it, or you will have to pay income tax and penalties on all of it.

Annuities can be bought in the private investment market. Just shop around for a life insurance agent. But remember the discussion on gender-based annuities in chapter 4—they are illegal as employment compensation (a pension), but legal in the private market.

Here's why, as a woman, you may want to think twice about an annuity. Twins Dan and Lisa each inherited $25,000 when their mother died. They purchased identical annuities from their family life insurance agent. Dan's paid him more each month than Lisa's, because of gender-based tables. The agent told them it was actually equal, because Lisa would draw hers longer than Dan. Lisa reminded the agent that there was only a statistical likelihood that she would outlive Dan, but a 100-percent likelihood she would need the same monthly income to survive. The agent shrugged. Lisa noted that the gender-based annuity tables penalized her by eight years—but the life insurance tables, which should have benefited her by the same number of years, in reality only gave her the benefit of three. A penalty of eight years and a benefit of three—she pointed out that things didn't even out. The agent shrugged again.

Of course, an annuity is more than just interest on your investment. It is different from merely putting your money in a bank and drawing interest. It is a bet with your insurance company. The insurance company takes the $25,000 (or whatever) and figures out your life expectancy. It invests it, and pays it back to you in installments, usually monthly or quarterly. The money paid back to you is a combination of investment income and your original $25,000. It is calculated to run out on the very day you die. If you live longer than that, you win the bet—the insurer continues to pay you until you do die. You get more out than you put in. If you die *before* your life expectancy, you lose the bet—the insurance company keeps the extra money it otherwise would have returned to you. Of course, you can make all kinds of annuity arrangements which vary these typical terms.

Annuity salespeople will dazzle you with "tax-deferred" annuities—the charts will make much ado over the difference between dollars put into tax-deferred annuities and dollars put into taxable ones. But beware. The illustrated rate of return probably does not include a deduction for various fees, nor does it point out that the annuity income will be taxable when received. You are almost certainly better off fully funding any employment-based deferred plan (including your IRA) than you are in a privately purchased tax-deferred annuity. Some investment advisors also say that no-load mutual funds are almost always a better investment in the long run than a fee-ridden, tax-deferred annuity. "No-load" funds traditionally charged no sales fee; however, hidden charges have been cropping up in some so-called no-loads, so be careful.

☑ **If you receive a lump sum from your husband's retirement package as part of your divorce settlement, you can roll it over into a tax-sheltered retirement account, such as an IRA. If you do not do so, it will be taxed as regular income the year you receive it.**

▶ *Ordering priorities.*

This is all very depressing, I know You've been heroically saving for college for the kids—and here I am telling you that you've got an even bigger job ahead of you. But stripped of their emotional baggage, higher education and retirement income become mere economic issues—if you can look at them with a dispassionate eye, certain truths will emerge.

Like comparative costs, for example. In 1989, four years (including room and board) at two world-renowned universities less than 50 miles from each other differed by $60,000—a nice jump-start on your retirement fund. Four years at Stanford was $90,000; four years at the University of California, Berkeley, $31,000. What this means is that one dollar invested at a public university could return (to you!) two for your retirement. Since a degree from a top institution will bring your child about the same income over a working lifetime whether it is public or private, the competition between you and the kids for the extra $60,000 takes on focus. Some financial planners go so far as to say that if you can provide your kids with an education at a major public university, any costs of a private education should come from them. In other words, these advisors feel that your obligation, if any, ends with a sound education which will yield an economic future for your child equal to any school in the country. If a private school is desired, the costs should be borne by the student—through work, loans and scholarships. The same analysis applies to private schools at any level.

In addition, there is the question of return on your tax dollar. Let's say the taxpayers in your state subsidize each public university student by $13,000 per year. If your son or daughter went to the state university for four years, you'd realize a "return" of $52,000 of your tax dollars—no small consideration—probably more than you'll ever pay in state taxes. And much, much more than the ·vilified welfare mother across town. As for the $60,000 difference in cost between a public and private university, the Rule of 72 tells us that if you invest it at 8 percent when you are 47, it will grow to $240,000 by the time you are 65! Go for it.

Maybe you are young and single, with no obligations other than to yourself. Think about buying yourself a retirement nest-egg instead of a new car every now and then. Drive your cars five years instead of three. If you do this for the first time when you are 30, you will save four "cars" by the time you are 65. Using the Rule of 72, and assuming each car saves you $15,000, you can see how the savings mount up—over $150,000 in your retirement fund when you are 65—and almost painlessly put aside. Try to put the funds into tax-deferred IRAs and 401(k)s.

Popular among tax-deferred accounts are "zero-coupon" bonds sold by the U.S. government. They are risk-free, and allow you to pay little now for a lot later. For example, an 8.95-percent zero-coupon bond purchased today for $174 will be worth $1000 in twenty years. Or $3,742 now will buy you $20,000 in 20 years. Zeros come in varying maturities (one to thirty years), so you can buy them to mature whenever you want—your 65th birthday, or whatever. I know, I know—you're thinking that $20,000 won't be worth anything in twenty years, so why bother? $20,000 will be worth $20,000 more than $0, that's what it will be worth. Call your nearest Federal Reserve Bank for more information.

DESPERATION MEASURES

The investment strategies discussed above are all well and good if you have disposable income to put into them. But women, even more than men, have heavy obligations in midlife and a lower income to meet them with. Divorced women often face funding the college education of the kids on their own, because child support usually stops at age 18. Or a woman may be unexpectedly widowed. For these and many other reasons, a savings nest-egg is out of the question for millions of midlife women. If you are among them, all is not lost. Here are some ideas if the situation looks bleak:

▶ *Deferred retirement.*
If all else fails, you may have to figure on working longer than you originally planned. Fortunately, mandatory retirement no longer applies to most jobs, so you can delay your retirement as long as you wish, and continue to accumulate pension credits if there is a plan. And remember, if you can delay drawing Social Security past age 65, you will get more than 100 percent of your full amount as a bonus for waiting. You cannot be discriminated against in pay or promotions because of your age. You statistically can expect a longer life after age 65 than your grandmother, or even your mother, so working a few more years might still leave you with the same number of retirement years at the end.

☑ **Stay with me on this one—it's a little complicated, but important for married women who intend to increase their Social Security by working past 65. If, because of the dual-entitlement rule, you end up qualifying for wife's benefits on your husband's account rather than your own retirement benefit, your extra working years will not translate into more Social Security dollars, because they are credited to your account, rather than to his. If your own benefit is higher than half of his (the wife's benefit) it's tempting to delay your retirement to increase your benefit. But when he dies, your widow's benefit will be 100 percent of his, so you may lose the advantage you gained by retiring late on your own account when you switch from your own account to your widow's benefit. It worked this way for Pam. She worked until she was 70, figuring that the extra Social Security in her check would be worth** the five extra years. When she retired, her Social Security check was $400 per month, more than her wife's benefit would have been at one-half her husband's $600, so she was delighted. Two months after she retired, her husband died, and Pam, under the dual entitlement rule, received the greater of her two entitlements, or $600 (100 percent of his benefit). Thus she was in no better position than if she had never worked those five extra years after her normal retirement date. Because few married women are entitled to more Social Security than their husbands, very few working wives will benefit from delayed retirement—at least after widowhood.

If you have not been in the paid labor market for a number of years, you may have to consider beginning a job in your fifties or sixties. Age discrimination is a fact, but entry-level jobs are easier to get than they have been for a long time, because the Baby Bust (now in their early twenties) has created a labor shortage in beginning jobs which will continue for years to come.

House-rich.

If, like many retired women, you will be "house-rich" but cash-poor, think of your house as your retirement asset. You could sell it, move into less expensive quarters, and live off the income from the sale. You could take in renters.

You certainly should investigate "reverse annuity mortgages" (RAMs), in which the lender pays you cash monthly against a growing mortgage. A fifteen-year RAM on $100,000 equity at 10 percent would bring a monthly income of $242. But be careful. A RAM which ends in a stated period of years (often ten) ends with foreclosure.

At 75, Marj found herself unable to live on her inflation-exposed resources. She applied for a RAM which would pay her $385 per month for ten years. Marj figured she'd be dead or in a nursing home by age 85, so she wasn't concerned. At 85, and in great health, she found herself tens of thousands of dollars in debt to the bank. The bank foreclosed, and Marj lived the rest of her years in a welfare hotel.

☑ **Try to get a Federal Housing Authority (FHA)– guaranteed RAM. In one type, the bank makes payments for life rather than a term of years, so foreclosure during the borrower's lifetime is avoided. The bank is repaid from your estate after your death— with the executor, perhaps, selling the house to raise the funds. But like many annuities, RAMs can be gender-biased. A woman can get a considerably smaller check each month than a man. An 80-percent RAM loan on $50,000 equity would bring a 65–74-year-old man $2,189 per year at 8 percent interest, but a similarly situated woman only $1,419. FHA RAMs are safe and attractive, and because they do not use gender-biased tables, women get the same monthly check as men. Call (800)245-2691 for information on FHA-participating lenders in your region.**

▶ *Life insurance.*
There are a couple of things you might try if you learn that there will be little or no pension survivor's benefit for you after your husband's death. Consider buying life insurance on your husband while he is still living. You'd need a benefit of about $100,000 to give you an interest income of $6,000 to $8,000 per year, but that may well exceed what a pension survivor's benefit would pay you. Of course, if your husband doesn't already have coverage, it can be relatively expensive, but compared to fifteen or twenty years without income, the cost comes into perspective. You want "term," not "whole," life—whole is ten times as expensive. Most term policies don't accept new customers over age 65, but some companies do offer that coverage—shop the Yellow Pages for an agent that can get if for you, or write Insurance Information Inc. for their list of several hundred companies and compare rates (there is a fee for this service—see Appendix II).

A better option might be to join an association that offers group policies. A group life policy might insure a 60- to 64-year-old non-smoking man for $250,000 for a premium of about $2,600 per year. Think of that for a minute. You would have to pay $2,600 per year for nearly 100 years before you'd spend $250,000. Since a 64-year-old, non-smoking man statistically has about fifteen years left, it sounds like a super deal. And indeed it is, provided he dies within that fifteen-year period. If he outlives his life expectancy you'd have done better investing the premiums yourself (remember the Rule of 72—you don't need 100 years to accumulate a fund of $250,000). Since you probably don't know how long he'll actually live, it is better to buy the insurance to ensure your retirement income.

Ideally, the insurance will be enough to replace the reduced or missing pension. The insurance benefit will originally be tax-free to you, but any interest it earns after you receive it will be subject to income tax.

Get life insurance on your husband before he turns 65. Many policies will then carry him at least until he is 70, invaluable protection for you during those years. If he's a non-smoker, shop for a policy that offers non-smoker rates—they are substantially cheaper.

▶ *Amortize savings or insurance proceeds.*
If you can't afford to endow your future with a $250,000 policy that will earn interest for you indefinitely, try this: figure out your life expectancy (at 65, for example, a woman's life expectancy is eighteen years). Life insurance agents have these charts—also a call to your reference librarian will probably get this information. Then buy a smaller policy that you can afford, and spend it down over your expected life.

Kirby and her husband Dale could not afford $2,500-per-year premiums for a $250,000 policy, but the more affordable $150,000 policy, which at 8 percent would earn about $12,000 per year interest, was not enough for her to live on.

She needed $18,000 per year, which, with her $7,000 Social Security, would allow her to maintain her lifestyle. They took the $150,000 policy, and Dale died when Kirby had a seven-year life expectancy. Kirby invested the $150,000, and withdrew $18,000 per year, which is more than the $12,000 annual interest the fund earned. In other words, she cannibalized the fund, but she had to in order to meet her needs. Because of the interest the fund earned (ever decreasing as the fund drew down), it took longer than her statistical life expectancy of seven years to exhaust the fund. Kirby died before it hit zero, so she won the bet. If she hadn't, she would have needed new alternatives. Either way, she would have been able to keep the wolf from the door for a substantial part of her retirement years, and that's a whole lot better than nothing. Obviously Kirby could have done the same thing with savings or a retirement lump sum.

If you have $150,000 invested at 8 percent, but draw out $15,000 per year, your fund will last twenty-one years. If you are an early retiree with expectations of Social Security, pensions, inheritances, and other income, you might consider this a chancy maneuver, as future expectations might not pan out, or medical costs might soar. If you take out $21,000 per year, your fund will exhaust in eighteen years; a $27,000 withdrawal will last twelve years. If investment earnings are a big part of your retirement plan, remember they aren't protected against inflation. You might plan to use the income from a fund until you are, say, 70, then switch to an amortization plan which will increase your income but exhaust your fund by the time you are 91. If you're still alive, there's always welfare.

▶ *Get smart for free.*
Do you feel lost whenever anyone says "business," or "finance," or "legal"? Here's a free self-education program for your spare time, which within a year will make you conver-

sant in these matters and ready to intelligently use an expert's advice.

Read the business and financial pages of your daily newspaper for one solid year. Every word. If an article is about a major corporation's bankruptcy woes, read it. If it is about a merger, read it. Read about "leading economic indicators," "blue chips," "commercial paper," "REITs," "the Fed," and "soft landings." *Of course* you will be bored. *Of course* you won't understand a word of it for a while. That's why you must do it. Every word.

Read economics columnists like Jane Bryant Quinn and Sylvia Porter. Listen to Bob Brinker's *Money Talk* weekends on the radio. Watch *Wall Street Week* and *Money World* on TV. These are consumer-oriented experts—their material is for you, not economists. Seek out similar free, public advisors (but not salespeople), and read, and listen and read some more. At the end of one year, you will be surprised how things have come together. You won't be an expert, but you will be informed enough to handle your affairs intelligently.

And don't forget Uncle Sam. I.R.S. publications explaining IRAs, SEPs, Keoghs, and 401(k)s are free for the asking. Other government agencies publish advice booklets by the thousands. The General Services Administration publishes a "Consumer Information Catalogue" which lists dozens of low-cost government publications with tips on resume preparation and starting up a small business, guides to health insurance, and the investor's bill of rights. Write to the Consumer Information Center, P.O. Box 100, Pueblo, Colorado, 81002.

THE PUBLIC AGENDA

Policymakers have a responsibility to provide a way for every income group to set up each leg of the stool. It is a disgrace for policymakers to say that pensions and Social Security were never meant to carry the full burden, while enacting laws that make it virtually impossible for middle- and lower-income workers to build the private-savings legs.

The private-savings leg depends on tax-protected programs. These are in place for the rich. The higher the tax bracket and the greater the amount of disposable income, the juicier the tax exemptions, deductions, and deferrals become. Study after study confirms that these programs mainly attract the folks they were designed to benefit—the well-compensated.

There is a tax device which favors the lower-paid—tax credits. Yet this is the one device which has *not* been used by Congress to encourage retirement savings. A tax credit is deducted directly from your income tax. If the credit is $2,000, and your tax is $3,000, you would pay the I.R.S. $1,000. This favors the lower paid, because it is a static amount. Two thousand dollars is two-thirds of the tax due in the example, but only one quarter of a tax bill of $8,000. Although both taxpayers benefit by $2,000, the poorer one has a proportional advantage.

A retirement savings program tied to a tax credit would be enormously helpful to the millions of Americans who are told by their government to save for their retirement, then denied the same opportunities and encouragements given the well-paid. To help midlife women, such a program must be as available to homemakers and widows as it is to workers. In other words, the credit should not be tied to employment earnings, as are IRAs.

CONCLUSION

If retirement policymakers in Washington are serious about putting all retired people on a firm footing, they will have to recognize the fact that almost 60 percent of people over 65 are women, a proportion which increases with age.

Plainly put, if the authorities want to solve the income problems of the aged, they will first have to solve the income problems of women, because the biases of the working and homemaking years are dragged into the retirement years through wage-based programs such as Social Security and pensions, and wealth-based programs such as IRAs. In this way, gender discrimination casts its ugly shadow over a lifetime, and clouds the future for the majority of America's aged—her women.

KEEPING TRACK OF YOUR OPTIONS

Until laws and policies accord women the same advantages as men, we will be left to do the best we can—leaping obstacles, skirting traps, and running for our lives. Paying attention is the key. Foresight is all important. And a heap of opportunism doesn't hurt. Read this checklist along with the one at the end of chapter 5 to fit the three legs together.

✔ **Do you have a fully funded IRA?**

✔ **If self-employed, do you also have a Keogh?**

✔ **Do you have or can you get a 401(k) or 403(b) or SEP/IRA?**

✔ **Did you leave your job before retirement age?**

✔ **Have you projected the effects of inflation?**

✔ **How much life insurance is on your husband? Is it term?**

✔ **Have you ordered your priorities with retirement in mind?**

✔ **Will you have a windfall you can convert to tax-favored savings?**

✔ **Do you have emergency savings that can be converted?**

✔ **Have you applied the Rule of 72 to savings or other funds?**

✔ Do you read every word of your newspaper's financial page daily?

✔ Do you read and listen to economic programs and columnists?

✔ If you don't have a pension, does your boss know about SEP/IRAs?

✔ Have you made the best use of your fringe benefit options?

✔ Will your home equity be your retirement plan?

✔ Do you understand reverse-annuity mortgages?

✔ Do you understand how you can amortize your own savings?

7

MINIMIZING THE GAPS IN YOUR HEALTH COVERAGE

In today's medical economy, to be without health coverage is to be without medical care. And women, over-represented in jobs without fringe benefits, are very much at risk. Also, more women than men are "dependents" on their spouse's employment group policy, since it's the husband who is more likely to have the more generous fringe benefits.

In this chapter we will look at health coverage from the point of view of both working women and homemakers. Along the way we'll learn about policy features such as deductibles and co-payments, the differences between individual and group policies, and how to make these features work for you. We'll see how women are especially disadvantaged when it comes to insurability, and why. And we'll identify rights and strategies to help even the uninsurable build a layer of protection between them and a medical catastrophe.

Women are especially likely to become uninsurable for health coverage at an absurdly young age. By their early thirties, many women have compiled a medical record which disqualifies them from obtaining health coverage outside of large group policies. Ironically, it is the health-savvy woman who falls into a trap. Here's how this hidden bias operates: let's say you and your twin brother are 33 and without medical symptoms whatsoever when you each apply for health coverage. You, because you take good care of yourself, have been to your doctor twelve times since you were 20—not because you were ill, but because you went for your annual Pap test and breast examination. During that time a benign breast lump was diagnosed, and a non-cancerous cervical lesion was treated. Your brother never went to the doctor in his twenties, because like you he had no medical problems whatsoever. Yet your health coverage applications look very different. You have an adverse medical record, and his record is clean. If you weren't so conscientious about your health, your record would be as clean as his, but because of your good medical habits, you will be denied health coverage, and your twin brother will obtain it.

Joyce was a typical midlife woman: her first job, when she was 22, had group health coverage, with no medical exam to qualify. At 41, Joyce changed jobs to one without health benefits. She declined the insurer's offer to continue in her old group at her own expense for eighteen months because she couldn't afford the $3,000-per-year premium. Later, when she decided to purchase an individual policy, Joyce was out of luck. No one would insure her, because of a history of harmless irregular heartbeats—even though she was ready, willing, and able to pay the $4,000 to $6,000 per year it would have cost her for a policy vastly inferior to the one she left behind, and even though her doctor told the insurers in writing of her excellent health. Joyce's only recourse was to go without insurance and keep her fingers crossed, or find a job with full health benefits. Joyce wasn't lucky. When she was 45, she learned she had breast cancer. They caught it in time, only because she included an annual mammogram in her budget and paid for it herself. But the surgery and chemotherapy cost her thousands. She depleted her IRA and a good part of her other retirement savings. During the twenty years before Medicare helped her pay (a little more than 40 percent of her medical costs), Joyce lost all her retirement savings to health care. When she retired at 65, Joyce had Social Security as her only income.

 When you leave your job, you will be offered a chance to continue in the group health policy for eighteen

months, as long as you pay the premium yourself, plus up to 5 percent administrative costs. You must make the election within the short time period offered, probably thirty days. If at all possible, find the money and sign on, even if it means borrowing or getting a cash advance on your credit card. It's a more important purchase than the new bedroom set you've been saving for. It may be the only health coverage you'll qualify for until you get another job, or get Medicare at age 65. After you've secured the coverage, you can search for more affordable policies. The premiums may be thousands of dollars per year, but even so they will be about half of what you'd pay for a non-group, individual policy with fewer benefits, presuming you can even qualify medically for one. This is your right under COBRA (see chapter 1).

In order to get the best health coverage, you need to understand what forms of coverage are out there and what they mean to you in practical terms.

Health coverage isn't free. Even if your employer pays all the premiums and the policy covers all benefits without deduction (unusual), you are paying for the coverage with a reduction in your wages. Premiums are paid either by your employer, you, or both. You make co-payments when you see the doctor (your health policy pays a percentage, and you pay the rest). Deductibles mean that your benefits don't begin until you've paid a certain amount, say $500.

✔ If your health benefits come from your job, you may not have much choice in selecting your plan. But some jobs offer a choice of plans. If so, you'd be wise to scrutinize the way each policy is financed. If you will be using the coverage often, a high-premium plan with low deductibles and co-payments might be less expensive than a low-premium plan. If you are basically healthy, the low-premium, high deductible plan might be just the thing. The point is, keep the financing mechanisms in mind when you compare policies—not just the benefits.

 Varieties of coverage.
If you qualify, you can get health coverage in a variety of ways. These include:

- Commercial health insurance policies

- Health Maintenance Organizations (HMOs)

- Blue Cross and Blue Shield

- Preferred provider plans

Traditional commercial health insurance policies (sold by insurance companies such as Aetna, Prudential, Cigna, etc.) are thought by many to be on their way out. They are usually characterized by lots of forms, high premiums, and gaps in coverage. Insurers report that as medical costs skyrocket, profits have turned to losses, and employers are increasingly reluctant to pay the high costs of commercial policies. Their advantage is that they generally allow you to use any doctor or hospital you want. You may pay premiums, co-payments, and deductibles.

More and more Americans are now members of HMOs. A fixed premium is paid to the HMO, in return for which the member is entitled to benefits. Preventive medicine is the key to the HMO. If HMO Medi-Wonderful takes in $300 per month for you but keeps you so healthy that it spends only $100 per month on your benefits, it is very happy. The lower the costs, the richer the providers, so generally speaking, the financial incentives driving HMOs are the reverse of those driving independent practicing physicians, who need to sell you that $5,000 hysterectomy if they are to pay for their Porsche. Medi-Wonderful prefers not to operate, giving rise to some who criticize HMOs for undertreatment. You are limited to a set group of providers (hospitals, physicians, therapists, pharmacists), but in some communities this can be quite comprehensive.

In many communities, Blue Cross and Blue Shield are the old standbys. In others, they have fallen on hard times. The "Blues" aren't insurance, technically speaking, but they function like it. Traditional Blue coverage pays around 80 percent of almost any doctor's "usual, customary, and reasonable" charges, and 100 percent of hospital costs after a deductible. The Blues are non-profit, but that doesn't mean much in the cost-conscious health-coverage world. The costs to you and the coverage offered can be comparable to traditional commercial policies, so be sure to look around. The Blues and many commercial carriers have formed specialized plans with cost containment in mind. In exchange for lower premiums, you are restricted to a list of "preferred providers" who have agreed to keep their billings down. There are a number of variations on this theme, but the important thing to you is that the lower cost is a trade-off for restricted choices.

Some people combine coverages. If you and your husband both are entitled to health coverage as a fringe benefit, carefully compare benefits so that you come out ahead. You might use the policy with the lower co-payment for routine office visits, and the one with a high lifetime maximum benefit for expensive hospitalizations and surgery. Carefully compare your policies to see if you might benefit substantially by keeping both of them before one of you chooses to drop the health coverage in favor of an alternative fringe benefit such as dental insurance. Dental work can be expensive, but it is rarely catastrophic.

▶ *Coverage packages.*

Commercial policies, the Blues, HMOs—all coverage can be packaged in a number of ways.

Generally speaking, the *employment group policy* is the best of the bunch, although there are exceptions. The employment group usually enjoys the highest benefits and the lowest premiums, even before the employer makes its contributions. Even if you have to pay full premiums, your employment group policy will usually be better and cheaper than anything else on the market.

A *continuation policy* like COBRA permits you to remain in the employment group for eighteen months to three years, depending on your status. With all the benefits of the group policy, including its lower premium, a continuation policy is often the next-best deal, even though you have to foot the full premiums yourself.

Use the short time you are entitled to a COBRA continuation wisely. Plan for the day it will run out. Find a job with good health benefits, or work on your employer to put one into place. Do not count on qualifying medically for an individual policy if you are a woman past 35.

If you are a member of an organization, you can try to qualify for its policy. *Association group policies* are generally more expensive than employment policies, offer fewer benefits, discriminate on the basis of sex and age, and often include a medical questionnaire to exclude existing conditions. Nevertheless, if you cannot obtain health coverage otherwise, don't ignore this possibility. It's well worth querying dozens of national organizations for information on their health coverage, and joining the one which is best, even if only for its coverage. You don't have to be a woman or old to join the Older Women's League, or the National Organization for Women (see Appendix II). Look around.

A variation on the association group is the *professional*, or *trade group policy*. Perhaps you are a member of the bar association, or a similar organization for real estate brokers, or a trade organization which offers group coverage to its members. These policies generally share characteristics with association group policies.

After you have run out your COBRA entitlement, you may be offered the chance to convert to an individual policy without qualifying medically. *Conversion policies* are written reluctantly by the insurance industry, on the reasoning that the only ones who will buy them are people in poor health.

The policies are usually that bad. Very low benefits, very high premiums. Still, better than nothing if you've nowhere else to go and you know you would flunk a medical test.

✔ **As with COBRA continuation rights, you only have a limited time to exercise your right to convert. Do it, even if you think you can qualify medically for better coverage later. You can always dump the conversion policy if something better comes along, and you will have taken advantage of a one-time window of opportunity to get coverage.**

The *individual policy* is usually not great, but better than the conversion policy. You must qualify medically for poor benefits and pay an astonishingly high premium. Nevertheless, there are some real jewels out there, if you look around (the Kaiser Hospital system, for example). Individual policies are generally better than conversion policies. But don't lose your right to convert because you believe you'll qualify medically for an individual policy. You could be wrong.

✔ **In some states the insurer cannot exclude existing conditions for longer than a limited period of time, say two years. If you find yourself excluded from coverage for major conditions, you should sign up for the policy as early as possible to start the clock running while you are still in good shape.**

If you can't do any better, you can always buy a lowly *indemnity policy*. These are the ones which promise a certain amount of cash per day when you are in the hospital. Insurance counselors view these policies with a jaundiced eye, because $100 per hospital day isn't going to do you much good if your $20,000 cancer treatments are mostly outpatient. Nevertheless, indemnity policies usually don't require you to qualify medically, and are relatively inexpensive. They pay out no matter what other coverage you have, something ordinary insurance programs may not do.

If all else fails, find a high-deductible association group policy that will accept you. I'm talking about a really high deductible, say $25,000. I know, I know—$25,000 sounds outrageous. But it does limit the nightmare. If no one else will insure you, your bad dreams are now limited to $25,000—not your entire net worth. You can self-fund the deductible with savings, and buy several indemnity policies to equal several hundred dollars per hospitalized day to take care of part of the deductible. This way you can bring your health coverage problem under control. It's not perfect, but it beats the alternative.

► ERISA plans.

The Employee's Retirement Income Security Act permits employers to offer their own health plan, through self-financing. The problem for consumers is that these plans, being creatures of federal law are exempt from state regulations which keep other health coverage providers in line. For example, in some states coverage must include mental health benefits, or recovery programs, or newborns, or developmentally disabled adults. ERISA plans are not required to offer any such benefits at all, and usually don't. If your employer's plan description mentions ERISA, or "employee welfare benefits," you probably have an ERISA plan and your coverage may have gaps. There's not much you can do about this, aside from applying pressure through your union or employee association, if you have one. Nevertheless, it is useful to know your employer has elected to avoid its responsibility under state insurance laws in order to save money on its health plan. This could be a lever at contract bargaining time.

► Government programs.

You've heard of Medicare and Medicaid, and maybe you believe they'll be your safety net if your medical expenses soar beyond your ability to pay. Think again. You have to be 65 or disabled (really disabled—on Social Security disability or with end-stage kidney disease) to get Medicare, and Medicaid is available only to the poor—the *very* poor. You have to be on welfare, or very close to it before Medicaid will step in—and that generally means assets under $2,000 and income under $400 per month. Absent Medicare or Medicaid, the only other resource is generally the county or city public clinic, and they will charge you if you are at all solvent.

▶ State plans.

Although Congress is dragging its feet in the area of health financing, several states have been pioneering various schemes to protect their citizens from catastrophic medical costs. These range from risk pools, which offer insurance to the otherwise uninsured, to mandatory coverage on the job. Call your state department of health to learn if your state can help you out.

▶ Job-related fitness programs.

There's an effort among some large companies to lower their health-coverage costs by establishing fitness programs for the employees. Some install gyms, tennis courts, and tracks, while others offer nutrition counseling. This is a good thing with a dark side, especially for midlife women.

Some people equate "fit" with "young" or "thin." At what point do age and sex discrimination rear their ugly heads? Many women are at their heaviest during midlife, a condition some attribute to the body's attempt to replace diminishing estrogen through estrogen-generating fat cells. The flight attendant's settlement with Pan Am, discussed in chapter 3, in which weight charts become more forgiving as the attendant ages, is an example of one group's recognition of midlife realities for many women.

☑ **Keep in mind the possibility of an age- or sex-discrimination suit if you suspect you were discriminated against in any way by an excessively fitness-conscious company. Under the guise of good health and lower medical costs, youth can be easily**

favored over age; or among midlife employees, the
athletic male favored over the sedentary but equally
healthy female.

▶ *Teachers and Medicare.*
Thousands of public school teachers are not covered by
Social Security. Again and again they vote to remain out of
the Social Security system, an option no longer available to
most of the workforce. This is very short-sighted. Not only
will the retired teacher need to supplement her pension
with a Social Security check, but many teachers fail to realize that Medicare is tied to Social Security. If you don't get
Social Security, you can still join Medicare, but in 1991 it
will cost you $177 per month in premiums.

☑ **If you're not covered by Social Security, you can
qualify for Medicare under your spouse's Social
Security benefit, even if you don't qualify for a wife's
cash benefit. If you aren't married, or are married to
someone who is also without Social Security coverage,
take on consultant jobs, or summer jobs until you earn
enough quarters to qualify. The Medicare premiums
charged to non–Social Security recipients increase
every year.**

▶ *The health-coverage prison.*
Most health plans cover a discrete geographical area. Out-
side of that, you are out of luck, except for emergencies.
HMOs, particularly, can be very local. What good are your
COBRA or conversion rights when you retire or move, if
you plan to move out of the area of coverage?

Gail's workplace offered three plans. Her choice, an
HMO, covered only a thirty-mile radius. The Blue Cross
plan covered the entire state, and the commercial policy
covered a 300-mile region. When Gail left her job to follow
her transferred husband, she could not exercise her
COBRA or conversion options because her HMO did not

service the area she was moving to. Had she been covered by the commercial policy, she would have been okay.

Daisy, on the other hand, planned a little better. She exercised her COBRA option on her large HMO even though she moved 500 miles away from its service area. She knew she'd be uninsurable in her new location, and would have to pay routine medical costs herself. But if she was struck with a calamitous illness, she planned to return to the HMO for hospitalization and treatment, even if it meant staying with friends or in a motel for the duration of outpatient treatments such as chemotherapy or radiation. When her COBRA eligibility ran out after eighteen months, Daisy converted to the HMO's individual policy, and continued her coverage, regarding it as a "stop-loss" which limited her exposure to costs she could anticipate and manage. Before you do something like this, make sure you check it out with the HMO. Some may not want to cover you outside their area even if it is only as a back-up.

If you plan to move out of your carrier's service area, you must plan ahead to secure your continuation or conversion rights. Find out if your employer's other plans cover the area you plan to move to, then join that plan. You may have to do this a year ahead of time, because many group policies only take new applicants during a short period once a year.

▶ *Special problems of homemakers.*
Not long ago, if your health coverage came through your spouse's job, you lost it when you lost the marriage. If you were divorced or widowed, out the window went your medical benefits; and if you were a woman past your middle thirties, you had very little chance of qualifying for an individual policy because of the medical exam. Then the Older Women's League (see Appendix II) took the lead in forcing states to permit the newly widowed or divorced spouse to remain in the group policy at her own expense. The premiums would be about one-half of what she would pay

individually, and she wouldn't have to qualify medically. After a handful of states passed helpful legislation along these lines, OWL and other women's organizations took the concept to Congress, and the result was COBRA. Under COBRA, workers are entitled to remain in the group policy at their own expense for up to eighteen months, or until they qualify for another group policy or turn 65. Former dependents can remain in for up to three years.

☑ **In the trauma of divorce or widowhood, it can be very easy to miss the short time limit for selecting the COBRA option. If you had an attorney handling your divorce or probate, and the COBRA deadline was missed, you have lost an opportunity worth thousands of dollars per year—if you're around 40, perhaps over $100,000 by the time you qualify for Medicare at 65 (unlike Social Security, you cannot take "early" Medicare at 62). This loss would make it worthwhile to see another attorney about a possible malpractice suit.**

A FEW WORDS FOR ALL OF US

Some health-coverage problems cut across the working woman–homemaker line. These include:

▶ *Higher premiums.*
While women pay much higher premiums than men, the silver lining for midlife women is that at about age 50 (in other words, menopause), the rates begin to equalize. After that, men's rates surpass women's until age 65, when with the onset of Medicare, policies charge unisex rates. This is also unfair, as unisex rates work against older women, generally healthier than older men.

▶ *Exclusions.*
Maybe you're not quite uninsurable. Carriers offer to insure you, but with "exclusions." Of course, what is ex-

cluded is what you'll probably need. Cancer if you've had a breast biopsy; heart disease if you've been treated for micro-valve prolapse, a benign heart condition common among women. But before you decide the policy is worthless, look at the fine print. Often the exclusion is only effective for a short period of time after you sign up—two years is common. In other words, if you aren't treated for the condition for two years, it is no longer excluded. If you haven't looked over your policy for awhile, get a current copy and really study it.

▶ *Self-insurance.*
If all else fails, self-insure. Establish a savings account for the premiums you would have paid an insurer. $3,000 per year will accumulate a medical nest-egg to stand between you and poverty. If you start this when you're 45, by the time you're eligible for Medicare you'll have well over a hundred thousand dollars. You can then switch part of your funds into retirement accounts. Your preparation for catastrophic health costs might even enrich your retirement at the same time it gives you peace of mind.

✔ **Your children have COBRA rights, too. If they're dependents on either parent's group health when they become ineligible because of age or marriage, they have the right to remain in the group, at their own expense, for up to three years. In some cases, a married child can obtain COBRA rights for his or her spouse and kids.**

LET'S JOIN THE TWENTIETH CENTURY

There's plenty written about the health policy fix we're in. It is enough, here, to make a couple of observations.

Medical coverage as public utility.

Some services or commodities are too important to be left to the vagaries of the free market. Power, water, and education are examples. We offer free, universal education through high school to every U.S. resident. Water, without which there is no life, is provided in most communities through public districts, or heavily regulated private suppliers. A free enterprise system of competing suppliers of water would be unthinkable. What would you pay for water, if you had to? It's very importance guarantees its universal availability at a reasonable (and regulated) cost. So, too, electricity and other essential utilities.

It is monstrous that medical care is not accorded the same status. As a vital commodity, it should be universally available, heavily regulated, and as close to free as possible. The United States is almost alone in the modern world in allowing its residents' medical needs to be a profit center, where the chips fall where they may, and the cost is whatever the market will bear. More than eight out of ten health policies are written for tax-subsidized employment groups, so the American taxpayer has every right to insist on a regulated product that will deliver the goods for every resident. The vital importance of the commodity, coupled with its government-granted monopoly status (through licensing) and tax subsidies makes medicine a proper candidate for public utility status. And public utilities, properly, are heavily regulated. They are not creatures of private enterprise.

Nationalized health coverage.

The time has come—almost everyone knows it. The only serious debate remaining among experts is over which form it will take. Will we follow Great Britain's model of full socialization, where the hospitals and clinics are owned by the government, and the medical staff, including doctors, are government employees? Or will it resemble Canada's system of private providers, paid by a provincial health plan subsidized by the national government? Canada provides more doctors and hospital beds per capita than we do, and at a much lower national cost.

We'll probably come up with something unique, although seeing what we've done with the current system does not inspire confidence. When you consider all the costs of our system (tax subsidies, health-insurance premiums, out-of-pocket costs, administrative expenses, Medicaid, etc.), we pay much more for our medical care than most countries (11.2 percent of U.S. GNP versus 8.6 percent in Canada and 6.1 percent in Great Britain), for a much shabbier system. The annual per capita health-care cost per Canadian is $1,580. We Americans pay $2,268. We have millions and millions uninsured. And the Canadians? Not one. Nor does our wasteful system buy us better medical care. One study compared U.S. life expectancy and infant mortality rates (the usual comparatives used by health statisticians to judge the quality of a society's medical system) with those of Canada, Great Britain, Japan, Sweden, and West Germany. The United States, the only one without a national health program, placed last in both categories.

An American national-health program should:

- Save us money.

- Raise our standards of health.

- Eliminate the problem of the uninsured.

- Relieve employers of health-coverage headaches.

- Provide long-term care, thus eliminating "spousal poverty."

- Eliminate Medicaid and county indigent clinics.

- Include virtually all medical conditions.

Congress has been derelict in its duty to the American public. By declining to enact a national health policy that would cover every resident, then refusing to make health coverage a mandatory benefit of every job, Congress in effect has delegated its responsibility for ensuring the nation's health care to American employers. As a result, 37 million Americans—one in six—are without health coverage. No other industrialized nation puts its citizens so at risk, with the lone exception of South Africa.

CONCLUSION

In the meantime, you'll have to use your wit to slay the health-insurance dragon. You can make estimates of what you'll need after retirement. But unlike retirement costs, your future health costs are unknown. Ironically, the healthier you are now, the more unknowable your future is. Someone with a chronic illness expects and plans for an expensive future. Someone with a terminal illness plans for the present and near future only. But healthy women, who enter midlife and old age expecting one-third more years than men have a planning problem of the highest dimension.

This makes the health-coverage debate of critical importance to midlife women. We have a tremendous stake in its outcome, if for no other reason than that we have more years to live under it than men of the same age. We midlife women must be vocal in our support of a responsible resolution to our nation's health-coverage crisis.

YOUR FINANCIAL HEALTH CHECK-UP

Review this list once a year. You don't want surprises. It's not right that you have to manipulate the system to gain needed protection, but with effort, you can at least turn your health nightmares into mere bad dreams.

✔ Do you have a copy of your policy (ask the group administrator)?

✔ Do you have group, conversion, COBRA, individual, or indemnity?

✔ If indemnity, have you tried everywhere for something better?

✔ Are you dependent on your husband's employment group?

✔ If so, what if he dies or you're divorced?

✔ Do you know whether you're medically insurable?

✔ Do you understand your COBRA rights as a worker or homemaker?

✔ What is your out-of-pocket annual premium cost?

✔ What are your co-payments (per visit)? Percentage or set amount?

✔ What is your deductible?

✔ What are your annual medical costs (include prescriptions)?

✔ Will you be able to self-insure that amount if you lose coverage?

✔ What about a catastrophe?

✔ How will you finance long-term care? For yourself? For a relative?

✔ Would paying for a nursing home bankrupt you?

✔ If you won't have Social Security, how will you pay for Medicare?

✔ Do you know what your carrier's service area is?

✔ What if you want to move from there?

✔ Do you have a medical problem which would be excluded?

✔ Have you checked if your state has a time limit on exclusions?

8

CARING FOR DAD, THE KIDS, THE HOUSE, THE JOB—AND YOU

This chapter is dedicated to the dedicated caregiver—and chances are your name is Woman. After the children are raised, many midlife women face the task of caring for an incapacitated adult relative, be it a parent, in-law, or husband. More than eight out of ten family caregivers are women—and their numbers will increase as the population in the upper age groups continues to swell.

If you're a caregiver, you don't need me to tell you about the grueling demands this task inflicts. Incontinency, aggressiveness, sleeplessness, loneliness—all impose their toll on the caregiver, whether she is with the person twenty-four hours a day or coordinates the situation from her office.

As a midlife woman, you are likely to be called upon to be a caregiver, yet you cannot count on having a caregiver when you get old.

Arranging, supervising, and providing the care for a parent, husband, or older relative is something most of us don't plan for. Yet you should assume caregiving is in your future and make plans for it now. This chapter will help you think through your options in terms of your own financial plans, your relative's financial abilities, how you can best manage their financial affairs (and how to save yourself a lot of legal grief), a little about trusts, joint tenancies, powers of attorney and other forms of management, nursing homes, home care and Medicaid, and long-term-care insurance. You will learn how to coordinate care from your office or from thousands of miles away, and how to plan for your own old age.

▶ ### A *word about guilt.*

When someone in the family begins to need personal care, in the door with the illness marches guilt. There is buckets of it to go around. The incapacitated person desperately wants not to be a burden. The family members who could, with some sacrifice, participate in the care but choose not to feel guilt over their reticence. The family members who are thousands of miles away feel guilt about that. And then there's you, the caregiver. You, the hero of the story, feel guilt too. You're shocked at your feelings of anger. You can't believe that at times you wish the person dead. You hate how you secretly feel that others could do more to help. The time you steal for yourself is paid for with self-recrimination—couldn't you give just a little more? You're disgusted with yourself—why do you dream of the day you'll be free?

You must understand that, through no fault of your own, you have been put in an agonizing situation. Because we don't have a national health service in this country, you have been invited by your government to provide the service that every other industrialized nation except South Africa provides for its citizenry as a matter of course. American health policy dictates that the long-term custodial care of the elderly must be provided primarily by the family. In practice, that means unpaid women.

For your own peace of mind, separate thoughts from deeds. There is no moral consequence to an unhappy thought. It's what you do about it that counts. Wishing someone dead is one thing; killing him is another. The first is a normal, inevitable, universal, and morally neutral recognition of a conflict situation. It's built into every one of us so that we can survive as a species. If you didn't recognize the conflict between the life you'd be leading under normal circumstances, and the life you're leading as a caregiver, something would be very wrong with you. So long as you don't abuse or neglect your charge, you should feel completely guilt-free about all your freedom fantasies. All caregivers have them.

But what if the unthinkable happens? Maybe you sense you have crossed the line, and actual abuse has entered the picture. It is not surprising that some caregivers give in to the pressure—but it must stop at once. I do not believe this is a situation for counseling, except possibly for a support group under some circumstances. The reason I reject counseling is that the problem is not with you, but with the situation. That must change, not your attitude.

Below we'll talk about the new field of geriatric care management. You need to talk to a geriatric care manager who can put together a package of assistance that will relieve the pressure on you. If none are listed in your Yellow Pages (look under "Senior Citizens," "Social Workers," etc.), try your local agency on aging, a senior center, or a hospital discharge planner.

Finally, do not be surprised at how other people handle their guilt. The individual who needs personal assistance may resent that fact so thoroughly that he or she works off the anger on you. Nothing you can do is enough. In addition, some brain disorders (Alzheimer's, strokes) have symptoms which include hostility and even aggressiveness. Your brothers and sisters who are not so involved in the care may surprise you by opposing everything you try to do. They may accuse you of neglect, mismanagement, theft, abuse, or trying to increase your share of the inheritance. It may help a little to know that this is common. That doesn't mean they are right; it does mean that you should not assume you are doing something wrong to incur their ingratitude. It does not mean that you have a bad family; it does mean you are all caught in a bad situation.

FULL-TIME CAREGIVING

Your family should meet as soon as it becomes clear that someone is going to need personal care. Formally. If a conference call is all you can manage, manage it. If you agree to be the caregiver, get these things straight:

Respite services.

First, you need at least four hours a day you can call your own. This is in addition to the times the person you're caring for is sleeping. Sleep time, as any caregiver can tell you, is not off time. Then you'll need weekends, or at least every other weekend, off. Tell your family you will need two weeks off every three months. Completely off. Out of the house. These will be expensive unless another family member can reliably fill in for you. You and the other family members must work out how to share the schedule and cost.

Retirement planning.

Then you need to think forward to the time when the caregiving ends. What will you live on? If room and board has been supplied by your ill parent, what will you do when the rest of the heirs decide to sell the house? Don't assume that, in their gratitude, they will give you the house or the right to live in it. Do not assume that there is something extra in the will for you, either. Get these things in writing. As a former probate attorney, I must tell you that property division after a death brings out the worst in people. Bluntly ask your kin how you're going to live when you're ten years older and ten years more unemployable, and missing ten years of Social Security and pension credits.

Compensation.

Is there any way your family can pay you for your services? Even an increased share of your future inheritance would be helpful for your own retirement. But be sure the will gets written, and that you see it. You can't be sure it won't be changed, but it's better than nothing. Perhaps you can be added to the house deed, or you can place a lien on it to compensate for your services when it's sold. One way or another it's important that the principle be established from the beginning: You will be providing an invaluable service to *everyone* in the family. It's better to clear up misunderstandings before they go too far. Too many families have been permanently embittered over a caregiver situation gone awry.

Of course, if it's your husband who needs the care, you will be considered the caregiver of choice as a matter of course. No one's going to feel you're relieving their burden. If you are the only child, the same assumptions will come into play. However, if you are merely the only daughter, or the closest daughter, or the daughter-in-law, or if everyone else lives miles away, you have a right to expect a sharing of the burden.

☑ **In some circumstances you could be compensated by public programs. Look in the Yellow Pages or call the local bar association's referral service for an elder-law attorney, or see Appendix II for the National Academy of Elder Law Attorneys. A geriatric-care manager may have the same information.**

▶ *The role of demographics.*

At the turn of the century, only 4 percent of Americans were over 65 and few midlife adults had a living parent. By the year 2000, 20 percent of us will be over 65, and that means the generation in the middle—called the "sandwich generation" by many—will struggle to put their kids through college, help their parents with medical crises, and plan for their own retirement.

In earlier generations, those that did have living parents generally had numerous brothers and sisters with whom to share the caregiving tasks. Today, it is not uncommon to have two living parents, two parents-in-law, a stepparent or two, and some ex-in-laws to be concerned about as well. The Census Bureau tells us that by the year 2000, four-generation families will be the norm. Great-great-grandparents will not be unknown. This means that assisting an older family member or friend will be the order of the day for the midlife generation.

And as the Baby Boom ages, it will have fewer children to draw upon for its own care. Today's 45-year-old probably has more "parents" to care for than did earlier 45-year-olds, and when he or she ages and needs care, will have fewer children as candidates to take on the task. In fact, 45 percent of today's midlife generation limited their families to one child or none at all. This "child-poor" group will challenge our long-term care system, which today is built upon assumptions of unpaid family (read female) caregiving.

Knowing this before the axe falls gives you an opportunity for some planning. First, to finance and manage the care of the elder(s) in your life; and second, to plan for your own care when the time comes. In this chapter we will talk about legal, insurance, and other strategies for midlife women who are or will be caregivers, as well as those who want to plan for the day when the need for care is their own.

THE REMOTE OR WORKING CAREGIVER

The full-time caregiver is a disappearing breed. Policymakers haven't figured this out yet, but full-time homemakers are rare in midlife America. It will not be so easy to find an "unpaid somebody" to take on twenty-four-hour care in the future. More and more, caregiving will be a matter of coordinating a variety of services from an office or afar. It will still be a woman, no doubt. But she will trade the tedium and grunt work of twenty-four-hour hands-on care for the panic and frantic frustration of hiring, firing, training, and supervising the variety of services and assistants her community offers. If these home-care or daycare services aren't available, she'll look to nursing home placement, and her life will become one of daily visits and phone calls to keep the staff on the ball, along with agonizing disappointment and guilt.

Services now available in some communities include:

- Prepared food brought to the home

- Adult day-care

- Personal attendant services, live-in

- Personal attendant services, part-time

- Chore and errand service

- Medical and hospital equipment rental

- Home hairstyling, massage, manicuring

- Short-term hospital stays to provide respite

- Respite service

- Escort service

- Bill-paying service

▶ *Geriatric care managers (GCMs).*
It may take a wizard to figure out the complexities of putting together a package that fits your situation. Fortunately, a new field is emerging which specializes in doing just that. Variously called geriatric care managers, case managers, geriatric social workers—all strive to do the same thing: look at the situation and the community, and make the pieces fit. Some GCMs are social workers, some are nurses, some are experienced in attendant services. Some work out of an agency, others are self-employed. As yet the field is unregulated, so anyone can hang out a shingle and call themselves a care manager.

☑ **Be very careful; the situation is obviously ripe for abuse. If an agency is involved, closely question them on their screening process, and how long they've been in business. Get references. Call your local district attorney for information (larger offices have elder abuse sections) and the Better Business Bureau, but be aware that the BBB is operated by the business** community and can be reluctant to act on complaints against its members. If the person will be handling money (paying bills, etc.) insist on a bond and do a credit check. Whether it's an individual or an agency, insist they be insured both for liability and their own personal injury. You're probably better off with someone who has a license to protect—an R.N. or licensed social worker. These individuals have a lot to lose if they misuse your trust. Use your common sense. Remove portable valuables, including personal jewelry, such as wedding bands. This is not to imply that you must view your attendant with distrust, but a little precaution will help avoid misunderstandings if something is mislaid, as often happens when someone works in a new environment.

When you've found a GCM you're comfortable with, you should expect at least these services:

• An assessment of the situation and family consultation

• A recommendation of appropriate services

• A continuing monitoring of the services and situation

• Frequent reports to the family

Some GCMs go further and provide at least some of the care themselves. Some provide bill-paying and budgeting services. Some chauffeur and escort the individual. Some step into your shoes and become a surrogate for the absent family. Most GCMs charge either a flat fee or an hourly rate, with a separate initial assessment fee. Expenses are usually extra, and the cost of the services they arrange for are not included. Still, with nursing homes running nearly $3,000 per month, coordinated GCM services will probably be less expensive.

In some areas, public agencies provide care management

for those with limited funds. Check with your local hospital discharge planner, or your state department of aging.

☑ **The nascent GCM profession is still sorting itself out, but there are a couple of professional organizations that screen their members and provide referrals; when interviewing GCMs, you might ask if they are affiliated with one of them. Send $1 and a self-addressed, stamped envelope to Children of Aging Parents, 2761 Trenton Rd., Levittown, PA 19056. Send a SASE to Aging Network Services (4400 East-West Highway, Suite 907, Bethesda, MD 20814) for information on their service, which includes an in-depth phone consultation with the family and a referral to a screened GCM (they charge a fee for this service). Finally, write the American Association of Retired Persons (see Appendix II) for their free booklet "Miles Away and Still Caring."**

PAYING FOR LONG-TERM CARE

▶ *The specter of long-term care.*
Nobody wants to pay for custodial, long-term care. Not insurers, not Medicare, not the taxpayers, not the individual, and not the adult children. Yet people are living longer, and the result is a shocking rise in custodial care costs. Projected increases for today's midlifers are mind-boggling. Optimistic forecasts predict that only 25 percent of the elderly will purchase long-term care insurance over the next thirty years, which means you can assume your parents will not be insured against catastrophic custodial care expenses; you can assume that most of your own generation won't purchase such insurance either.

Long-term-care insurance.

Long-term-care insurance differs from ordinary health insurance in that it pays for nonmedical services, such as custodial nursing home care. Ordinary health insurance does not pay for custodial care, nor do Medicare and most Medicare supplement policies. ("Medi-gap" is the popular name for policies that fill in some of the gaps left by Medicare.) Ten years ago only one or two companies wrote long-term-care insurance. Today you have many to choose from, and under a variety of models. Most are indemnity policies (they pay $50 or so per day), exclude anyone over 80, are limited to two or three years, and escalate in cost steeply with age. If a 70-year-old buys one today, at age 78 when she needs it, her $50 per day won't go very far. In other words, the risk of inflation is on her.

☑ Watch out for policies which exclude "mental disorders." These are targeted to exclude Alzheimer's sufferers, a population much in need of custodial care.

There are better policies, which put the risk of inflation on the insurer. These offer a percentage (perhaps 70 or 80 percent) of cost. Most long-term-care policies have an unfortunate institutional bias. They will only pay a nursing home, not home or respite care. Insurers are worried that everyone will want a "maid," so everyone will make a claim for home services. Obviously, this forces more people into nursing homes than need be because it's the only way to pay for the care. But some policies will cover home health services as well. Investigate associations, such as the American Association of Retired Persons (AARP), the Older Women's League, and other senior organizations, with their group policies in mind.

You want a policy that will come as close to possible to this:

- 75 to 80 percent of daily nursing home costs

- Coverage for at least four years

- Home health coverage

- No required hospitalization before benefits begin

- A level premium (no increase with age)

- No mental disability or Alzheimer's disease exclusions

- At least $250,000 lifetime maximum benefits

I don't believe you will find a policy that promises custodial nursing home or home care for life. Those available at present have a time limit, generally under four years, or a dollar maximum that amounts to the same thing. Statistically, very few folks survive longer than two years in a nursing home, so a four-year or $200,000 limit might suffice.

Many medi-gap policies advertise that they provide nursing home coverage, but their promise comes close to fraud. A close reading of the policy will probably reveal that "custodial" care is excluded. The policy may say "convalescent" care only (meaning that if the prognosis does not include a ready cure, the coverage is nonexistent), or it may say it covers the kind of care that qualifies for Medicare (another way of saying custodial care is excluded). A true long-term-care policy will clearly say that it includes custodial care. Call the Older Women's League and AARP, and see Appendix II for other organizations.

▶ *Medicare and Medicaid.*

Medicare is the medical financing program authorized by the Social Security Act for persons over 65 or severely disabled. If you are eligible for Social Security, either on your own record or your husband's, you also qualify for Medicare at $177 a month (in 1991) less than someone who doesn't qualify for Social Security. Medicare does not pay for all medical costs. It is estimated that it picks up less than half the total costs of the over-65 population. If you're caring for someone over 65, you should make it a point to go to Social Security for information on Medicare and its benefits. Use it for all it's worth. Medicare provides unlimited home visits for medical reasons (shots, therapy) but very little for institutional care. Medicare accounts for only about 2 percent of nursing-home payments in this country, because it excludes custodial care. It will pay for a limited number of "skilled" nursing days in a nursing home after a hospital discharge, but if the need is custodial only, count Medicare out. Medicaid (welfare), on the other hand, pays over half the nursing home costs in the nation. You can be any age, but you must be *very* poor to qualify. Call your local Social Services department to learn how to qualify.

✔️ **You are not legally required to pay your parents' medical bills. If you are going broke paying for home attendants and other home services, you should consider transferring your ward to a nursing home. After he or she has spent their assets—except the home, generally—to the qualifying level, Medicaid will pay the entire cost, and you can save your money for the day you will need it for your own home care. It's unfortunate that Medicaid favors institutionalization over home care, but it does. Weigh this option carefully, because if your parent or husband is alert, entering a nursing home may be so traumatic that it verges on the unthinkable. On the other hand, if he or she is "out of it," it may be an acceptable option. Be sure to check whether Medicaid will place a lien against the person's estate for repayment (in most cases, that means the home). If your retirement plans include inheriting the equity in your parental home, be sure you have a conference with an attorney expert in elder law as soon as you even suspect a long-term-care situation is developing in your family.**

▶ *Healthy wives, frail husbands.*

The caregiver lives in an expensive world. Personal attendants, special diets, prosthetic devices, prescriptions, special beds, wheelchairs, home health visits—all come at a high price, and it's usually out of pocket. Private medical coverage seldom pays anything for home care, and Medicare, if the patient is over 65, won't pay for anything not directly medically related. When the time comes for the nursing home, chances are overwhelming that the costs will be paid for out of the family assets. Since most nursing homes cost at least $25,000 per year, most caregivers can't pay out of ready cash. They dip into life savings to foot the bill. When the life savings have been spent down to a certain limit, the nursing home costs will be picked up by Medicaid. When, as is usual, the first spouse to fall gravely ill is the husband, the marital assets must be spent to pay for his care until the couple is poor enough to qualify for Medicaid. This differs among the states, but for a married couple it is generally $12,000 to $60,000 in assets (adjusted annually), excluding the home. The husband then dies, leaving the wife with fifteen or twenty healthy years to live in poverty. The experts refer to this as spousal impoverishment, but a more accurate name would be wifely impoverishment.

☑ **Don't be tempted to give the assets away in order to qualify for Medicaid earlier. The application will be denied if property was given away within thirty months of the application, unless the gift was to a qualified recipient, such as a spouse or a blind or disabled child. There are ways to legally manipulate your assets so as to minimize your exposure to the spend-down process. One way is to plough the assets into the home, since it is exempt from consideration as an asset. For example, if the house has a $12,000 mortgage, paying it off instead of spending $12,000 on the nursing home will lower the housing costs for the individual remaining at home, and not affect the Medicaid application. You could put on a new roof, or** do other needed maintenance. **Household goods qualify as well. You can replace your ancient appliances (but you might have a problem buying art or antiques). Don't do any of this without expert advice; Medicaid rules are in constant flux.**

Carleen and Dean, a couple in their early fifties, had fully financed their three children's college education, saved for their retirement, and in every way acted responsibly in their planning. They had a $200,000 house, $100,000 invested for income, and health insurance. Dean was a salesperson, and Carleen was a homemaker, active in civic affairs.

Unexpectedly, Dean had a stroke after his morning workout, and was gravely impaired, requiring full-time care. Fortunately, his company gave him early retirement. Dean and Carleen's postretirement income was $800 per month from investments, and $1500 per month from his pension. Their expenses equaled their monthly income.

Everyone helped Carleen at first, but after two years, people stopped coming by. Three years after Dean's stroke, Carleen had a heart attack and could no longer care for him at home. Carleen put Dean in a nursing home, at a cost of $2,700 per month, $400 per month more than her monthly income, and $1,700 more than her bare-bones budget of $1,000 for her own needs. In three years, Carleen spent more than $61,000 of their investments, thus lowering the investment income from $800 per month to $300. As a result she had to spend more of her investments to meet her own needs. She quickly spent them down, until she reached her state's minimum asset level, which, like most states, was around $12,000 (some states go as high as $60,000).

At this point Medicaid stepped in to help pick up Dean's nursing home costs. Carleen was permitted to keep around $800 per month to live on (in a few states she could have kept as much as $1,500 per month); the rest went to the nursing home.

Now reverse the scenario. All the income and expenses are the same, but this time it's Carleen who needs long-term care, and Dean who will need income to support himself at home. When Medicaid begins to pick up Carleen's nursing home expenses, Dean gets to keep his entire $1,500 per month pension for his own use, because it is in his name. It doesn't take a genius to figure out the gender bias in this one. Men are more likely than women to have substantial income assets in their own names (pensions, Social Security), so men keep more money to meet their own needs when their wives are on Medicaid than women do when their husbands are.

✔ **It's best to apply for Medicaid as soon after admission to the nursing home as possible. This is because the marital assets are calculated as of the day of admission, not the date of application. In other words, if the couple has $80,000 in assets on the day the husband enters the home, but spends them down to $10,000 before applying, the wife has lost her chance to insulate a greater portion of them from the spend-down.**

Six years after entering the nursing home, Dean died. His pension continued for Carleen, but dropped to $750 per month. This was not enough to pay taxes and insurance, so she lost the house. Her entire net worth was the $12,000 she had been permitted to insulate from the spend-down. Carleen lived fifteen more years—in poverty—because she had the bad luck to be married to a sick man.

✔ **There are sophisticated legal techniques to protect assets, including the use of trusts and asset exemptions, which are known to lawyers who specialize in elder law, a new field which encompasses the minefield of entitlement programs, pensions, health policies, and long-term care. It is imperative that you seek advice as soon as you think someone in your family is facing a chronic, debilitating illness.**

In an area rife with bitter options, there is one strategy which really tears at the gut. A wife of thirty or forty years may be forced to divorce her ailing husband to escape the life of poverty stretching before her. It's unbelievable that government policy would so penalize married women with sick husbands, but the fact is, financially, many are better off divorced than married to a "custodial case." If the husband goes into the nursing home when the assets (excluding the home) are $200,000, in many states a divorce court will award the wife $100,000, and most will at least give her more than the $60,000 maximum (adjusted annually) allowed by a few states' Medicaid regulations. Alimony from his pension can also be awarded, which could exceed the maximum of $1,500 per month permitted in a few states.

Rosie and Pete, married 30 years, have $40,000 in savings and a house. Rosie also has $100,000 she inherited from her mother. When Pete enters the nursing home, the entire $140,000 must be spent down to the applicable level (approximately $12,000–$60,000) before Medicaid will begin paying. If Rosie divorces Pete, she will probably keep all of her $100,000 inheritance, plus up to half of the $40,000. In dollars and cents, she's much better off.

Of course, mentally—don't even ask. But women are divorcing ailing husbands, especially when their husbands are not aware of their surroundings. Many consider it a technical divorce only, for fiscal purposes, and jointly plan it. It would not surprise me to hear that some remarry secretly after Medicaid has been established—even though they could be penalized for fraud. Again, Medicaid regulations vary among the states. For heaven's sake, don't go filing divorce papers until you've had competent legal advice from an attorney who knows Medicaid law.

☑ **Medicaid does permit an exception to the asset and income limits. If you get a court order for support which allocates more income to the "well" spouse, Medicaid authorities in some states may honor it. In other words, the wife goes to court and sues her husband for support, because she is left destitute when his $1,500 pension is paid to the nursing home. Some courts have awarded almost the entire pension to the** wife in these circumstances, well more than the allotment she could receive under Medicaid rules. Again, don't go filing lawsuits until you've checked it out.

WHEN IT'S TIME TO LEAVE HOME

The elder-care industry is booming, and with the over-80 population the fastest growing in the country, its day has just dawned. As a caregiver, you will have more options as more and more businesses get in on the game—but until a satisfactory financing method is created, you will be limited to what you can afford. Medicare, Medicaid, traditional health insurance, long-term-care insurance—all have narrow rules and broad exclusions, which more often than not add up to no dollars at all.

Finances aside, the commercial out-of-home care spectrum includes:

- Senior residential communities

- Adult day-care centers

- Board-and-care homes

- Life-care facilities

- Skilled nursing homes

- Traditional acute-care hospitals

- Mental hospitals

The *residential community* usually requires the applicant be competent and ambulatory. An apartment and meals are usually included. Most have an arrangement with a nursing home, so that, if it becomes necessary, the resident can be transferred there. This can be a problem, of course, if the resident (or her family) and the institution do not agree on the need. Some offer an intermediate level—a floor of apartments, for example, with in-room meals and nursing supervision.

Adult day-care is just what it sounds like. Older people with some difficulties in managing themselves can spend several hours per day in adult groups, supervised by social workers or medical professionals who engage them in group activities. If you have a job and are responsible for your parent or spouse, adult day-care may relieve you of anxieties, if you can find a way to pay for it. A good long-term-care policy might pick up some of the cost, and Medicare and Medicaid might help under some circumstances. Call some facilities in your community to find out how they are usually financed.

Board-and-care homes take ambulatory residents, are usually not as well regulated as skilled nursing homes, and may be difficult to finance.

Some retirement facilities, in return for a substantial lump-sum payment, will promise to *care for you for life*. This is a variation on the annuity concept discussed earlier. If you die early, the facility "wins"; if late, you do. Some people have been very satisfied with this kind of arrangement. Others have met disaster when the facility went bankrupt, or defrauded them. You need very objective advice before turning over large sums. How long has it been in business? Does it offer a refund within a reasonable time for dissatisfaction? Is there a monthly charge that can increase unchecked? What happens if the resident needs skilled care? Some states control these contracts by law, requiring refunds of the "life" deposit if the person moves out or dies early in the arrangement.

The *nursing home* provides round-the-clock care for those who need it. In addition, it offers skilled medical procedures such as tube feeding, oxygen, and medical supervision. You should visit several before you even contemplate placing a relative in one. There is a delicate balance between the needs of the caregiver and the dreadful situation of many nursing home residents—not necessarily through neglect or abuse (although both happen) but because of the realities of living with so many very ill people. Nursing homes cost between $25,000 and $50,000 per year, which is why every year a million Americans are forced into destitution paying for the care. There is a federal "Patients' Bill of Rights" which protects nursing home patients in many ways. Ask your nursing home administrator for a copy, or your local health or social service department. In addition, some states have augmented the federal rights with stronger provisions of their own.

The traditional *acute-care hospital* is not the place for long-term custodial care. Medicare won't pay for it, and you don't want to, either. Some rare conditions are still treated in county long-term facilities (a few people remaining in iron lungs because of polio, for example) but otherwise, your local hospital is not your long-term-care facility. Nevertheless, many insurance carriers require an acute-care hospital stay before they'll begin paying for skilled services in a nursing home, so a trip to the hospital is often a financial, although not a medical, necessity.

Saddest is the warehousing of older people in *mental hospitals*. People with Alzheimer's disease and other dementias are often unwelcome in nursing homes, because of disruptive behavior. When a resident becomes too tough to handle, nursing homes have been known to haul them in an ambulance to the door of the local "locked" ward, and dump them. Likewise, if a tenant begins to leave the stove on and otherwise act "dangerous" to herself or others, the landlord or next-door neighbor may be the dumper. The mental facility has little choice but to admit them, and begin commitment proceedings if no other alternative can be found.

Choosing from this smorgasbord of possibilities is tricky. What appears to be a nicely graduating set of options is in fact riddled with inappropriate rules. Placing your mother in a skilled nursing home may be overkill if all she really needs is someone to watch her while you're at work. Nevertheless, if her insurance will only pay for nursing-home care, you may have no choice. This kind of wasteful mismanagement of our health resources is at its worst when it comes to long-term custodial care.

And women occupy four of five nursing-home beds, constitute four of five family caregivers, and make up nine of ten long-term-care workers. Women are very nearly the long-term-care universe.

Unfortunately, women don't make long-term-care policy. Male policymakers and industry representatives are proposing solutions which consider cost-avoidance the highest priority, probably because they don't really see themselves at personal risk. Even progressive proposals rely on an unpaid caregiver as the central figure. Women must embrace long-term care—all aspects of it—including the caregiver, the exploited personal care attendant and nursing aides and the cared-for—as a women's issue of compelling importance.

✔️ **If you're involved in a nursing-home placement, look over the contract very carefully. Studies confirm that nursing-home admissions contracts can be full of illegal and improper clauses. You can't rely on common sense to tell you what's legal, because laws and regulations differ among the states, but there are ways you can check. Begin by asking your state agency on aging for the legal services for elders office closest to you, then call them. Write the nursing-home consumer's group listed in Appendix II for information.**

MANAGING THE AFFAIRS OF ANOTHER

If you are close to someone advanced in years, sooner or later you'll probably consider helping them manage their financial affairs. Sometimes the problem is merely physical—Aunt Colleen can't get to the bank anymore, and needs someone who can sign for her. Sometimes it's sporadic—your father has days when he fades a little, but most of the time he's just fine. You both think someone should be in a position to act for him when he's not himself. Or, in the worst-case scenario, the problem can erupt quite suddenly. Your mother, in tip-top mental and physical shape by all appearances, has a stroke and becomes almost entirely unaware of her surroundings.

Many families approach these situations informally. For the confined person or the occasionally confused parent, often the decision is made to put someone on the financial accounts as "cosigner." Here, legally speaking, is where the problems begin, for there is no such thing as a mere "cosigner." Every signator has a legal role, usually one of joint ownership, regardless of the informal intentions of the signers. You and Aunt Colleen feel that adding your signature to her bank accounts has no significance beyond convenience. There is no disagreement between you that the funds remain entirely hers. The law, however, sees it differently. You and she are joint owners of the account, and the form of ownership you so casually enter into matters a lot, legally speaking. The common forms of joint ownership of financial accounts are:

- Joint tenancy with rights of survivorship

- Tenancy in common

- Community property or tenancies by the entireties (spouses)

In a *joint tenancy*, the survivor gets the joint property. In other words, if you added your name to Aunt Colleen's account under a joint tenancy, you will get the entire account when Aunt Colleen dies, regardless of Aunt Colleen's express wishes, even her will. If Aunt Colleen willed all her possessions to your three cousins, the joint-tenancy account will go to you, anyway. You can turn it over to your cousins if you like, but you are not obligated to. Perhaps, as so often happens, you feel morally entitled to the funds because you spent more time with Aunt Colleen in her difficult later years than did your cousins. Family strife is a common consequence of the unexpected results of joint tenancy accounts carelessly entered into. If you are a cosigner on someone's account, ask the bank to confirm what form it takes. In most states, unless the account expressly states that it is a joint tenancy, then it is a tenancy in common.

Joint tenancies are useful if you know what you're doing. Because the property automatically passes to the surviving joint tenant(s), it does not go through probate. This avoids a costly, often lengthy procedure, but there can be drastic tax consequences when you use joint tenancies on appreciating property, such as stocks and real estate, especially for married couples. See your estate planner or tax advisor. Some people use joint tenancies to leave a gift after death in secret. A special friend you don't want named in your will, for example—secret lovers come to mind, or children born out of wedlock.

A *tenancy in common* has very different characteristics. When Aunt Colleen dies, her share of the account will go to her heirs, not to you. If you have funds in the account, you had better have a written agreement between you as to the proportion, so that on her death, only her part goes to her heirs. If the account was originally hers, it may be difficult to prove after her death that you added some of your own funds. It's better not to commingle funds, but if you do, have a written agreement spelling out whose is what. Without evidence to the contrary, a tenancy in common account may be presumed by a court to belong to the tenants in common in equal shares.

Community property and *tenancies by the entireties* are forms of joint ownership for married couples—who can also hold property as joint tenants and tenants in common. Because of the reciprocal rights married people have to marital property, these forms of ownership become tricky when marital property has been converted. For example, if the husband took $25,000 from the community property account and set up a joint tenancy for his mistress, she can be compelled after his death to give the community share back to his widow.

The point to all this is: be alert to what you're doing when you sign onto someone else's account.

A joint account is only one way of assisting your mom, and not always the most appropriate one. The array of other legal devices available to you include:

- Ordinary powers of attorney

- Durable powers of attorney

- *Inter vivos* (living) trusts

- Conservator of the estate

- Guardian of the person

- Civil commitment

From top to bottom these range from the least expensive and least intrusive to the most expensive and invasive of the ward's rights. All are discreet legal instruments, designed to do a particular job. They do not duplicate each other—but unfortunately, many people, including some lawyers, take a meat-axe approach to a particular problem, and prescribe the wrong legal instrument. Let's see what these devices can do for you:

The *ordinary power of attorney (POA)* removes the problem of an implied co-ownership. It is an agency relationship, with the principal being the account owner, and the agent (called the attorney-in-fact) being the cosigner. Since there is no presumption of shared ownership, POAs do not have the estate and potential liability problems joint tenancies and tenancies in common carry. But there is a major problem with ordinary POAs. They are valid only so long as the principal is mentally competent. In other words, she must be competent when she authorizes the POA, and remain competent throughout its use. If she should become incompetent, the POA ceases automatically. This makes ordinary POAs less than useful for older folks, when an incapacitating illness can strike quite suddenly—before alternative arrangements can be made.

This flaw in the traditional POA led to the development of the *durable power of attorney*. There are two types of durable POAs. In the first, the POA becomes immediately effective, and continues in force despite a later incapacity. In the second, the POA "springs" into existence when the incapacitating event occurs (called a "springing power"—a touch of lawyerly poetry, I guess). Until then, it is not in force. For both types, the principal must be competent when she originally signs the instrument. There is no way around that requirement, which makes POAs out of the question for people already greatly confused. But for minor incapacities, the POA is a useful, safe, and cheap alternative to the joint account.

✔️ **Although you can get POA forms at the stationery store, it is better to go to each financial institution and execute POAs on their own forms. They paid their lawyers to draw up the forms, and most will refuse to honor anyone else's. The institution is not required to honor your POA, although, if you do it their way, most will.**

The refusal of many institutions to honor a "general" POA makes them less than useful if what is really needed is full authority to manage all aspects of the individual's financial affairs. An *inter vivos* trust can enable the trustee to buy, sell, trade, and otherwise manage all or part of the individual's holdings. This kind of trust is popular with estate planners, because it avoids probate and probate fees. Although you can buy do-it-yourself books to help you set up your own simple trust, expert advice is best, unless the estate is very small and simple. It should cost somewhere between $600 and $2,000 to set one up. Depending on the circumstances, the trustee can be one person, two or more co-trustees, the lawyer, a bank—even the person setting up the trust herself, assuming she's mentally competent. Like the POA, the individual must be competent when she sets up the trust, which puts trusts out of the picture if the person has a sudden stroke, with no advance planning. Inter vivos trusts are also commonly referred to as living trusts.

This is where *guardianships and conservatorships* enter the picture. These are instruments of last resort, appropriate only when advance planning using one of the other tools was not possible. They are expensive and intrusive. The court is involved, a competency review is made (even if it is called something else), and the individual loses much of her autonomy. There is a wide variation among the states in these devices. In at least one state, guardianships for adults have been abolished, and the term conservatorship is used exclusively. In others, a guardian makes personal decisions for the ward (such as where he or she will live), whereas a conservator has authority only over the estate. Still others use "guardians of the person" and "guardians of the estate." However it is worded, the upshot is this: the individual no longer has the rights you and I have. Depending on the authority granted by the court, the ward may or may not be able to vote, write a will, decide to marry, and make his or her own medical decisions. It's a sad fact that many lawyers, faced with a worried family, recommend guardianship prematurely, partly because it's what lawyers are familiar with (courts, and all that)—and partly because it covers all bases. Lawyers feel most comfortable when all future contingencies can be covered in one instrument, and guardianships do that. All too often, they are overkill.

The extreme remedy is *mental commitment*. Seldom, if ever, is full-blown commitment appropriate for an older person. Commitment differs from guardianship in that the individual can be locked up. Some mental health experts estimate that between 50 and 90 percent of the nation's 1.5 million nursing-home residents have mental disorders, but are being improperly drugged, restrained, and ultimately warehoused. Mental health wards of public hospitals are inappropriately filled with older folks who have been dumped there by nursing homes or landlords or neighbors. You don't want this for your family member, so please plan ahead by setting up POAs and/or a trust.

When Aunt Donnell was 80, she had a light stroke, which affected her mobility. She needed physical assistance only—she was fine mentally—so you became a tenant in common on her bank accounts so that you could transact business at the bank for her. This arrangement was ideal until Aunt Donnell needed more help from you. When she needed you to sign for her on all accounts, you decided a power of attorney was appropriate. You were careful to get a durable power of attorney so that, if she worsened mentally, you would still be able to handle her affairs. At age 85, Aunt Donnell began to have times when she faded mentally, although most times she was just fine. You both felt a trust was appropriate at this point, because you could manage her affairs, including her real property holdings out of state, despite her increasing disability. You also liked the probate avoidance characteristics. For the last year of her life, Aunt Donnell was in another world. But you continued to have authority, as her trustee, to manage her financial affairs, so her capacity was not an issue. When she died, you simply distributed her assets to the persons she designated when she set up the trust.

But Donnell's sister, Marilee, suffered a different fate. She and her children did no advance planning, so when Marilee had a sudden stroke and became permanently and totally mentally incapacitated, it was too late to set up joint accounts, POAs or a trust. Only a clumsy, expensive guardianship would do.

A trust is not the perfect substitute for a guardianship under all circumstances. A trustee, for example, does not have the authority to determine where the person will live. In other words, a trustee cannot place Aunt Donnell in a nursing home over her objections; a guardian can. A guardian with the proper authority can make medical decisions for Donnell; a trustee cannot. Nevertheless, for most families a well-thought-out trust can avoid a guardianship or, at the very least, delay the day.

☑ **The lesson is obvious. If you have an older family member, even if that person is perfectly all right, get legal instruments in place to minimize the need for the meat-axe guardianship approach later on.**

MEDICAL DECISION MAKING

Are you prepared for this? Your grandmother is on life-support. Your mother is certain she would like a dignified death—in blunter words, pull the plug. Your uncle disagrees. He wants everything possible done for her. The hospital staff is paralyzed. They cannot act either way, because your grandma didn't leave instructions.

There is a general notion out there that the next of kin can legally direct physicians in this situation. Informally, yes—legally, no. Ever since two California physicians were charged with murder for following what they thought were the family's instructions to discontinue nutritional support, medical staffs have been increasingly reluctant to be guided by informal methods.

▶ *Medical directives.*

Most states have created devices which allow an individual to write down their own preferences in advance. But there is not coherence between the states. If you execute a California "Durable Power of Attorney for Health Care," will it be recognized in Louisiana when you fall ill during Mardi Gras? Will your New York "Living Will" protect you in Utah? Will a "Natural Death Act" instrument work outside its state of origin? These questions are only now being answered on a case-by-case basis. Your safest bet is to assume the instruments will not travel between states until established otherwise. Even within the state, doctors frequently ignore these instruments if the wording is vague or the legal protections for the physician are scanty.

☑ **Despite the problems, definitely have your older family members consider signing your state's variation. Be**

sure it makes its way into the medical record.
Specifically talk it over with the regular doctor. But
remember, if after careful consideration your relative
declines to sign, don't force the issue. No decision can
be more personal. If he or she is more comfortable
letting things unfold as they may, you'll just have to
live with that.

Some medical directives simply state what the person
wants done. Others appoint a surrogate decision-maker who
will make the decision at the appropriate time. If you are a
caregiver, you may or may not want to be the surrogate.
Often family members are too close to the situation, so a
trusted friend is preferred. There is also the problem of (let's
face it) a conflict of interest when the surrogate is also an
heir. The law worries that granny might be shuffled off prematurely in order to stop the medical spend-down of her
assets or to hasten an inheritance.

For these reasons, states encrust medical directives
with plenty of formalities. It will not be enough to
write out your instructions informally, or call a family
meeting and explain your feelings. Your doctor can tell
you what your state requires. Then follow the
directions to the letter. Even then, in all states, the
physician can refuse to follow the directive. In some
states, he or she must appoint another physician who
will carry out the instructions; in others, the directive
is simply ignored.

PLANNING FOR YOUR OWN FUTURE

Saving for your own nursing-home care is more a matter
of planning than great expense.

Nursing-home insurance.

Some policies feature a "level" premium. That means that if
you buy the insurance at age 50 for $200 per year, you will

be charged the same premium when you're 75. Look the policy over very carefully before you buy it, though—there are very few good ones.

▶ ### Group-living plans.

I know a group of close friends in their forties, all single, who plan to sell their homes when they retire and pool their funds. They figure to have in excess of a million dollars. They will buy a comfortable group home, then invest the rest in a kind of endowment fund. The income from the endowment will pay the salary of a personal attendant or nurse, should one be needed. Group homes will be common by the time today's midlifer retires. The ingenious feature of the plan is its built-in personal assistance feature, which will work to delay or even obviate institutionalization. Brothers and sisters can make the same plan; even unrelated people can. A real-estate attorney can help you work out the ownership formalities.

▶ ### Medical directives.

Execute one. They are not just for older people—you can be hit by a car tomorrow. Be sure it gets into your doctor's files, and don't forget to discuss your wishes with close relatives and friends. If married, be certain you and your husband are very clear about all this, and know where the directives are kept.

▶ ### A warning about long-term investments.

We will have a national health plan in this country before today's 45-year-old is 65. Only Congress hasn't figured this out yet; everyone else knows it's coming. For this reason, don't spend much money on any scheme which promises to pay off in the distant future when you need nursing-home care. Although it's too early to tell, very likely long-term-care costs will be a component of the health system, so you don't want to shift resources now into something which will be included in your coverage twenty or thirty years down the line.

▶ *Nomination of guardian.*

Some estate planners like to "nominate" a guardian or conservator when their clients make a will. Some experts feel
that the presence of a nomination in your estate plan makes
it all the more likely a guardianship will be sought. It's like
you planned for one, so why not? On the other hand, if you
have strong preferences regarding your choice for this role,
you'd probably better spell it out. Gay and lesbian couples,
for example, should nominate guardians to avoid family
members from overcoming their preferences later on. The
court will not be bound by your nomination, but will accord
it great respect.

▶ *Barrier-free housing.*

When you're planning your retirement dream house, make
sure it won't work against you as you age. Too many people
end up in old folks' homes just because their own home
becomes their enemy. One level, wheelchair access, bath-
room plumbing that can be fitted later for safety, a location
convenient to accessible public transportation, a separate
room for a personal attendant—all these considerations can
make the difference between your retirement home being
your "final resting place" and a way-station along the road
to the nursing home. Half of all women (only a third of all
men) over 65 spend some time in a nursing home. Careful
advance planning can put you in the happier half.

☑ **Don't overlook the Independent Living Movement
founded by disabilities-rights advocates. Their
perspectives and techniques are relevant to anyone
with physical limits, very much including the aging.
Some centers provide consultations. The aging
movement has much to learn from the disabilities
movement, in terms of access issues, autonomy issues,
and political action.**

▶ *Who will be your caregiver?*

Do you have children? Will they live near you when you're
old? You can make their lives easier by thinking through

various scenarios which include you as the person needing services. How can you compensate the one with the heaviest involvement? Can you sweeten their inheritance? Can you learn about GCMs and other services in your area—making lists of them for your children? If you have no kids, can you make a reciprocal agreement with an old friend? Obviously, you want to get things straight with your husband or partner, but remember, you are more likely to be his caregiver than he yours.

WHAT SHOULD BE DONE

Refer to the previous chapter's recommendation regarding a national health plan. It's as simple as that. All nationalized health plans include long-term care, and ours should as well. One benefit of such a plan would be the elimination of the patchwork quilt we have today. Under a comprehensive, universal health plan we would no longer need Medicare, Medicaid, medi-gap policies, long-term-care policies, ordinary health insurance, county clinics, and the whole array of inefficient and costly devices we now call our health-care system. Adult day-care, home care, acute care, and custodial care would be available as needed, rather than utilized, as now, according to which one is financed by an individual's coverage.

CONCLUSION

There is a natural tension between the needs of the caregiver and the needs of the person requiring assistance. Family care is different from paid care in a number of ways. With paid service, the question of who is in charge becomes important. Does the person with disabilities hire, fire, train, pay, and supervise the attendant? Does he or she decide how much, and what type of service is appropriate? Or does the government, through public programs such as Medicaid and in-home support services? Or does the doctor, in authorizing home nursing? The disability rights movement argues that the user of the service should rightly be in charge, not the provider or the payer. Does this argument for basic civil rights become less relevant when the service user is very old, and questionably competent? Does it matter when the caregiver is an unpaid family member?

Think through these angles in your own situation. Be sensitive to the independence of your family member, but don't forget your own needs. Perhaps never will you need more wisdom and balance.

BEING PREPARED

Of course you want the best for your parents and other loved ones if they need your help. Everyone does. The thing is, it can happen very suddenly—a stroke can turn your lives upside down overnight. You don't really have the luxury of waiting until someone shows signs of fading before you make some plans. Most things on this list won't cost you anything but time. And when the moment arrives, you'll be so glad you took that time.

✔ **Does your parent's health policy cover custodial care?**

✔ **How many children do you have? How many daughters?**

✔ **Are you the likely caregiver for your parents?**

✔ **Have you talked this over with them and your siblings?**

✔ **Have your parents signed a medical directive? Have you?**

✔ **Are the directives in your medical files?**

✔ **Have you talked about end-of-life medical decisions?**

✔ **If you have a power of attorney, is it a *durable* power?**

✔ **Do you have any "convenience" joint accounts?**

✔ **Are they tenancies in common or joint tenancies?**

✔ Are you sure you know the difference?

✔ Have you had a consultation with an elder law attorney?

✔ With a geriatric care manager where your parents live?

✔ Have you ever been in a nursing home? Visited three?

✔ Do you understand Medicare and Medicaid?

9

CHECKING UP
ON THE REST
OF YOUR LIFE

You are going to do something terrific for yourself.

Right now, take a look at your calendar and find one free day. From sun up to sundown, this one's for you. If it's at all possible, plan a day at the beach, or the lake, by the river, in the country, or in the park. If a day at home is most appealing, plan to shut off your phone.

This will be a banner day for you, because on this day you will plan for your second life. It's like the day you were born, only this time you're way ahead of where you were then. You've got four decades of experience and the wisdom that brings, plus the answers to some very big questions. You probably know who your children are, and what they will need from you in the next decade. Ditto a spouse. You now know whether your parents will live into old age, and you have an idea what their circumstances will be. You know the state of your assets halfway through your life, and whether you're basically healthy or chronically ill. This time around, you're much closer to your dream than when you first started out.

Make this day as special as can be. Splurge a little on a picnic, or lunch at a favorite cafe (but go alone—today you're your own best friend). Get bubble bath or bath oils for a relaxing end to the day. Buy a split of champagne or a special mineral water for bedtime. Let your imagination go free in planning your day—make it as special as possible, but free of distractions. The only one you'll be talking to will be you.

For this one day, you will think through every aspect of your economic life. You'll be making a list, and checking it twice. You'll let your mind roam over all the alternatives, even the unthinkable ones. You want to leave no possibility unexplored just because it's unpleasant.

Unlike your male colleagues, chronological midlife for you may not be at the midpoint of your career. Your strategies have to be a little different—sometimes very different—if you are to surmount the gender differences laid down by biology, society, and the law. Women, due to re-entry and job mobility, have more career starts in their worklives than do men. And because of late starts or low retirement benefits, today's midlife women intend to stay in the paid labor force longer than men of the same age. A 45-year-old man may be hungering for early retirement because he's had it after twenty years with the firm; but you, with only five years on this job under your belt, and precious little in retirement savings to look forward to, plan to work until you're 70. The differences call for very different strategies, and you'll have to ask yourself different questions.

Get yourself a full pad of paper and let's get started. Use the morning to think through the questions below. After lunch, we will plan your second life.

TAKING INVENTORY

These questions are in broader strokes than the ones that ended each chapter. You should begin by reviewing the chapter lists, then answer each of the following questions in writing on a fresh page.

- Where have you been and what have you done?

- In five years, where do you want to be living?

- In five years, where do you want to be working?

- In five years, how much do you want to be earning?

- Answer the same questions for ten years and twenty years.

- What do you want to be doing when you're 50? 65? 75? 85?

- Are you vested in a pension? Do you have this in writing?

- Will you be a victim of pension integration?

- Will you lose pension benefits because of the fractional rule?

- How are you protected against inflation?

- Will you have a survivor's benefit from your husband's plan?

- Can you increase funding of tax-deferred devices?

- How much Social Security will you get if you quit at 50? 65?

- What will you do if you lose your health benefits?

- List all your relatives over age 65.

- For each one, list everyone who could care for them.

- Do you appear on any of those lists?

- If so, how are you going to manage financially? Physically? Emotionally?

- List your own children. How many will care for you?

- Are you married?

- Do you live in a common-law or community-property state?

- Do you know what your share of the marital property is?

- Do you know for sure whose name is on every asset?

- If divorced, will your ex-husband pay the kids' college costs?

- Are you planning to remarry? Are you sure you will?

- Have you considered education in terms of cost-effectiveness?

- Will you have divorced-wife's Social Security? When?

- Will you have a pension survivor's benefit after your divorce?

- Have you checked your own credit rating?

- Do you have a will? Does your husband?

- Are they recent? Have you seen his?

- Are you sharing your life with someone you can't marry?

- Have you shared assets?

- If so, are they tenancies in common or joint tenancies?

- Have you contracts and wills to replace marriage rights?

• Are you counting on an inheritance as your retirement plan?

• If so, do you know (for sure) your status under the will?

• How much will be left after four years in a nursing home?

• Do you have stepchildren?

• If so, have you thought out their inheritance? College?

• What about your own kids from a former marriage?

• Do you have a large equity in your home?

• Is that your retirement plan? Is it well-insured for all perils?

Now have your nice lunch, and don't worry your way through it. You are already ahead of nearly every woman your age in America. After lunch we'll identify your challenges.

TAKING CHARGE

This part of your day is for planning. Take a look at your pages from the morning. Sort them into three piles:
(1) Those that will pose no problem.
(2) Those that may.
(3) Those that will.
Throw the first pile away. Take another look at the second pile. Sort it into two piles:
(A) Those that have the potential to be major problems.
(B) Those that would be manageable without major planning.

Throw pile (B) away. Sort pile (3) into two piles:

(C) Those that you can handle economically.

(D) Those you can't.

Keep both these piles. You now have (A) and (D) to concentrate on, and (C) to absorb any resources left after planning for (A) and (D).

Reread the chapters which address the problems you identified in (A) and (D). Make a ballpark estimate of how much each problem might cost you (e.g., four years of a nursing home for your dad might be $125,000; or $10,000 per year stands between you and an adequate retirement). Chapter 6 gives savings ideas for retirement, many of which can be used for anything else you need. List all possible solutions, even if you don't like them.

Start matching funds to problems. If you buy a car every five years instead of three, how much will you save before the anticipated problem arises? Enough to solve it? Remember compounded interest and the Rule of 72 explained in chapter 6. Will life insurance on your husband replace a missing survivor's benefit for you? Call some agents and find out the cost. Would a quality public university for your daughter save enough for you to self-insure against a major medical catastrophe? All of these questions are obvious, and you've thought of them in one way or another many times. The goal here is to get them all together in one place and at one time, and think them through as part of a whole—the whole rest of your life, in fact. If you can finance Gail's college education by prematurely retiring your IRA, what will be the impact on your stepson John's hopes for a loan to buy his first home? Your own retirement? Will a private education for Sid cost your mother a home attendant? Your hypothetical responsibilities will seem enormous when you first look at them all at the same time. But this is a necessary first step in allocating resources and ordering priorities.

Play around with your piles of problems and your lists of solutions, and see which fit. As you eliminate problems, list the solution on the page, and set it aside. In a couple of hours, you will either have solved every problem remaining in your life or—much more likely—have some problems left over that defy solution. Even if you have done no more than accurately identify all the challenges, it's a tremendous start. But as you paint the picture of the rest of your life, patterns will begin to emerge. Not all tasks occur simultaneously; some will be resolved before others take shape. Resources used for the one can be shifted to the other. Naturally, you should leave ample room for the GOK factor (God Only Knows). GOK will happen—good and bad, but you definitely should have a much clearer picture of what you'll need in the years ahead, and approximately when. Obviously, it would be quite unrealistic to think you can find all the answers in one afternoon. But you can identify the problems, price them, give them an approximate timeframe. Your battle will be more than half won.

Keep the unsolved problems in the forefront of your thinking over the next several months. Do not shove them aside as unsolvable. As you read and learn more about economic matters, you will begin to see ways out. Some problems from pile (B) won't materialize; use the resources elsewhere.

Finally, every year on the day before your birthday, do a miniversion of this. Plan for a morning for yourself, capped with a special lunch. Review your list. Make changes. Update. Customize the list—will you have responsibility for someone with developmental disabilities? Factor it in. Do you have stepchildren? Consider them, too. Do you have a chronic illness? List the ramifications.

You should feel good about yourself as you soak in that evening bath. Identified demons are demons half-slain. You spent your first lifetime fighting the demons that were given you at birth: ignorance, dependency, and want. As you begin your second lifetime, you have much more control. You have education, skills, and experience—bought and paid for in lifetime number one. Now get busy on your plan of action, and enjoy that most precious of possible gifts, that pearl beyond price that all the queens of history couldn't buy—a second lifetime to plan for and cherish.

Live well, plan well, be good to your neighbor, and cherish Mother Earth—and let the prime of your life be the time of your life.

DO YOUR OWN
LEGAL RESEARCH

One of the great joys of being a lawyer is knowing that an hour or two in the law library will tell me whether I really have to accept a damaged sofa because I signed a receipt stating it was in "good" condition; or if I really can't see my medical records; or if the nursing home can hold my grandmother to a contract she didn't understand. What power! And you can have it, too. You don't need to go to law school in order to learn enough about legal research to do a competent job yourself. A good enough job, anyway, to let you know if what you really need is a good lawyer. Take this chapter to your local law library, and let's get started on this mini-course to conquer the law.

Two years ago your doctor (Dr. Maladie) noticed a mole on your hand, and recommended it be excised. All she told you was that it should come off, and it would probably leave a very visible scar. You're a little vain about your hands, and decided against the excision because of the scar.

Dr. Maladie made no comment when you declined the procedure. A year later, she again recommended excision, without explaining why she was concerned. Again, you declined. Two months ago you met a dermatologist at a cocktail party, who immediately spotted the mole, and scared you half to death. "It looks like melanoma—a lethal form of cancer," he said. "Have it off at once, or your life could be very short."

You immediately went to surgery, and lost much of your hand, as well as most of your use of it. You can no longer make your living as a secretary, and it will be months or years before you know if they caught it in time. In addition, you lost your health insurance when you lost your job, and, because of the malignancy, you are now uninsurable. You face your future uninsured, disabled, and fearful of a recurrence of cancer which could put you on welfare for the rest of your (perhaps foreshortened) life.

You are furious at Dr. Maladie for not warning you. If you'd known a deadly cancer was a possibility, you would have had it excised immediately—when it was small, and with only minor surgery and an excellent prognosis. You blame her for your loss of livelihood, your disability, and your exposure to catastrophic medical costs—not to mention the threat of early death.

You know that malpractice suits are America's way of compensating victims of medical negligence. This is the only way our country distributes the risk—by charging the entire medical consumer population (patients) through the increased fees they pay because of their doctor's malpractice premiums. In other words, you have to sue your doctor in order to get the insurance to compensate you for the harm done by medical negligence.

But was Dr. Maladie negligent? If not, she's not liable, and you'll bear your losses on your own. After all, she did recommend removal of the mole. Twice. It was you who declined the minor surgery. But you feel she should have given you the whole story. You think she was negligent in not warning you of the dire consequences of refusing the simple, safe procedure.

☛ **For anything as important as this, you should proceed directly to an appropriate attorney. You should *never* rely on your own research to resolve the question of negligence or a large tax liability, or a fraud suit against your broker, etc. Lawyers have an abundance of information in their arsenals that you could never turn up, even in a thorough research effort. The statutes of limitations vary from days to years, depending on the claim, so you can't take chances on losing an important right because you dithered away the time limits in the law library. For the sake of example, we will proceed as though you decided to see if you had a case before you consulted a lawyer.**

You live in California, so you will focus your research there. The system is analogous for all the states, and the materials are similar, so the California example will serve Alabamans and New Yorkers equally well. Call your courthouse, your general library, the nearest law school, or your lawyer to locate the public law library nearest you.

Familiarize yourself.
When you first get to the law library, spend some time just strolling around the open stacks. Note that shelves and shelves are devoted to multi-volume sets of books. A closer look will distin-

guish them from each other: *Pacific Reporter, Northeast Reporter, Atlantic Reporter, American Jurisprudence, Federal Supplement, Supreme Court Reporter, United States Code.* The list goes on and on. Look through some of the "reporters." Take down a couple of volumes of the United States Code—the federal statutes. Find your own state's statutes, and look them over, too. Find the card catalogue, and notice that it is similar to ones you've worked with before. When you've oriented yourself, let's get to work on your malpractice problem.

Legal encyclopedias.
You know what your grievance is, but you don't know the legal buzzwords to describe it. Looking around at the sea of books, you rightly assume that unless you come up with a few magic code words to focus your search, you will spend the rest of your life reading lawbooks.

A legal encyclopedia is a good place to start your research if you don't already know the section of the statutes or regulations you need. The encyclopedia will tell you all about your topic, and help you define your problem in legal terms. An encyclopedia is a good start—but it is not designed to be your only source. There are two legal encyclopedias, published by the two main competitors in the world of legal publishing: West Publishing Company, and Bancroft Whitney–Lawyer's Cooperative. We'll call the publishers West and BW for convenience.

West's encyclopedia is *Corpus Juris Secondum (CJS)*; BW's is *American Jurisprudence 2d (AmJur)*. Each set is divided into broad topics like Divorce, Wills, Tenants. Look through the topic list to see which ones seem best to fit your situation. You can eliminate such topics as Taxation, Husband & Wife, and Securities. Others are possibles, such as Physician & Surgeon, Negligence, Hospitals, Malpractice. *AmJur* and *CJS* indexes define topics differently, so browse through each set until you feel more comfortable with one of them, then stick with it.

You'll follow many leads that don't pan out. Don't be discouraged—legal research is like that for all of us. Soon you'll begin to zero in on your subject. You'll learn about "informed consent," for example, that requires doctors to disclose all risks of treatment to their patients before gaining their consent to proceed.

You wonder how up to date the material is—after all, the volume was copyrighted ten years ago. What's happened to the law in the meantime? Any new developments? At the back of each volume of CJS and AmJur is a paperback supplement tucked into a pocket—the "pocket part." These are published annually, and update the main volumes. Always, *always* update your legal research by checking the pocket part, or use the other updating methods we'll learn about. In the encyclopedia's pocket part you will quickly bring your information on informed consent to within a year or two of your research.

But wait, you think. "Consent" isn't precisely the issue here. Dr. Maladie didn't fail to inform me before she treated me—she failed to inform me of the consequences when I *refused* treatment. Does that fit under the informed consent doctrine?

Maybe yes, maybe no. It's one of those exquisitely arguable points beloved of law professors and bar examiners. You want to know how your state's courts have developed the law of informed consent, so you jot down some of the cases recited in the encyclopedia's footnotes (from any state—pick those which seem most relevant to your situation). It is important to include the case citation—the string of numbers and letters following each case name.

Case citations.

Griswold versus Connecticut, 381 U.S. 479, 85 S. Ct. 1678, 14 L.Ed.2d 510 (1965). There is nothing complicated or mysterious about these numbers. They simply describe the volume and page number in which you'll find *Griswold*, the 1965 case which established that state laws forbidding birth control violated the constitutional right of privacy. Note that there are three separate strings of numbers and letters, separated by commas. These designate three different sets of books in which you can find the U.S. Supreme Court's *Griswold* opinion. Remember West and Bancroft-Whitney? They are represented here, along with a third publisher. Take the second series of letters/numbers. It means that in volume 85 of the *Supreme Court Reporter* (published by West) at page 1678 you will find the *Griswold* opinion, augmented by helpful cross-referencing material inserted by West. Likewise, in volume 14 of *Lawyer's Edition* (second series), on page 510, you will find the exact same words of the Supreme Court that you found in West's *Supreme Court Reporter*, except that BW has added its own cross-references. Volume 381 of the *United States Reporter* at page 479 contains the same opinion, with yet a third publisher's editorial additions. You can use any set to read *Griswold*, but we will use the West citations throughout this mini-course, because

West materials dominate legal publishing, and their cross-referencing system is ideal for beginners.

The West key-number system.

"Case reporters" are where appellate opinions are published.
These opinions form the legal precedents which bind lower
courts, or persuade sister courts. An opinion from the Florida
Supreme Court will not bind a lower court in Kentucky, but if
well argued, it could persuade the Kentucky court to adopt the
same position, provided there is no Kentucky precedent which
already binds it. Likewise, a pronouncement from a federal district
court will not bind a New Mexico appellate court, but it could
persuade it. Of course, the United States Supreme Court is
Queen of the Mountain, so its opinions bind all courts in the
land.

Case reporters are those shelves and shelves of books called
Federal Reporter, Northwest Reporter, California Reporter, and so
forth. Some cover the appellate opinions of a region (*Pacific, Atlantic*) and others confine themselves to one jurisdiction (*New
York Supplement, Federal Supplement*). The U.S. Supreme Court is
in the three reporters represented by the *Griswold* citation, above.

Take a look at 85 *Supreme Court Reporter* 1678. It begins with a
brief summary of Estelle Griswold's conviction for counseling others on contraceptives in the course of her duties with Planned
Parenthood. The summary is followed by a series of numbered
paragraphs, each headed by a topic and a number preceded by the
symbol of a key. These topics and key-numbers are the wonderful
cross-referencing method devised by West to virtually every appellate opinion in the country that has discussed your point of interest—the constitutional right to privacy, in the case of Ms.
Griswold. These "headnotes" are not a part of the appellate opinion, which follows "Mr. Justice Douglas delivered the opinion of
the court."

Note that, in *Griswold,* all the topics are "Constitutional Law"
except one which also includes "Abortion." In many opinions,
the topics are more varied. Take a look at *Griswold*'s headnote
number 5, which carries keynote number 82. Keynote 82 is just
West's way of saying section 82 of their topic, Constitutional
Law. In other words, look up "Constitutional Law" in the state
and federal digests (see pages 246–247) and you will find all the
cases in the land that have discussed the first amendment's implied right of privacy under keynote 82.

Now, look up some of the cases you collected from your encyclopedia search. In the West reporter, jot down the topics and key numbers from the headnotes that seem to come closest to your situation. In the next step we will unlock the door to the magic kingdom of law.

Case digests.

Find the multi-volume sets of "digests." There are regional digests (covering the same regions as the regional case reporters), and some specific ones, such as *California Digest*, and *U.S. Supreme Court Digest*. The West digests are collections of headnotes from all the cases in the region or state or jurisdiction covered by the digest. The Connecticut Supreme Court's *Griswold* decision will be in the *Atlantic Digest*, but the U.S. Supreme Court's decision is in the *Supreme Court Digest*. If you look up Constitutional Law keynote 82 in the *Supreme Court Digest* you will find *Griswold*, along with all other cases which preceded and succeeded it in discussing the first amendment and the right to privacy.

If you look in the *California Digest* under "Physicians & Surgeons Key number 15," you will find medical malpractice. Subsection (8) focuses you in on "disclosure to patient," which seems to you to be on track with your communication problem with Dr. Maladie. If you wanted to see what Georgia courts had to say about medical disclosure, you would go to the *Southeastern Digest*, Physicians & Surgeons Key number 15(8), and find them all. *The Federal Practice Digest 3d* likewise will zero you in on federal opinions. And if you're really ambitious, go to the *General Digest* and look up Phys & Surg 15(8) for the law of all state and federal courts on the point, collected by the decade. The elegance of the West key-number system is that once you've got the appropriate topic and key-number, you have access to all law on that point in the country.

For now, stick with the California Digest. You'll see references to *Cobbs versus Grant*, the leading California case establishing the right of a patient to informed consent. But even more on target is *Truman versus Thomas*, 27 C. 3d 285, 165 Cal. Rptr. 308, 611 P.2d 902 (1980). As with *Griswold*, there are three publications reporting *Truman*. We'll use West: volume 165 of the *California Reporter*, page 308. Read *Truman*, and you'll find you're close to the answer to your question. The *Truman* plaintiffs were children whose mother died at age 30 from cervical cancer. Her physician had recommended she have a Pap smear, and she declined. He did not explain the possible consequences of her refusal of this safe, inexpensive procedure. The question before the California Supreme Court was whether a patient had the right to an informed *refusal*, as well as the established right to informed *consent*. The court answered yes.

Are you on the way to a medical malpractice attorney about your mole? Not yet. How do you know if *Truman*, decided in 1980, is still good law? Was it overruled by the U.S. Supreme Court? Did the California legislature pass a law in effect overturning the California Supreme Court? Did the California Supreme Court later overrule itself? Did organized medical associations rise up in protest and get a law passed which, in effect, overruled *Truman*? How are you to know? Fortunately, there's Shepard's.

Shepard's citators.

Shepard's citators are extremely useful tools for updating opinions and countless other research tasks. The editors have taken every state and federal opinion, and listed every other federal and state opinion which has mentioned it. In other words, if any other court in the United States has mentioned *Griswold* in reaching its decision, *Shepard's* will point you to it. This means that courts which have followed the precedent set in *Griswold*, as well as those which disagreed, will be listed. If the U.S. Supreme Court later overruled itself, *Shepard's* will tell you that, too. Find the *Shepard's United States Case Citations* (be sure you are in the right volume—*Shepard's* also has United States Statute citations, as well as cases and statutes for every state). Under any of *Griswold*'s three citations, trace the decisions listed under its volume and page number. You'll quickly see that *Griswold* was a very important case, as hundreds of other cases have cited it. One in particular may interest you: the West citation is 93 Supreme Court Reporter 705, perhaps the most controversial decision in the annals of American law: *Roe versus Wade*. Read *Roe versus Wade* for an example of a badly divided court sweating out the woman's constitutional right to privacy first enunciated in *Griswold versus Connecticut*.

In the California *Shepard's*, find *Truman versus Thomas*, and reassure yourself that none of the cited cases overturned it. In the front of *Shepard's* the little letters which precede some of the citations are decoded: "o" for "overruled," "f" for "followed," others for "questioned," "criticized," and "distinguished." *Shepard's* is updated frequently, so in order to bring your research to within weeks of the present, you must search through the supplementary paperback volumes shelved with the hardbound main volumes.

Your research is not yet complete. You've found a case which seems right on point, but you haven't yet looked at any statutes. You will have to see if federal or state legislators have had a say in the matter before you can be confident you can sue Dr. Maladie for violating your right to an "informed refusal." Quite often, legislators react to controversial pronouncements of the courts by enacting a statute which rules the other way. In other words, after the *Truman* decision, the California Medical Association no doubt lobbied the California legislature to enact a statute making it clear that the right of informed consent does not include the right of informed refusal. You need to know if the legislature acquiesced.

State statutes.

State statutes are produced by a variety of publishers, so indexing and updating may vary with the state. For *Truman,* look in the California codes, published either by BW or West. Look in the indexes under Medical, or Malpractice, or Negligence—as with most legal research, taking time to learn the index will bear fruit. Shepard's statute citators will tell you which cases have considered the statute, so you can learn how courts have interpreted it. Remember to update—statutes are updated by pocket part, periodic paper supplement, or by loose-leaf replacement pages, depending on the style of the publication. This is an essential step—legislators are always busily amending and repealing statutes on the books.

Federal statutes.

All federal statutes are contained in the *United States Code,* a multi-volume set of books. You can use either the *United States Code Annotated (U.S.C.A.)* or *United States Code Service (U.S.C.S.).* Both sets include much more than the bare statutory language, and both are well indexed.

Federal statutes are usually cited like this: 28 U.S.C. §61. This means Title 28 of the *United States Code,* section 61. In *U.S.C.S.* and *U.S.C.A.,* the statutory language is followed by cross-references, including digests of appellate court opinions which have considered the section, and other materials included by the publisher as helpful aids.

Regulations.

Once you've found the right statutes and cases and updated them with the pocket parts and *Shepard's*, you are ready to focus on your issue in greater depth. *The Code of Federal Regulations (C.F.R.)* contains all the regulations used by the alphabet soup of federal agencies such as the I.R.S., FAA, EPA, FDA, EEOC, and, of course, Social Security. Your particular research problem may well involve a regulation rather than a statute. Your state has regulations, too. Ask the law librarian to help you find them.

Treatises.

Finally, as you can imagine, hundreds, perhaps thousands of volumes have been written by legal scholars on particular areas of law. Probate, trusts, wills, contracts, divorce, Social Security, tax, negligence, crimes—you name it, someone has written about it at length. These treatises can be very useful as both an overview and a detailed look at a particular area of law.

Legal periodicals.

In addition, law schools and other bodies publish law reviews on a periodic basis, where legal esoterica is ground down to its finest possible point. The *Index to Legal Periodicals* is arranged by subject and author, and will point you to the articles which concern your area of law. For example, 14 *U.C.D. L.Rev.* 1105 means that in volume 14 of the *University of California (Davis) Law Review* on page 1105, the *Truman* doctrine of informed refusal is discussed in depth.

Just for practice.

Here are some (West) cites for you to practice on (whether the opinion is from your state or not).

• *McCarty versus McCarty*, 101 S. Ct. 2728(1981). Patricia McCarty was denied the right to part of her former husband's military pension (an excellent example of how you must always follow up—the McCarty decision was, in effect, overturned by Congress after outraged pressure from military wives).

- *O'Brien versus O'Brien*, 489 N.E.2d 712 (1985). A New York court says that Dr. O'Brien's earnings from his medical practice were part of the marital property, since his former wife put him through medical school, and awards her a share in his future earnings.

- *Gideon versus Wainwright*, 83 S. Ct. 792(1963). A poor prisoner in Florida establishes the indigent defendant's right to legal counsel.

- In re *Heather P.*, 250 Cal. Rptr. 468(1988). A mother regains custody of her child on a technicality (never underestimate technicalities).

☛ If you are among the millions of people who volunteer time to various public service organizations, you may want to spend time developing legal research skills to further your cause. Or perhaps you are intrigued by our legal system and want to learn more about it. Here are two ways to get you started:

For a hands-on legal research course for the general public, try the University of California Extension's correspondence course, designed for anyone in any state or country who has access to a law library with American legal materials (I'm the instructor). Write to the Correspondence Division, University of California Extension, Berkeley, CA 94720, and ask about *Researching the Law*.

In addition, NOLO Press of Berkeley, California, publishes a do-it-yourself legal research book for non-lawyers. Call them and ask for Stephen Elias' *Legal Research*. They will send it to you through the mail for under $20. See Appendix II.

RESOURCES

The following organizations and agencies have long been working on issues of relevance to midlife women. Contact them for consumer information, or to join their efforts for reform.

Alzheimer's Disease and Related Disorders Association
70 East Lake St.
Chicago, IL 60601
(800) 621-0379
(educational materials on Alzheimer's and other brain disorders)

American Association of Retired Persons (AARP)
Women's Initiative
1909 K St. NW
Washington, DC 20049
(202) 872-4700
(all issues of interest to people over 50)

American Association of University Women (AAUW)
1111 16th St. NW
Washington, DC 20036
(202) 785-7700
(promotes the advancement of women in education and learning)

Center for Women Policy Studies
2000 P St. NW, Ste. 508
Washington, DC 20036
(202) 872-1770
(education and policy analysis on women's issues)

Children of Aging Parents
2761 Trenton Rd.
Levittown, PA 19056
(215) 945-6900
(education, referrals, and support for caregivers)

Consumer Information Center
P.O. Box 100
Pueblo, CO 81002
(low-cost government publications)

Displaced Homemakers' Network
1411 K St. NW, Ste. 930
Washington, DC 20005
(202) 628-6767
(support and education for divorced and widowed homemakers)

Ex-Partners of Servicemen/ Women for Equity (EXPOSE)
P.O. Box 11191
Alexandra, VA 22312
(support and advocacy for military divorced wives)

Insurance Information, Inc.
Hyannis, MA
(800) 472-5800
(compares insurance rates for a fee)

Hot Flash
P.O. Box 816
Stonybrook, NY 11790
(newsletter for midlife and older women)

Hysterectomy Education Resources (HERS)
422 Bryn Mawr Ave.
Bala Cynwyd, PA 19004
(215) 667-7757
(publishes a newsletter, educates on hysterectomies)

National Academy of Elder Law Attorneys, Inc.
655 North Alvernon Way,
Suite 108
Tucson, AZ 85711
(602) 881-4005
(attorneys experienced in Medicaid, estates, pensions, guardianships)

National Citizens' Coalition for Nursing Home Reform
1224 M St. NW, Room 301
Washington, DC 20005
(202) 393-2018
(consumer advocates on long-term-care issues)

National Committee to Preserve Social Security and Medicare
2000 K St., NW, Ste. 800
Washington, DC 20006
(202) 822-9459
(educates and advocates on Social Security and Medicare)

National Insurance Consumer Orgaᵢization
121 N. Payne St.
Alexandria, VA 22314
(insurance reform, will analyze your policy for a fee)

National Organization for Women (NOW)
1000 16th St. NW, Ste. 700
Washington, DC 20036
(202) 331-0066
(women's rights generally)

N.O.W. Task Force on the Rights of Women in Marriage
Dorothy Jonas and Bonnie Sloane
see NOW above
(marital rights)

National Osteoporosis Foundation
2100 M St. NW, Ste. 602
Washington, DC 20057
(202) 223-2226
(educational materials on osteoporosis)

National Pension Lawyer Referral Service
Pension Rights Center
918 16th St. NW, Ste. 704
Washington, DC 20006
(202) 296-3776
(referral service for pension lawyers)

National Senior Citizens Law Center
1815 H St. NW, Suite 700
Washington, DC 20006
(202) 887-5280
(analysis and education on pensions, Social Security, health, etc.)

(NSCLC western office)
1052 West 6th St., Ste. 700
Los Angeles, CA 90017
(213) 482-3550

National Women's Political Caucus
1275 K St. NW, Ste. 750
Washington, DC 20005
(202) 898-1100
(promotes women's political careers)

NOLO Press
950 Parker St.
Berkeley, CA 94710
(800) 992-NOLO
(800) 640-NOLO (Calif.)
(415) 549-1976 (inside 415 area code)
(self-help law books for non-lawyers)

Nursing Home Information Service
National Council of Senior Citizens
925 15th St. NW
Washington, DC 20005
(202) 347-8800
(information and referral)

Older Women's League (OWL)
730 11th St. NW, Ste. 300
Washington, DC 20001
(202) 783-6686
(advocates and educates on all midlife and older women's issues; chapters)

Pension Rights Center
Women's Pension Project
918 16th St. NW, Ste. 704
Washington, DC 20006
(202) 296-3776
(consumer information and advocacy on pension policies and practices)

Social Security Administration
Office of Public Inquiries
6401 Security Boulevard
Baltimore, MD 21235
(301) 594-1234
(public information on Social Security, SSI (welfare), Medicare and Medicaid)

U.S. Department of Labor
Office of Pension and Welfare
Benefit Programs
200 Constitution Ave. NW
Washington, DC 20210
(enforces federal pension law (ERISA))

Widowed Person's Services
American Association of
Retired Persons
1909 K St., NW
Washington, DC 20049
(202) 872-4700
(support and outreach for the newly widowed)

Adult day care, 204, 211, 215, 229.
See also Caregiving
Age discrimination. See Age
Discrimination in Employment
Act; Employment discrimination
Age Discrimination in Employment
Act (ADEA), 64–76, 105–107.
See also Employment
discrimination
Alzheimer's disease, 201, 208–209,
217, Appendix II. See also
Caregiving
Alimony. See Spousal support
American Association of Retired
Persons (AARP), 207, 208, 209,
Appendix II
Annuities, 167–168. See also
Pensions; Retirement savings
401(k)s, 19, 157–163, 166, 170,
176
403(b)s, 154, 157–163, 166
gender bias in, 95, 167–168, 173
life care, 216
pensions, 129, 133
and remarriage, 167
tax-deferred, 168
Appearance discrimination, 82–83.
See also Employment
discrimination
Attorneys. See also Appendix I
do-it-yourself lawbooks. See NOLO
Press, Appendix II
divorce, 28–32, 54
elder law, 55, 203. See also
Appendix II
employee benefits, 163
employment law, 68–69, 78,
105–106
fees, 27–28, 31–32, 105
how to find, 30–31
malpractice, 138, 192
pension law, 128. See also
Appendix II
probate 51, 55

Bona fide occupational requirement
(BFOQ), 66–67. See also
Employment discrimination;
Title VII

Cafeteria plans, 161–162. See also
Retirement savings
California Senate Task Force on
Family Equity, 31–32
Canada, health system, 194–195. See
also Health insurance; National
health program
Career assets, 11–13, 22–24. See also
Marital property
Caregiving, 199–232. See also Family
roles; Jobs
acute-care hospitals, 217
adult day care, 204, 215–216, 229
Alzheimer's disease, 201, 208, 209,
217, Appendix II
checklist, 231–232
compensation, 202–203
demographics, 203–204
divorce, 213–214
durable powers of attorney for
health care, 47, 225–227
family conflict, 200–202
family leave, 97
financial, 207–215, 218–225
fringe benefits, 162
geriatric care managers, 3, 201,
203, 205–207
guardians and conservators, 221,
223–225, 228
guilt, 200–201
home care, 204–211
life care, 216
long-term-care insurance, 207–209,
211, 215, 226–227, 229
Medicaid, 209–215
Medicare, 209–211
medical directives, 225–227
mental hospitals, 217, 223–224
national health program, 195, 200,
227, 229

Caregiving *(continued)*
    nursing homes, 204, 208–218
    personal property management,
        219–225
    reform, 229–230
    residential programs, 215–218
    respite services, 202, 205, 208
    retirement planning, 123, 202
    Social Security credits, 140
    spousal support, 213–215
    wives, 203, 211–215
    women, 218
Checklists
    caregivers, 231–232
    divorce, 33–34
    employment, 89–90
    health insurance, 197–198
    homemakers, 109–110
    marriage, 58–59
    pensions, Social Security, 151–152
    plan for life, 234–237
    retirement savings, 179–180
Children of Aging Parents, 207,
        Appendix II
Child custody. *See also* Divorce
    domestic partners, 47
Child support, 13–17. *See also*
        Divorce; Spousal support
    age of majority, effect of, 14
    college costs, 2, 9, 12, 15–16
    credit, 43
    sale of home, 28
Civil Rights Act of 1964, 2, 63–70,
        72–76, 82, 105–107, 126. *See
        also* Employment discrimination
    history of, 63–64
    pensions, 126
COBRA (Consolidated Omnibus
        Budget Reconciliation Act), 183,
        186–187, 190–193. *See also*
        Health insurance
    children, 14
    divorce, 14, 17–18
College costs, 12–16, 163, 169–170.
        See also Divorce; Retirement
        savings
Common-law property, 36–43, 48–54,
        220–221. *See also* Community
        property; Marital property;
        Marriage
Commonwealth Commission, The, 2
Community property, 36, 39, 41–43,
        49–54, 55–57, 220–221. *See also*
        Common-law property; Marital
        property; Marriage

Comparable worth, 78–80. *See also*
        Employment discrimination; Jobs
Conservators, 221, 223–225, 228. *See
        also* Caregiving
Consolidated Omnibus Budget
        Reconciliation Act. *See* COBRA;
        Health insurance
Convalescent home. *See* Nursing
        homes; *See also* Caregiving
Cost-of-living adjustments (COLA's),
        125. *See also* Pensions; Social
        Security
Credit, 3, 43–44, 163
    credit bureaus, 44
    Equal Credit Opportunity Act,
        43–44
    Fair Credit Reporting Act, 81
Default divorce, 29. *See also* Divorce
Deferred compensation plans,
        157–163, 166. *See also* 401(k)s;
        403(b)s; Retirement savings
Disparate impact, 66–68. *See also*
        Employment discrimination
Displaced homemakers. *See* Divorce;
        Homemakers; Jobs; Widows
Dissolution. *See* Divorce
Divorce, 7–34. *See also* Marital
        property; Marriage
    age as factor, 7
    attorneys, 27–32
    caregivers, 213–215
    checklist, 33–34
    child custody, 47
    child support, 2, 9, 12–17
    college costs, 9, 12–16
    credit, 43–44
    default, 29
    fault-based, 8–11
    health insurance, 12, 14, 17–18,
        191–192
    homemakers, 10–28
    IRAs, 169
    long-term care, 213–214
    methods, 29–30
    military wives, 17
    retirement, 18–20, 27
    retirement income, 9, 17–20,
        25–27, 112, 129–130, 135–138,
        143, 145–147. *See also* Pensions;
        Social Security
    sale of home, 12, 26–28
    Social Security, 145–147
    standard of living, 12, 15, 23–24, 27
    state differences, 12–13, 16–17,
        25–26, 136–137
    trial, 30

Divorce Revolution, The (Weitzman), 16, 21–23

Department of Labor, United States, 107, 124, 127, Appendix II

Do-It-Yourself Divorce, 29. *See also* NOLO Press, Appendix II; Divorce

Do-It-Yourself Wills; Trusts, 54. *See also* NOLO Press, Appendix II

Domestic partners, 46–47, 132. *See also* Marital Property; Marriage

Domestic relations. *See* Divorce; Marriage

Dower, 37, 39–40, 48. *See also* Marital property; Marriage

Dual entitlement rule, 19, 144–146, 171–172. *See also* Social Security

Durable power of attorney for health care, 47, 225–227. *See also* Caregiving; Medical directives; Powers of attorney

Early death benefit. *See* Pensions

Earnings sharing, 149–150. *See also* Social Security

Education
   investment in, 98–99
   re-entry, 98–99
   self, 175–176. *See also* College costs

EEOC. *See* Equal Employment Opportunity Commission

Employees' Retirement Income Security Act (ERISA), 115–124, 127–132, 134–138. *See also* Employment discrimination; Pensions
   health insurance, 188
   marital property, 55–57, 135–138

Employers. *See also* Employment discrimination; Jobs; Pensions
   matching contributions, 158, 160, 162
   resumes, 99–101
   retirement savings, 156–158, 160–162

Employment agencies, 104. *See also* Employment discrimination; Jobs

Employment discrimination, 61–90. *See also* Homemakers; Jobs
   age discrimination, 61–77, 95, 104
   Age Discrimination in Employment Act (ADEA), 64–76, 105–107

appearance discrimination, 82–83
   bona fide occupational requirement (BFOQ), 66–67
   checklist, 89–90
   class actions, 72–75
   comparable worth, 78–80
   disability, 80–83
   disparate impact, 66–68
   EEOC, 69–71, 75, 76, 85, 104–107
   employment agencies, 104
   evaluations, 70–71
   experience requirements, 66–67
   family roles, 96–97
   fitness, 68, 80–82, 189–190
   foreign employers, 76
   homemakers, 95, 97, 101, 104–106
   professionals, 61, 79–80, 83–84
   reform, 86–88, 106–108
   retaliation, 70, 73
   retirement, 71–72
   self-employed, 95
   sex discrimination, 63–88
   sexual harassment, 69–70
   sex-segregated occupations, 78–80
   state laws, 65, 76–78
   Title VII, 64–70, 72–76, 105–107
   unions, 85

Enhanced earning power. *See* Marital property: Career assets

Equal Credit Opportunity Act, 43–44. *See also* Credit

Equal Employment Opportunity Commission (EEOC), 69–71, 75–76, 85, 104–107. *See also* Employment discrimination; Jobs

Equitable distribution. *See* Marital property. *See also* Divorce

ERISA. *See* Employees' Retirement Income Security Act

Fair Credit Reporting Act, 81

Fair employment practices. *See* Employment discrimination

Family roles. *See also* Caregiving; Employment discrimination; Homemakers; Jobs
   jobs, 84, 92–93, 96–97
   retirement income, 96–97, 123

Fault-based divorce, 8–11. *See also* Divorce

Fiduciary duties. *See* Marriage

Forced share. *See* Marriage. *See also* Inheritance; Widows

403(b)s, 19, 157–163, 166, 170, 176.
See also Retirement savings
Fringe benefits. *See* Employment
discrimination; Health insurance;
Insurance; Jobs; Pensions

Gay partners. *See* Domestic partners
Gender bias, 2
annuities, 95, 167–168, 173
health insurance, 181–182, 192
IRAs, 164–165
marriage laws, 56–57
Medicaid, 212–213
pensions, 125–126, 147–150,
177–178
reverse annuity mortgages (RAMs),
173
Geriatric Care Managers, 3, 201, 203,
205–207. *See* Caregiving
Guardians, 221, 223–225, 228. *See
also* Caregiving

Health insurance, 181–198. *See also*
Insurance
Alzheimer's disease, 208–209
association groups, 186, 188
Blue Cross, Shield, 184–185, 190
Canadian system, 194–195
checklist, 197–198
COBRA, 12, 14, 17–18, 182–183,
186–187, 190–193
Congress, 189, 195–196
continuation, 12, 14, 17–18,
182–183, 186–187, 190–193
conversion, 186–187, 190–191
divorce, 2–3, 12, 14, 17–18
exclusions, 95, 187, 192–193, 209
fitness discrimination, 80–81,
189–190
gender bias, 181–182, 192
group policies, 182–183, 185–187,
188, 191
HMOs, 184–185, 190
homemakers, 191–192
indemnity policies, 187–188, 208
individual policies, 182, 186–187,
191
long-term care, 207–209, 211, 215,
226–227, 229
medi-gap, 208–209
medical record, 181–182, 187, 191
national health program, 193–196,
227, 229
other countries, 195–196
pre-existing conditions, 95, 187,
192–193

reform, 193–196
self-employed, 94–95
self-insurance, 193
types of policies, 184–189
widows, 18
Health Maintenance Organizations
(HMOs), 85–185, 190. *See also*
Health insurance
Hochschild, Arlie: *The Second Shift,*
97
Home
barrier-free, 228
collectives, 227
divorce, 12, 26–28
long-term care, 210–212
reverse annuity mortgages (RAMs),
172–173
Homemakers. *See also* Caregiving;
Marital property; Marriage;
Pensions; Retirement savings;
Social Security; Widows
checklist, 109–110
civil rights laws, 105–106
divorce, 8–28
employment discrimination, 95, 97,
101, 104–106
health insurance, 191–192
IRAs, 163–166, 177
job reform, 106–108
long-term care, 211–215
paid experience, 101–104
paid work, 91–110
pensions, 128–135
resumes, 99–101
retirement income, 111–113,
128–135, 143–146, 149–150,
171–172. *See also* Pensions;
Retirement savings; Social
Security
spousal support, 9–17, 20–22,
27–28
Social Security, 128–129, 139–141,
143–146, 149, 171–172. *See also*
Social Security

Immigration Reform and Control Act
of 1986, 101
Individual Benefit Statement, 125. *See
also* Pensions
IRAs (Individual Retirement
Accounts), 19, 154, 162–170,
176–177. *See also* Retirement
savings
Inheritance. *See also* Marriage; Trusts;
Wills

between spouses, 36–37, 39–40, 48–55
domestic partners, 47
forced share, 40, 48–53
intestacy, 53–55
long-term care, 214, 226, 229
unmarried, 47
Insurance. *See also* Health insurance
annuities, 95, 167–168, 173
disability, 94–95
employee benefits, 161–163
health. *See* Health insurance
long-term care, 207–209, 211, 215, 226–227, 229
liability, 94
life, 3, 9, 123, 132, 168, 173–175
medicare supplement (medi-gap), 208–209, 211, 229
Integration. *See* Pensions; Social Security
Inter-vivos trusts. *See* Trusts. *See also* Caregiving
Intestacy, 53–55. *See also* Marriage; Wills

Job discrimination. *See* Employment discrimination. *See also* Jobs
Jobs. *See also* Employment discrimination; Pensions; Retirement savings; Social Security
checklists, 89–90, 109–110
consultants, 92–95
employment agencies, 104
family roles, 84, 92–93, 96–97
health insurance, 94, 182–186
homemakers, 106–108
interviews, 104
part-time, 92–93, 116–117
professional, 96
re-entry, 106–108
reform, 106–108
resumes, 99–101
self-employment, 91–96
sex-segregated occupations, 78–80
training, 98–99
Joint tenancy, 47, 49–50. *See also* Caregiving

Keogh plans, 19, 94, 163, 176. *See also* Retirement savings

Law library. *See* Appendix I
Lawyers. *See* Attorneys
Legal research. *See* Appendix I
Lesbians. *See* Domestic partners. *See also* Marriage
Life care, 215–216. *See also* Caregiving
Life expectancy. *See* Longevity
Life plan, 233–239
Living trusts. *See* Trusts. *See also* Caregiving
Living wills, 225–227. *See also* Caregiving, Medical directives
Longevity. *See also* Pensions; Retirement savings
annuities, 95, 129, 167–168
health planning for, 196
inflation, 166–167
retirement income, 124–126
Long-term care. *See* Caregiving; Insurance

Management and control. *See* Marital property
Mandatory retirement, 72, 97, 171. *See also* Employment discrimination; Jobs; Pensions; Retirement
Marital property, 20–28, 35–46, 48–55. *See also* Divorce; Marriage; Pensions; Widows
career assets, 11–13, 22–24
common-law, 36–43, 48–54, 220–221
community property, 36, 39, 41–43, 49–57, 220–221
Congress, 55–57
debt, 27, 45–46
dower, 37, 39–40, 48
equal division rule, 27
equitable distribution, 12–13, 27, 36, 39, 49
fiduciary standards, 44–46
inheritance, 25, 36–37, 39–40, 48–55
intangible assets, 13, 23–26
management and control, 41–43, 45–46, 55–57
marriage, 35–57
long-term care, 211–215
pensions, 18–20, 26, 51, 55–56, 134–138
reform, 32, 55–57
separate property, 36, 42, 50–52
tenancy by the entirety, 41

Marital property *(continued)*
title theory of property, 39, 42, 51, 56
widows, 40, 48–54
Marriage, 35–59. *See also* Divorce; Marital property; Widows
checklist, 58–59
common-law, 36–43, 48–54
community property, 36, 39, 41–43, 49–57, 220–221
domestic partners, 46–47
dower, 37, 39–40, 48
English tradition, 36–40, 48
fiduciary duties, 44–46
forced share, 40, 48–53
inheritance, 36–37, 39–40, 48–55
lesbians, 46–47
married women's acts, 38, 40, 56–57
pensions, 39, 55–56
vows, 38
Married women's acts, 38, 40, 56–57. *See also* Marriage
Mediation (divorce), 29. *See also* Divorce
Medicaid, 188–189, 195. *See also* Caregiving
long-term care, 209–215, 229
gender-bias, 212–213
marital property, 55, 211–215
Medical data bases, 81–82. *See also* Employment discrimination
Medical directives, 47, 225–227. *See also* Caregiving
Medicare, 94, 188–190, 192. *See also* Caregiving
long-term care, 207–211, 215
reform, 229
teachers, 190
Medicare supplement insurance (Medi-gap). *See* Health insurance; Insurance. *See also* Caregiving

National Academy of Elder Law Attorneys, 203, Appendix II
National Association of Private Geriatric Care Managers, 207
National health program, 193–196, 200, 227, 229
National Pension Lawyer Referral Service, 128, Appendix II
Natural death acts, 225–227. *See also* Caregiving; Medical directives
No-fault divorce, 2, 7–13. *See also* Divorce

Nursing homes, 204, 208–218. *See also* Caregiving

Older women. *See also* Divorce; Homemakers; Pensions; Social Security; Widows
divorce, 7, 17, 32
remarriage, 47
what constitutes, 4
Older Women's League (OWL), 191–192, 208–209, Appendix II

Part-time work, 92–93, 116–117, 145. *See also* Employment discrimination; Jobs; Pensions
Pension Benefit Guaranty Corporation (PBGC), 126–127. *See also* Pensions
Pensions, 111–180. *See also* Employees' Retirement Income Security Act; Retirement savings; Social Security
annuities, 129, 133, 167
appeals, 128
caregivers, 123, 202
checklist, 151–152
Civil Rights Act of 1964, 128
cost-of-living, 125
credit, 43–44
divorce, 12–13, 26–27, 112, 129–132, 135–138
domestic partners, 132
early death benefit, 130–131
ERISA, 115–124, 127–132, 134–138
forfeitures, 114–115
gender bias in, 125–126, 147–150, 177–78
homemakers, 128–135
Individual Benefit Statement, 125
inflation, 113, 124–126, 166–167, 175
IRAs, 19, 154, 162–170, 176–177
integration, 112, 117–119
lump-sums, 132, 167, 175
management and control, 55–57
mobility, 97, 119–125, 147, 156
marital property, 39, 55–56
part-time work, 116–117
Pension Benefit Guaranty Corporation (PBGC), 126–127
plan features, 116–124
reform, 147–150
retaliation, 128
remarriage, 134–135
retirement discrimination, 71–72

state and local, 131, 148
Summary Annual Report (SAR), 127
Summary Plan Description (SPD), 116, 119, 124
survivor's benefit, 129–138, 173–174
vesting, 119–123, 127, 147–149, 156, 162, 165
voluntary contributions, 162
unmarried, 132
Personal Earnings and Benefits Estimate Statement, 141. *See also* Social Security
Poverty
divorce, 32
older women, 2
pensions, 134
Powers of attorney, 221–225. *See also* Caregiving
durable powers of attorney, 222–225
durable powers of attorney for health care, 47, 225–227
Probate, 50, 51
Property. *See* Marital property

Respite services, 202, 205, 208. *See also* Caregiving
Resumes
falsifying, 101
homemakers, 99–101
paid experience, 101–104
volunteer work, 100
Retirement. *See also* Pensions; Retirement savings; Social Security
deferred, 171–172
discrimination, 71–72
mandatory, 72, 97, 171
phased, 97–98
Retirement income. *See* Pensions; Retirement savings; Social Security
Retirement savings, 153–180. *See also* Pensions; Social Security
amortizing, 174–175
annuities, 129, 133, 167–168, 173
borrowing from, 163, 166
cafeteria plans, 161–162
checklist, 179–180
college costs, 169–170
deferred compensation plans, 157–163, 166
divorce, 19, 169

401(k)s, 19, 157–163, 166, 170, 176
403(b)s, 154, 157–163, 166
home equity, 172–173
IRAs, 19, 154, 162–170, 176–177
Keogh plans, 19, 94, 163, 176
reform, 176–178
reverse mortgages, 172–173
tax-protected, 153–166, 176–177
Reverse annuity mortgages, 172–173. *See also* Annuities; Retirement savings
Right to die. *See* Medical directives. *See also* Caregiving
Rule of 72, 159, 170, 174. *See also* Retirement savings

Second Chances (Wallerstein): 7, 15–16
Second marriages, 50–52, 54, 134, 137
Second Shift, The (Hochschild): 97
Separate property, 36, 42, 50–51, 53. *See also* Marital property; Marriage
SEPs (SEP-IRAs). *See* Simplified Employee Pensions
Sex discrimination. *See* Employment discrimination; Gender-bias; Title VII
Sexual harassment, 69. *See also* Employment discrimination
Simplified Employee Pensions (SEPs), 156–158, 161–162, 176. *See also* Pensions; Retirement savings
Social Security, 111–113, 117–119, 138–147. *See also* Pensions; Retirement savings
checklist, 151–152
credits, 140, 143
delayed retirement, 171–172
divorce, 19, 27, 112, 146–147
dual entitlement rule, 19, 144–146, 171–172
earnings, 161
earnings sharing, 149–150
good-faith wife, 19
homemakers, 128–129, 139–141, 143–146, 149, 171–172
integration, 112, 117–119
Medicare, 190, 209–210
part-time work, 93, 145
reform, 147–150
retirement age, 141–143, 145–146
teachers, 190
widows, 143–147, 149, 171–172

Social Security *(continued)*
wives, 144–147
zero-years, 141, 146, 149
Spousal impoverishment, 210–215.
See also Caregiving; Medicaid
Spousal support
credit, 43–44
homemakers, 9–17, 20–22, 27–28
justifications for, 21–22
long-term care, 214–215
survivor's benefits, 18–19. *See also*
Divorce; Marital property;
Survivor's benefits
Survivor's benefits, 18–19, 129–138,
173–174. *See also* Pensions;
Social Security

Taxes. *See also* 401(k)s; 403(b)s;
Keogh plans; Retirement savings
annuities, tax-deferred, 168
annuities, tax-sheltered (TSAs). *See*
403(b)s
fringe benefits, 157
joint tenancies, 220
retirement savings, 154–166, 170,
176–177
Social Security (FICA), 93–94,
(SE), 140
Tax-protected savings. *See* 401(k)s;
403(b)s; Keogh plans;
Retirement savings
Tax-sheltered annuities (TSAs). *See*
403(b)s; Retirement savings
Title VII. *See* Employment
discrimination

Trusts, 47, 50, 52, 54, 221–225

Unions, 85, 128

Volunteers, 101–104

Wallerstein, Judith: *Second Chances*, 7,
15–16
Weitzman, Lenore: *Divorce Revolution,
The*, 16, 21–23
Welfare
and credit, 43–44
and divorce, 12
widows, 144–145
Widows, 48–54. *See also* Inheritance;
Marriage; Trusts; Wills
at common-law, 36–37, 40
credit, 43–44
fiduciary standard, 45–46
health insurance, 191–192
inheritance, 36–37, 39–40, 48–55
long-term care, 214
marital property, 40, 48–54
retirement income, 128–135,
143–147, 149, 171–172
Social Security, 143–145, 149,
171–172
welfare, 144–145
Wills, 47–52, 54, 219–220. *See also*
Inheritance; Marriage; Trusts
Wrongful discharge. *See* Employment
discrimination